JOURNAL FOR THE STUDY OF THE OLD TESTAMENT SUPPLEMENT SERIES
251

Editors
David J.A. Clines
Philip R. Davies

Executive Editor
John Jarick

COPENHAGEN INTERNATIONAL SEMINAR
4

General Editors
Thomas L. Thompson
Niels Peter Lemche

Associate Editors
Frederick H. Cryer
Mogens Müller
Hakan Ulfgard

Sheffield Academic Press

The Tragedy in History

Herodotus and the Deuteronomistic History

Flemming A.J. Nielsen

Journal for the Study of the Old Testament
Supplement Series 251

Copenhagen International Seminar 4

For Lene

Copyright © 1997 Sheffield Academic Press

Published by Sheffield Academic Press Ltd
Mansion House
19 Kingfield Road
Sheffield S11 9AS
England

Printed on acid-free paper in Great Britain
by Bookcraft Ltd
Midsomer Norton, Bath

British Library Cataloguing in Publication Data

A catalogue record for this book is available
from the British Library

ISBN 1-85075-688-0

CONTENTS

A growing number of scholars regard the Hellenistic period as central to the formation of the Old Testament historical traditions. As a piece of historiography recounting the history of a whole people or nation corporately and explaining the causes of the final state of things, the so-called Deuteronomistic History stands unique compared to extra-biblical, Near Eastern literature prior to the Hellenistic Age. Among Hittite, Babylonian, Assyrian, Egyptian, Syro-Palestinian and Persian historiographic texts, there seems to be nothing comparable. Instead, a close extra-biblical literary parallel to the Deuteronomistic History is furnished by the Greek historiographer Herodotus. In both works the material is subordinated to a causal and corporate progression of events. The causes of the Persian defeat in Hellas and of the Israelite exile respectively are explained, in both cases, as models for proper behaviour in the writers' own age as well as in the future.

In the following, Herodotus' position in the Greek literary tradition with regard to the Presocratic 'physicists' and the Ionian historiographers is emphasized, and it is demonstrated that Herodotus also continues an epic tradition exemplified by Homer. Consequently, as a historian, Herodotus writes 'poetically', and as a poet Homer writes 'historically'. Thirdly, Herodotus is heavily influenced by the Attic tragedy to which a close affinity is demonstrated around several literary motifs. 'The Herodotean Tragedy' is specified in detail based on two logoi in which the tragic form seems to be most essential as well as conspicuous: the stories about Croesus and Xerxes. Whereas the Croesus story plays through the metaphysical themes dominating the whole work of Herodotus, the story of Xerxes demonstrates that the Persian war is ultimately caused by divine, inscrutable volition.

Subsequently, Herodotus and the Deuteronomistic History (DtrH) are compared, and in the light of the said exposition of the Herodotean tragedy, the comparison is made from a perspective which has hitherto been less favoured in the scholarly literature on Old Testament historiography: the tragic mode of presentation. I shall argue that a tragic form like that of Herodotus can be demonstrated in DtrH and identify several common tragic themes as well as a 'deuteronomistic' tragic leitmotif.

The book is a slightly revised edition of a *speciale* delivered at the Copenhagen University in 1994. Thanks are due to my teachers for their interest and much encouragement. In particular, I wish to mention Niels Peter Lemche who originally suggested to me to write about Greek and Old Testament historiography. I also thank the editors of *The Copenhagen International Seminar* series and Sheffield Academic Press for agreeing to publish my work. The Danish Research Council for the Humanities generously granted the financial support that made it possible to Janne Elisabeth McOwan to undertake the unenviable task of translating the text from Danish. Frederick H. Cryer kindly read through the English manuscript. All have contributed by pointing out a number of obscurities and mistakes, though I am, of course, solely responsible for any surviving imperfection.

I dedicate the book to my wife, Lene, who was never short of good advice and heartening remarks in spite of the fact that her loving patience was severely tried in the course of my writing.

All translations of ancient texts are my own, unless otherwise indicated.

ABBREVIATIONS

AASF	Annales Academiae Scientiarum Fennicae
AB	Anchor Bible Dictionary
ABAW.PH	Abhandlungen der Bayerischen Akademie der Wissenschaften, Philosophisch-historische Abteilung, Neue Folge
AOS	American Oriental Series
ADPV	Abhandlungen des Deutschen Palästinavereins
AfO	*Archiv für Orientforschung*
AKuG	*Archiv für Kulturgeschichte*
Antike	*Die Antike: Zeitschrift für Kunst und Kultur der Altertumswissenschaft*
Arca	Arca: Classical and Medieval Texts, Papers and Monographs
ASNSP	*Annali della Scuola Normale Superiore di Pisa: Classe de Lettere e Filosofia: Serie III*
ATANT	Abhandlungen zur Theologie des Alten und Neuen Testaments
Bib	*Biblica*
BWANT	Beiträge zur Wissenschaft vom Alten und Neuen Testament
BZAW	Beihefte zur *ZAW*
CAH	Cambridge Ancient History
CB	*The Classical Bulletin*
CBQ	*Catholic Biblical Quarterly*
ClW	*The Classical Weekly*, since 1957: *The Classical World*
ConBOT	Coniectanea biblica, Old Testament
CP	*Classical Philology*
EeC	Etudes et commentaires
EETh	Einführung in die evangelische Theologie
EPRO	Etudes préliminaires aux religions orientales dans l'empire Romain
FOTL	The Forms of the Old Testament Literature
FRLANT	Forschungen zur Religion und Literatur des Alten und Neuen Testaments
HAW	Handbuch der Altertumswissenschaft
HGym	*Das humanistische Gymnasium*
Hist	*Historia: Zeitschrift für alte Geschichte*
Hist(L)	*History: The Quarterly Journal of the Historical Association*
HSCP	*Harvard Studies in Classical Philology*
HSM	Harvard Semitic Monographs
IBKW.S	*Innsbrucker Beiträge zur Kulturwissenschaft, Sonderheft*
JARCE	*Journal of the American Research Center in Egypt*
JCS	*Journal of Cuneiform Studies*

JHS	*Journal of Hellenic Studies*
JLCR	Jordan Lectures in Comparative Religion
JNES	*Journal of Near Eastern Studies*
JPh	*The Journal of Philosophy*
JSOTSup	*Journal for the Study of the Old Testament*, Supplement Series
KAT	Kommentar zum Alten Testament
KTA	Kröners Taschenausgabe
LCL	Loeb Classical Library
LSJ	Liddell-Scott-Jones, *Greek–English Lexicon*
MVAeG	Mitteilungen der Vorderasiatischen-Aegyptischen Gesellschaft
OBO	Orbis biblicus et orientalis
Or	*Orientalia*
OrAnt	*Oriens antiquus*
OTL	The Old Testament Library
OTS	*Oudtestamentische Studiën*
PEQ	*Palestine Exploration Quarterly*
Philological Monographs	Philological Monographs Published by The American Philological Association
Poetica	*Poetica: Zeitschrift für Sprach- und Literaturwissenschaft*
REA	*Revue des Etudes Anciennes*
RhM	*Rheinisches Museum*
SBLTT	SBL Texts and Translations
SC	Sources chrétiennes
SCO	*Studi classici e orientali*
SHANE	Studies in the History of the Ancient Near East
SHAW.PH	Sitzungsberichte der Heidelberger Akademie der Wissenschaften, philosophisch-historische Klasse
SJOT	*Scandinavian Journal of the Old Testament*
SKG.G	Schriften der Königsberger Gelehrten Gesellschaft, Geisteswissenschaftliche Klasse
SÖAW.PH	Sitzungsberichte der österreichischen Akademie der Wissenschaften in Wien, philosophisch-historische Klasse
StBT	Studien zu den Bo azköy-Texten: Herausgegeben von der Kommission für den Alten Orient der Akademie der Wissenschaften und der Literatur
TBü	Theologische Bücherei
TCS	Texts from Cuneiform Sources
ThW	Theologische Wissenschaft: Sammelwerk für Studium und Beruf
TRu	*Theologische Rundschau*
TWAS	Twayne's World Authors Series
UaLG	Untersuchungen zur antiken Literatur und Geschichte
UCP.CS	University of California Publications, Classical Studies
UGAÄ	Untersuchungen zur Geschichte und Altertumskunde Ägyptens
VAB	Vorderasiatische Bibliothek
VTSup	*Vetus Testamentum*, Supplements
WBC	Word Biblical Commentary

WdF	Wege der Forschung
YNER	Yale Near Eastern Researches
ZA	*Zeitschrift für Assyriologie und verwandte Gebiete: Neue Folge*
ZAW	*Zeitschrift für die alttestamentliche Wissenschaft*
ZPE	*Zeitschrift für Papyrologie und Epigraphik*

Chapter 1

INTRODUCTION

That historiography was practised in ancient Israel as early as the time of the united monarchy may be regarded as a 'classical' statement in Old Testament scholarship. For example, S. Mandell and D.N. Freedman (1993: 84-86) summarize what they term 'the *communis opinio*', stating that in the beginning was M. Noth's '*Grundlage* (G), which may well have been an oral, poetic composition of the twelfth to the eleventh centuries BCE, relating the or at least *an* established account of the Sons of Israel and their forefathers'.[1] Then a tenth-century written Yahwistic redaction (J) and a ninth-century Elohistic redaction (E) followed, and in the late eighth century they are supposed to be combined to form a 'JE Epic' (R^{JE}), which was given some form of 'overriding redaction' by the Priestly Redactor (P) in the sixth century. In the seventh century, the Deuteronomist (D) wrote a separate work, now part of Deuteronomy, and later in the same century the Deuteronomistic School or the Deuteronomistic Historian (Dtr^1) authored or compiled the Deuteronomistic History (DtrH). This work was then redacted by a subsequent, exilic (sixth-century) redactor (Dtr^2) and combined with the Tetrateuch to form what Mandell and Freedman term 'the "First Bible" or the "Essential Bible" or the "Fundamental Bible"' (Mandell and Freedman 1993: p. 85).

However, the idea of historiography dating back to the time of the united monarchy has long puzzled historians such as those whom G. von Rad, quite inappropriately, referred to as 'secular historians'. In 1930 E. Meyer indicated his surprise by stating that the historiographic literature is 'the most striking product of the early monarchy', unparalleled among other peoples of the ancient Near East.[2] As a matter

---

1. Mandell and Freedman 1993: 98. For this *Grundlage*, see Noth 1948: 40-44.
2. 'Das überraschendste Erzeugnis der ersten Königszeit ist die geschichtliche Literatur, die sie geschaffen hat.' One of the striking characteristics of this historio-

of fact, more recent research, largely ignored by Mandell and Freedman, has suggested that 'Israelitic' historiography belongs to a much
later era than has previously been suspected. For example,[3] I. Finkelstein (1988: 22) indicates the late monarchic period, J. Van Seters
(1975; 1983; 1992; 1994) the period of the exile, whereas the Persian
period has been suggested by P.R. Davies (1992) and T.L. Thompson
(1992), and N.P. Lemche (1993) moves as far forward as the Hellenistic period (cf. Bolin 1996). The writing down of the Israelitic
historical tradition did not, according to Thompson, begin until the
post-exilic period, in other words towards the end of the sixth century
BCE, and the process was not completed until the middle of the second
century BCE (Thompson 1992: 315-16, 356). This perspective makes a
comparison with the Greek historiographers possible. The beginning
of Greek historiographic tradition, or rather, that which has come
down to us, is represented by Hecataeus (sixth century BCE), whereas
its first milestone may be said to be Herodotus who died some time
after 430 BCE[4] and thus may be credited with the oldest historical
work in Greek preserved in its entirety and with dimensions comparable to the continuous account comprised by the Tetrateuch and the
Deuteronomistic historical work.

  N.P. Lemche has suggested that the Greek historians might be
considered as forefathers of Jewish historiography of the post-exilic
period.[5] J. Van Seters (1983: 8-54) and B.O. Long (1984: 15-30) have
likewise indicated various similarities between the historiography in

---

graphic literature is 'ein novellistischer Charakter, ähnlich so manchen Erzählungen
bei Herodot und dann wieder bei Xenophon' (Meyer 1953: 284-85). Von Rad (1944:
33) mentions E. Meyer as an important example of a 'Profanhistoriker'.

  3. For the following list, see Lemche 1996: 111.

  4. Regarding the problems of dating Herodotus, see Jacoby 1913: 229-232;
Fornara 1971. The last events he records took place during the Peloponnesian war in
431 and 430 BCE. He knows about the Theban attack on Plataea (7.233), the expulsion of the people of Aegina (6.91), the invasion of Attica (9.73), and the execution
of envoys (7.137); Levi 1985; How and Wells 1928, II: 180. Fornara (1971) suggests as late a date as 414 BCE (the Peace of Nicias), but approximately 426–425 is
far more often advanced—cf. Fornara's references and Immerwahr 1985: 427.

  5. Lemche 1991: 156-73; cf. pp. 169-70: 'It may even be argued that instead of
considering Old Testament history writing a unique feature of ancient Oriental society... it would be preferable to turn to the Greek historians and consider the older
among them to be also the forefathers of the Jewish history writers of the post-exilic
period.'

the Old Testament and that of Herodotus and have called for comparative readings of these texts.[6] Thus it seems reasonable to consider to how great an extent Herodotus may have been among the sources of inspiration for the Old Testament historiography. Scholars of Herodotus frequently emphasize that he was the first historiographer.[7] In the light of more recent Old Testament scholarship, it has become legitimate to examine whether this classical understanding of Herodotus as *pater historiae*[8] may be valid in what in relation to the classic Greek and Roman world may be termed an extended geographical area. The impression that Herodotus in his opus, unique in its own time,[9] created a new genre, or at the very least fostered the idea of one,[10] makes it relevant to extend the historiographic frame of reference of the classics from Hellas and Rome to the Near East. Was Herodotus also the first historiographer when compared to ancient Near Eastern literature? The historical works written by the Egyptian Manetho[11] and the Babylonian Berosus (third century BCE),[12] clearly influenced by

6.   Van Seters 1983: 39: 'the Old Testament and Herodotus share a great deal in common and ought to be studied together'. Fehling (1989: 11) states that 'the Israelites had developed a genre of historical writing which in places is remarkably similar to that of Herodotus. This is particularly true of *Samuel* and *Kings*.' Likewise, O'Brien (1989: 17) recognizes that the Deuteronomistic Historical Work has more points of resemblances to Herodotus than to the historiographic genres of the ancient Near East.

7.   Lateiner 1989: 227: 'Historiography as we know it was then created at one time and by one man, Herodotus.' Von Rad (1944: 1-2) emphasizes the difference between historical documents and historiography, the latter being characterized as 'eine besondere Form des Kausalen Denkens und zwar in Anwendung gebracht auf eine größere Abfolge politischer Geschehnisse... So sind es nur zwei Völker, die im Altertum wirklich Geschichte geschrieben haben: die Griechen und lange Zeit vor ihnen die Israeliten.'

8.   Cicero, *De legibus*, 1.5 (text and translation: Keyes 1928). Regarding the classical authors on Herodotus, see Myres 1953: 17-19.

9.   Lateiner 1989: 223: 'Herodotus's original inquiry was... the invention of the first complex prose work in European literature.'

10.   Fehling 1989: 252-53: 'Herodotus's imagination has anticipated possibilities such as source-criticism, epigraphy, comparative linguistics, and ethnology, which have had to wait for modern science to make them a reality. And, we may safely add, the way he envisages these possibilities makes it perfectly clear that he had no practical experience of them whatsoever.'

11.   For the basics facts concerning Manetho, see Helck 1979. Text and translation: Waddell 1940.

12.   Spoerri 1979; Lehmann-Haupt 1938. Fragments: Schnabel 1923: 249-75.

Hellenistic culture, should be noted in this connection. It is also a well known fact that both Jewish and Greek literature from the fifth century BCE onwards developed under similar circumstances caused by the Persian empire (Momigliano 1990). A. Momigliano adduces two examples of Jewish historiography's dependence upon Greek historiography, and he finds his parallels to the Jewish examples, which are from the book of Daniel and the book of Judith, in the work of Herodotus.[13]

The above-mentioned appeal from Van Seters and Long to make comparative readings of Herodotus and the Old Testament has recently been followed up by S. Mandell and D.N. Freedman (Mandell and Freedman 1993). In their opinion, Ezra is the man responsible for what is termed 'Primary History', that is, the Pentateuch combined with the Former Prophets. At the time of Ezra, this Primary History had long since been completed, so 'his work was that of selection and presentation rather than compilation, much less editing or composing' (Freedman 1990: 317). By and large, Ezra's work corresponds to our extant text of the 'Primary History' (Mandell and Freedman 1993: 89). Ascribing such a pivotal role in the genesis of Old Testament historiography to Ezra, is, however, a serious weakness in Mandell and Freedman's reading of what they term the 'Primary History'. Historically speaking, it is not easy to get a grip on Ezra.[14] Comparing such a legendary figure with an indisputably historical person such as

---

13. Momigliano 1981: 30-32. His parallels are: 1) The notion of a succession of universal empires, as the author of the Book of Daniel knew it, is unparallelled in the ancient Near East and is to be found for the first time in Herodotus' work and subsequently in the writings of such historians as Ctesias, Polybius, Aemilius Sura, and Dionysius of Halicarnassus. 2) Herodotus' account of the defence of the Pass of Thermopylae, Hdt. 7, contains so many similarities to the book of Judith with regard to structure and contents that the author of the latter must have been acquainted, directly or indirectly, with Herodotus' work.

14. See Grabbe (1991) and Garbini (1988: 151-69) for some important problems regarding this legendary figure. C.C. Torrey's old *dictum* might be apposite, though he has long been anathema to the prevailing consensus regarding the sources for Ezra–Nehemiah and their authenticity (Torrey 1896: 65): 'The result of the investigation as to the historical content of Ezra–Neh. has thus been to show, that aside from the greater part of Neh. 1–6 the book has no value whatever, as history... [The Chronicler's] work, whatever else may be said of it, certainly throws no light on the history of the Jews in the Persian period.' As regards Torrey's view on Ezra as a fictitious character without any basis of fact, see Torrey 1896: 57-62.

Herodotus[15] is highly problematic. Mandell and Freedman's comparison results in a false alternative: either of the two men must have looked over the other's shoulder. The choice is easy for Mandell and Freedman: Herodotus had some knowledge of Ezra's work, as Herodotus knew Aramaic, whereas Ezra 'is not known to have had a command of Greek or even to have had interaction with the Greek world'.[16]

The first thing that comes to mind when faced with this 'solution' is the question why, if he had any knowledge about this work of Ezra, Herodotus does not mention anything at all about Israelite matters, although he does refer to a Palestinian Syria as well as Palestinian Syrians.[17] The next thing is that Mandell and Freedman's ideas about Herodotus' (and Ezra's) knowledge of languages are the result of mere guesswork. We do not know anything at all about these two gentlemen's linguistic abilities. This applies to Mandell and Freedman's other ideas about Ezra as well. They are not verifiable, but mere guesswork, shots in the dark. Rather than their false alternative, a real alternative should be taken under consideration: is the 'Primary History' among the sources of inspiration for Herodotus, or is it vice versa? This alternative does not presuppose that either author/compilator read the other work personally. Rather, the work that is identified as the earlier one should be viewed as being part of a greater, literary context to which the later work also belongs.

The present work deals with a comparison of Herodotus and Old Testament historiography as represented by the so-called Deuteronomistic Historical Work (DtrH). This is inspired by J. Van Seters's statement that DtrH might be the most ancient example of Israelitic historiography which has come down to us.[18] I am unable to say

---

15. Regarding Herodotus' biography, see F. Jacoby's meticulous investigation (Jacoby 1913: col. 205-247).

16. Mandell and Freedman 1993: 175. The idea that Herodotus knew Aramaic is connected with a corresponding idea that he made journeys in the Persian Empire in whose western parts Imperial Aramaic was the *lingua Franca*. But Schmid (1934: 557-58) rightly emphasizes that Herodotus did not know any foreign languages.

17. ἡ Παλαιστίνη Συρίη/Συρίη ἡ Παλαιστίνη (καλεομένη): Hdt. 1.105; 2.106; 3.91; 4.39. According to Herodotus, the western part of the Persian Empire was inhabited by three peoples: Persians, Assyrians, and Arabs. Obviously, he had never heard about Israelites.

18. Van Seters 1983; Van Seters 1992, particularly p. 332. See also Mayes 1983: 139-49; Rendtorff 1977: 166-69. Schmid (1976: 167) puts the Yahwist 'in der Nähe der deuteronomisch-deuteronomistischen Traditionsbildung und literarischen Arbeit',

whether Van Seters is actually right.[19] In fact, one cannot be sure that there ever was such a thing as 'The Deuteronomistic History'. To demonstrate that this work existed (Noth 1943) is just as possible as demonstrating that it never existed (Westermann 1994: 13-78). However, what one can do, and what will be done by the present writer, is to accept Noth's Deuteronomistic Historical Work as a working hypothesis[20] and deal with an existing text block within the Hebrew bible, consisting of Deuteronomy, Joshua, Judges, Samuel and Kings.[21] An initial, cursory reading of this continuous text block showed such an astonishing number of similarities to Herodotus, that I felt that reading these books of the Hebrew bible in conjunction with Herodotus would be a rewarding exercise. It would be possible to compare many aspects of these works; I have chosen one which Van Seters has not discussed in his comparison of Greek historiography with that of the Old Testament (Van Seters 1983: 8-54), namely what might be called 'the tragic mode of presentation'. It is a well-known fact that Herodotus' work bears traces of the Attic tragedy of the fifth century BCE. In the following, I hope to demonstrate that one of the many aspects of the Deuteronomistic history is its tragic view of the relationship between God and humanity.

Firstly, Herodotus' Greek context will be depicted through Ionic natural philosophy, the epic tradition and the Attic tragedy, before I attempt a more particular description of the Herodotean tragedy. Secondly, the Deuteronomistic history will be seen in connection with historiography in the ancient Near East, whereupon it will be discussed from a tragic point of view as well. I intend to use Herodotus as a 'mirror' for the Deuteronomistic history, and hope to be able to demonstrate to what extent tragedy in the Deuteronomistic history resembles Herodotus' tragedy.

as the theology of this author cannot be much older than that of the Deuteronomist (p. 175). Levin 1993: 430-34 places J between Deuteronomy and Joshua–Kings. However, it should be mentioned that such opinions are not universally held. For example, Berge 1990 dates the Yahwist to the tenth century BCE, that is 'zur Zeit des davidisch-salomonischen Großreiches... vor der Bedrohung des Großreichs durch äußere und innere Feinde' (p. 313).

19. Cf. T.L. Thompson's criticism that Van Seters's dating is based on a *circulus vitiosus*; Thompson 1995: 107-108.

20. I have borrowed this wording from Nelson 1981: 13.

21. For a very similar term, 'The Deuteronomic History', applied to this text block in its existing form, cf. Polzin 1980: 18.

Chapter 2

HERODOTUS

Herodotus' historical work may look like 'a mere collection of loosely woven tales',[1] but is actually a stringent literary composition. Its leit-motif may be described as agonistic. This can already be noticed in the proem[2] and the following stories about the abduction of women (1.1-5). The introduction concludes with the following statement: '…but having pointed out the man whom I myself know to have been the first to commence unjust acts against the Greeks, I will proceed further into the story…' (1.5.3). The person referred to here is Croesus, the protagonist of the subsequent 'Croesus prologue' (1.6-45)[3] which relates the history of the kingdom of Lydia from the time when Croesus' ancestor Gyges came to power in Sardis until Croesus' subjection of the Ionian coastal towns and his treaty with the Ionian islands. At this zenith of Croesus' power, the sage Solon from Athens visits the king, and they discuss the philosophical aspects of the changes of fortune. Croesus' subsequent attack on the Persians may be regarded as a new section of the history. In the course of this section,

---

1. This is the reputation opposed by Immerwahr (1966: 17).

2. Unlike Immerwahr (1966: 17-18), I refer, by this term, solely to the famous long introductory sentence giving the author's name and a short description of the character of the work: 'This [is] the setting forth of the research of Herodotus the Halicarnassian, [provided] in order that the actions of men should not be extinguished by time and that great and marvellous deeds accomplished by Greeks as well as barbarians should not be without renown, everything else [included], but especially the reason why they warred against each other' (Ἡροδότου Ἁλικαρ νησσέος ἱστορίης ἀπόδεξις ἥδε, ὡς μήτε τὰ γενόμενα ἐξ ἀνθρώπων τῷ χρόνῳ ἐξίτηλα γένηται, μήτε ἔργα μεγάλα τε καὶ θωμαστά, τὰ μὲν " Ἕλλησι, τὰ δὲ βαρβάροισι ἀποδεχθέντα, ἀκλεᾶ γένηται, τά τε ἄλλα καὶ δι' ἣν αἰτίην ἐπολέμησαν ἀλλήλοισι.)

3. Immerwahr (1966: 81-88) designates 1.6-94 *The Croesus Logos*, as Croesus may be regarded as the protagonist in this entire passage.

the Persians expand their borders to where they were at the start of the Ionian revolt and the Persian wars (1.46–3.38). By way of introduction to the account of the Persian king Darius' ascent to the throne and his consolidation of the empire, the story of the Lacedaemonians' unsuccessful attack on the island of Samos (3.39-60) is inserted. The last of the Persian defeats recounted by Herodotus, the battle of Mycale, likewise took place near Samos (9.90-108). Thus these two accounts of warfare result in a ring composition,[4] Samos being the ultimate boundary of Persian expansion. In the next section (3.61–4.27), the Persian king Darius consolidates his kingdom, then mounts an unsuccessful campaign against Scythia. Following this, he makes conquests in Thrace and Thessaly by way of preparation for the invasion of Hellas, and thus the battle-lines for the subsequent battles are drawn up. The Ionian revolt (5.28–6.42) becomes the pretext for the Persians' attack on the mainland, and in three 'battle-series' (6.43-140; 7.1–8.125; 8.126–9.108) the Persians' attempts to conquer Hellas are defeated. The epilogue (9.108-122) tells of the Hellenes' home voyage after the last of the battles, that of Mycale, an example of the traditional motif of the return of the warrior in Greek literature.[5]

This account contains an overwhelming number of digressions, the shortest ones being only a few lines in juxtaposition to the main subject,[6] whereas the longest, concerning Egypt (Hdt. 2.2-182), fills the better part of 80 pages in B.A. van Groningen's edition (Groningen 1949: 96-175). As to the agonistic leitmotif which is introduced from the very beginning of Herodotus' work, one would easily feel led astray, were it not for the fact that by means of these digressions Herodotus tells the history of the Greek states, starting approximately two generations prior to the Persian wars. Concurrently, the Persian empire is described and its growth accounted for (Gomme 1954: 87-94), the whole being built around a framework consisting of the account of the Persians' vain attempt to subject the liberty-loving Hellas.

In his thorough description of Herodotus' paratactic style, H.R. Immerwahr differentiates between the external and internal

---

4.   I have borrowed this term from Immerwahr (1966: 54).

5.   See Lesky (1963: 98-103) for this *nostoi*-tradition, of which the Odyssey is doubtless the most outstanding example.

6.   We hear, for instance, about Cambyses' mother Cassandane that '...[she had] died earlier, and Cyrus had mourned deeply and had ordered all his subjects to mourn...' (Hdt. 2.1).

organization of the work. Herodotus has himself explicitly designated the external structure by his use of 'framing sentences', that is 'repeated introductory phrases or sentences at the beginnings of sections of the narrative, and...summary ones at the ends'. This makes what Immerwahr terms a 'ring composition'. Using these 'framing members', it is possible to divide the work into a number of units. With some reservation, Immerwahr terms these units *logoi*,[7] following the practice of M. Pohlenz (1937). S. Trenkner describes these units as *novelle*, that is 'a[n] imaginary story of limited length, intended to entertain and describing an event in which the interest arises from the change in the fortunes of the leading characters or from behaviour characteristic of them; an event concerned with real-life people in a real-life setting'. The *novella* differs from edifying fables and from myths and legends, both of which maintain religious or historic truths, and yet again from fairy-tales which in contradistinction to the realistic *novella* 'feed upon the marvellous' (Trenker 1958: xiii-xiv). The internal structure derives 'in part from the motifs found in popular story telling, early ethnography, Greek wisdom literature, and the moral patterns of tragedy' (Immerwahr 1966: 12). Various aspects of this internal structure will be discussed shortly.

Herodotus and Ionian historíe[8]

Ionian Natural Philosophy
After the versatile Thales of Miletus (first half of the sixth century BCE; von Fritz 1967a: 37-39), Ionian natural philosophy, in the form that has come down to us, may be said to be characterized by attempts at constructing whole philosophical systems. This undertaking was begun by Anaximander of Miletus, a young contemporary of Thales. Anaximander's attempt at establishing the history of the Earth from its genesis to its end, as well as the development of all living creatures, served, according to K. von Fritz, as the framework for the earliest attempts at systematic geography and critical historiography (von Fritz 1967a: 39-47). It is possible that Anaximander was the first

---

7.   This does not reflect Herodotus' own terminology, where *logos* is merely used in the sense of '"story" or "argument", i.e. to indicate contents'; Immerwahr 1966: 12-15.

8.   In the following, it would be possible to include the *Corpus Hippocraticum*; Schmid 1934: 554-55, including n. 10.

Greek to make a map of the world using a Babylonian model, but this is a moot point.[9] Anaximander's framework lent itself to chronological and spatial elaborations, that is historical and geographic studies such as those of Hecataeus (von Fritz 1967a: 48; 1967b: 32-33). In his cosmology, Anaximander talks of an originative substance, *to ápeiron*, 'the Indefinite' (Kirk, Raven and Schofield 1983: 105-122).[10] From this substance, something originated that produced a pair of opposites, fire (heat) and mist (cold). The world as we know it is maintained due to the fact that *to ápeiron* keeps the balance between fire and mist. This control is carried out by virtue of the law of retribution. The only fragment of Anaximander in existence deals with this subject, albeit cryptically: 'And the source of coming-to-be for existing things is that into which destruction, too, happens, according to necessity; for they pay penalty and retribution to each other for their injustice according to the assessment of Time'.[11]

At the turn of the fifth century BCE, Heraclitus of Ephesus advanced another system based upon the idea of *logos*, the subtending coherence of things (Kirk, Raven and Schofield 1983: 181-212). The *logos* may be interpretated as the unifying formula or proportionate method of arrangement of things, what might almost be termed the structural plan of things both individual and in sum. At the same time, *logos* was also an actual constituent of things, in many respects co-extensive with the primary cosmic constituent, fire. In other words, the arrangement of things would not be fully distinguished from the thing arranged, but would be felt to possess the same concreteness and reality as the thing itself. Evident pairs of opposites possess an essential unity. Opposites can a) inhere in, or be simultaneously produced by, a single subject;[12] or b) they may be different stages in a single invariable

9. The main source is Eratosthenes' statement according to Strabo 1.1.11 (text and translation: Jones 1917). Fehling (1989: 144) regards Strabo's account as hypothetical and based on the mention of Aristagoras' bronze map in Herodotus (5.49.1). Fehling's point of view may be compared to the discussion in von Fritz (1967b: 28-29).

10. With regard to the difficulties in interpretating Anaximander's term, see Kirk, Raven and Schofield 1983: 109-111.

11. This is the translation of Kirk, Raven and Schofield 1983: 118 n. 110. How much of this little fragment can be actually traced to Anaximander is uncertain; see the discussion, p. 118.

12. The same thing produces opposite effects upon different classes of animate objects (seawater is drinkable and salutary for fishes but undrinkable and deleterious

process.[13] The unity of things lies beneath the surface and depends upon a balanced reaction between opposites. The total balance in the cosmos can only be maintained if change in one direction eventually leads to change in the other. Fire is the archetypal form of matter. The world order as a whole can be described as a fire of which measures are being extinguished in order to form the two other main world-masses, sea and earth, corresponding measures being re-kindled. Changes between fire, sea and earth balance each other, the *logos* or proportion remaining the same.

Xenophanes of Colophon (second half of the sixth century BCE) concentrated his philosophy for the most part on theological questions. His work may be considered a reaction to the Ionian theories and to the Ionian Homer, whose gods Xenophanes regarded as immoral (Kirk, Raven and Schofield 1983: 163-80). Opposing Homer's anthropomorphic polytheism, Xenophanes maintained that the gods are in no way similar to mortals either in body or in thought. It is not given to any mortal to know the entire truth about the gods, and indeed about any other subject Xenophanes discourses upon, as the gods have not revealed everything to the human race.

The above-mentioned examples clearly show the resemblances between Ionian natural philosophy and Herodotus. The likeness to Xenophanes is obvious, when Herodotus (2.53) states that Homer and Hesiod were the first to teach the Greeks about the gods, and again when he makes the Persians criticize the anthropomorphic gods of the Greeks (1.131; Pohlenz 1937: 104). The idea of dynamic equilibrium dominates in the cosmologies of Anaximander and Heraclitus, Anaximander expressing the principle of eternal retribution and Heraclitus the principle of *logos*. We shall see that the idea of a dynamic equilibrium is also expressed by Herodotus, where the influence of the Attic tragedy may be found as well.

for men); different aspects of the same thing may justify opposite descriptions (the act of writing combines the straight, in the whole line, and the crooked in the shape of each letter). These and the following examples are from Kirk, Raven and Schofield 1983: 188-89.

13. Such pairs of opposites are 'living and dead', 'the waking and the sleeping', 'young and old'.

Historiography

Herodotus refers to many poets, but we find definite references to only one prose-writer, Hecataeus of Miletus (second half of the sixth century BCE to the first half of the fifth).[14] We have traces of both geographic and historical works from his hand. In his description of the earth (the titles *Períodos Ges* and *Periégesis Ges* are extant), he has in two books, later referred to as 'Europe' and 'Asia', enumerated the peoples of the Mediterranean with their geographic localities (von Fritz 1967a: 51-65). Hecataeus designates the various territories by the name of their inhabitants, and he also enumerates the different communities in each territory. Thus K. von Fritz's reading of the extant fragments of Hecataeus. Using Herodotus' criticisms of his predecessors' conceptions of geography,[15] von Fritz arrives at the conclusion that the Earth, according to Hecataeus, was circular and flat being surrounded by the river Oceanus. The surface of the earth comprised a northern semicircle, Europe, and a southern semicircle, Asia and Libya, the semicircles being separated by rivers having their sources in Oceanus. Hecataeus' geographical work should be regarded as of enormous importance, as he dealt systematically with the geographical knowledge that had been accumulated by Ionian travellers during several generations, and he may even have extended and defined this knowledge through his own travels and observations.[16] He incorporated his knowledge in the existing framework by defining the points of the compass and by seeking natural boundaries (the rivers) thus dividing the earth into geometric figures.

14. For Hecataeus, see Pearson 1939: 25-108. Herodotus' references: 2.143; 5.36; 5.125-26; 6.137. Herodotus does also mention Thales of Miletus (1.74-75; 1.170), but it seems unlikely that he actually was a writer, cf. Kirk, Raven and Schofield 1983: 86-88, especially p. 88: 'The evidence does not allow a certain conclusion, but the probability is that Thales did not write a book.' Momigliano's statement that Herodotus regarded Hecataeus as his only 'authoritative predecessor' does seem an exaggeration (Momigliano 1978: 3). Judging by the many poetical references, it would seem that Herodotus regarded the poetical tradition as an authority in line with Hecataeus.

15. Hdt. 4.36 and 4.42 in conjunction with Hecataeus, fragment 18a (Jacoby 1923: 11).

16. This is the opinion of von Fritz (1967a: 63, including n. 69), who employs the word 'zweifellos', although we actually only have one account of these voyages, namely Hdt. 2.142. Regenbogen (1930b: 68) has abstained, perhaps wisely, from commenting upon Hecataeus' voyages.

In classical literature, Hecataeus' historical work is referred to either as *Heroologíai, Historíai* or, more often, as *Geneelogíai* (von Fritz 1967a: 66-76). He uses genealogies to establish the chronology of the distant past which is solely the era of the heroes. He reconstructs this era by means of the legendary tradition, subjected to his own rationalistic criticism. The legends are purged of miraculous events, and he even attempts to trace the original legend down through the various versions. His criterion of truth consists of a *katholou*: the unusual in any given story is discounted, so that only the ordinary or trivial remains. Hecataeus was, as far as we know, the first person to employ systematic principles upon the collected knowledge of the past and the first to evolve rationalistic criteria that could be used for evaluating the plausibility of historical traditions.

In the period between Hecataeus and Herodotus, at least the following historians are important: Acusilaus of Argos, a contemporary of Hecataeus, recounted local legends and tales, without any indication of rationalistic criticism (von Fritz 1967a: 80-82). He concerned himself principally with a systematic account of divine genealogies and of the history of the legendary age. This systematic account resulted in correlations between the various groups of legends, until they at last came together in the Trojan war. Pherecydes of Athens wrote a work in ten volumes, said to date from the early fifth century (von Fritz 1967a: 83-87). Pherecydes' work may be termed a manual of mythology, although he may also be said to have given rise to a geographic systematization, as he evolves etymologies of contemporary names of tribes, countries, and communities from legends. Pherecydes is mainly concerned with the distant past, but occasionally he attempts to bridge the gap between the distant past and the more recent past by means of genealogies. He is the first person known to have attempted this. As far as we know, he was also the first to have compiled all available historical and mythographical material. The prolific Hellanicus of Lesbos (fifth century BCE)[17] attempted, in those of his works that we have several traces of,[18] to organize the legendary material genealogically and chronologically by synchronizing the various genealogies, making them merge in the course of the generation prior to the

17. Von Fritz 1967a: 479-506. The extant fragments are cited under 24 titles, but these titles may refer to a somewhat smaller number of works; Pearson 1939: 155-56.

18. Quoted as *Phoronis, Asopis, Atlantias, Deukalioneia* and *Troika*.

Trojan war. The actual legends are rather overshadowed by these comprehensive genealogies. The treatment of the legends is character- ized by the same type of rationalistic criticism as Hecataeus employed, but Hellanicus, as opposed to Hecataeus, does not even mention the miraculous versions of the legends he recounts. In the geographic– ethnographic works we find the same attempt at collecting the greatest amount of data and compiling it systematically.

Historians prior to Hellanicus mainly reconstructed the distant past (von Fritz 1967a: 93-94). However, starting just before the middle of the fifth century, we have evidence of historians whose subject, being their own geographic locality, also included the more recent past. In a history by Ion of Chios (c. 483 BCE to c. 423), the transition from legend to history is barely perceptible (von Fritz 1967a: 94-95). He is the first author known to have written of the recent past which had not become legendary. Xanthus of Lydia is the only known Hellenic histo- rian from the middle of the fifth century to have used what may be official, quasi-annalistic sources in his account of the history of Lydia until the time of the kingdom's subjection to Croesus (von Fritz 1967a: 97-98). Antiochus of Syracuse, slightly younger than his con- temporary Hellanicus, was probably the first person to write a history of the Greeks in the west and of the Greek western settlements (von Fritz 1967a: 507-518). Like Hellanicus, Antiochus collected and recounted local traditions in a systematic manner. He, however, dealt with the 'historic' past to a greater extent than did Hellanicus, and although he dealt with eponyms, he also tried to trace leaders of the work of colonization who were not eponyms.

Herodotus' predecessors among historiographers may be divided into two groups: those who mainly occupied themselves with the dis- tant past and those who attempted to bridge the gap between the dis- tant and the recent past. Both groups, however, may be regarded as compilers, as their work consisted of the systematic collection and dis- semination of the greatest possible amount of facts and stories con- cerning the past. These stories often underwent rationalistic criticism, although this was not always the case. Herodotus' historical work, as the following will show, may very well be included in this historio- graphic tradition.

Herodotus—Poet and Historian

Herodotus was both a poet and an historian.[19] As an historian, he explored the world he lived in, and as a poet he created his own model of the world. To do so, he continued the traditions known from Ionian prose as well as the Greek epos and the Attic tragedy.

Herodotus and Homer[20]

F.W. Walbank emphasizes that Greek historiography and the Attic tragedy have a common root in the epic tradition. Thucydides wrote about the same 'facts' in his *archaiología* as Homer or Euripides did, and he did not question the historicity of his mythical personages.[21] According to F. Jacoby, the main source for the early history of the Greek people was the so-called Panhellenic *epos* (Jacoby 1949: 202). History and tragedy are 'linked together in their common origin in epic, in their use of comparable and often identical material, and in their moral purpose' (Walbank 1969: 229). As early as the first century CE, we find the term *homerikótatos* applied to Herodotus in Pseudo-Longinus (13.3).[22] M. Pohlenz regards the term as typical even earlier and finds it applicable, as Herodotus' prose continues the Homeric epic style (Pohlenz 1937: 212). Herodotus' philosophy resembles Homer's. Human beings are given a mixture of good and evil,[23] and both authors depict tragedy as being initiated by a god.[24] Herodotus mentions most of the poets known to his contemporaries, Homer being naturally included amongst them,[25] and he

19. Cf. Fehling 1989: 155: 'scholars... believe that the only possible alternative to Herodotus the scientific historian is Herodotus the fraud and they fail to recognise that the real alternative (which does not even rule out the historian) is Herodotus the poet'.

20. Text and translation used for the *Iliad* and the *Odyssey*: Murray: 1924-25; Murray: 1919.

21. Thuc. 1.2-19 (text and translation: Smith 1928); Walbank 1960: 221.

22. Text and translation: Fyfe 1995. The basic facts on this work may be found in Blume 1979: col. 733-34.

23. Hdt. 1.32; 7.46; Homer *Il.* 24.525-30 may be mentioned as examples.

24. Homer: Apollo (*Il.* 1.9). Herodotus: the deity who sent Xerxes a deceptive dream (7.12-18).

25. How and Wells (1928: I, 21 n. 2), mentions the following poets: Hesiod, Olen, Archilochus, Alcaeus, Sappho, Solon, Aristeas, Simonides, Pindar, Phrynichus and Aeschylus, and furthermore the oracular poets Musaeus and Lysistratus

speaks, as a matter of course, of 'all' the poets.[26]

Apart from these resemblances and references, there is a linguistic and stylistic influence attributable to Homer. F. Jacoby warns against exaggerating this influence (Jacoby 1913: col. 491), but W. Aly gives examples of atypical vocabulary, morphology and style in Herodotus' work which he interprets as deliberate Homeric quotations.[27] Laudable as Aly's work is,[28] it is, however, difficult to ascertain Herodotus' use of 'foreign' dialect, as Aly presupposes the existence of a 'pure' Ionian dialect which does not seem ever to have existed.[29] Aly is of the opinion that there was no particular reason for Herodotus to quote Homer as such. The fact that Herodotus expresses himself poetically at given points in the narrative is in accordance with traditional usage (Pohlenz 1937: 212-13). This phenomenon L. Huber designates 'Rezeption' in contradistinction to 'Imitation', that is artistically rephrased quotations from Homer. Certain passages acquire a double meaning, as Herodotus deliberately plays upon his readers' awareness of particular passages of Homer (Huber 1965b: 30-35). A particularly marked occurrence of this is seen in the Croesus-narrative (Hdt. 1.86-91), where the many quotations from Homer and the entire Homeric structure are far more than merely an artistic decoration, in that they create a backcloth for Croesus' and Cyrus' speeches by associating them in the readers' mind with Agamemnon and Achilles.[30] The most

as well as Aesopus, Anacreon and Lasus. To these names, two references to the cyclic poets must be added: *Cypria* (Hdt. 2.117) and *Epigoni* (Hdt. 4.32). Herodotus doubts that these poems are composed by Homer; Chiasson 1982: 156 n. 2. Herodotus refers to Homer in the following passages: 2.23; 2.53; 2.116-17; 4.29; 4.32; 5.67; 7.161.

26. 6.52.1: '...ὁμολογέοντες οὐδενὶ ποιητῇ...'; 2.156.6: '...Αἰσχύλος... μοῦνος δὴ ποιητέων τῶν προγενομένων ἐποίησε γὰρ "Αρτεμιν εἶναι θυγατέρα Δήμητρος...'.

27. Aly 1969: 266-73; the first edition appeared in 1921. Aly's examples can be supplemented with Huber 1965b: 30, including n. 9.

28. See Huber's 'Nachwort': Huber 1969.

29. Huber 1965b: 30. Cf. Rosén (1962: 231-53), which places Herodotus' language among the dialects known from Chios and Halicarnassus.

30. Huber 1965b: 34-36. Huber demonstrates the following Homeric features in the Croesus-story: On the pyre, Croesus cries out Solon's name ἀνενεικάμενόν τε καὶ ἀναστενάξαντα, Hdt. 1.86.3. This application of the word ἀναφέρω is rare, but parallelled in Homer, *Il.* 19.314: ἀνενείκατο. Thereby, the audience is reminded of Achilles' mourning his dead friend and his own infatuation, *Il.* 19.315-37. Listening to Croesus relating Solon's words that no living man should be called

critical events in the account of the Persian wars are likewise related to the Homeric account.[31] In this manner, the Persian wars are shown as no less important than the Trojan war, the Persian-Greek conflict being a repetition of the war between Achaeans and Trojans.

Thus H. Strasburger rightly points out that the historian's task is not intrinsically different to that of the poet. Both hymn the doings of mankind, τὰ κλέα ἀνδρῶν.[32] The historian deals with ἔργα

happy, Cyrus regrets having put Croesus on the pyre, Hdt. 1.86.5-6; here the lis-tener, being familiar with Homer, recalls Achilles' reconciliation with his foes: it is a rule applying to himself as well as these foes that ὡς γὰρ ἐπεκλώσαντο θεοὶ δειλοῖσι βροτοῖσιν/ζώειν ἀχνυμένοις... *Il.* 24.525-26. According to Hdt. 1.87.3, the god of the Hellenes has urged Croesus to the campaign—likewise Agamemnon accuses the gods of having caused his infatuation and thereby his and Achilles' dispute, *Il.* 19.86-87. Croesus' words to Cyrus, ἀλλὰ ταῦτα δαίμονί κου φίλον ἦν οὕτω γενέσθαι (Hdt. 1.87.4) allude to Agamemnon's speech, *Il.* 9.17-28: here, too, everything comes to pass according to divine decree. The god destroys great cities, just as, according to Herodotus, the divine being promised Croesus that his attack on Cyrus would destroy a great kingdom. The gods make man fulfill their will by means of propitious signs and oracles. This is what makes the gods infatuating and deceitful (*Il.* 9.21; Hdt. 1.90.2). The oracle's message to Croesus (Hdt. 1.91.1) τὴν πεπρωμένην μοῖραν ἀδύνατά ἐστι ἀποφυγεῖν καὶ θεῷ, is Homeric: μοῖραν δ' οὔ τινά φημι πεφυγμένον ἔμμεναι ἀνδρῶν (*Il.* 6.488); compare *Il.* 16.441 and *Il.* 22.179.

31. Huber 1965b: 36-39. Note the following examples: According to Hdt. 5.97, the Athenian dispatch of 20 ships in support of Ionia is the beginning of the Persian wars. In this way the Athenians are associated with Paris, the instigator of the Trojan war, *Il.* 5.62-64. In Xerxes' council (Hdt. 7.5) young Xerxes, having succeeded his famous father, is on the point of making a name for himself (Hdt. 7.5.2), thus allud-ing to Telemachus in a similar situation (*Od.* 1.95; 3.78). Mardonius' putting for-ward as an argument for war that Xerxes' foes should learn to abstain from attacking him, associates the Persian king with the infatuated and thoughtless Agamemnon (*Il.* 1.185-86) and Hector (*Il.* 8.515). Artabanus, the warner, is akin to Nestor (*Il.* 1.250-74; 9.96-113) and Polydamas (*Il.* 12.211-12; 18.254-83), the latter being accused of cowardice, just as Artabanus himself (Hdt. 7.11). Agamemnon's dream (*Il.* 2) is the obvious parallel for Xerxes' deceitful dreams (7.12-19), the wording and the connexion between the king and the sceptical adviser (cf. Nestor, *Il.* 2.77-83) being Homeric. Finally, the crossing of the Hellespont, the all-important border in Herodotus' opus, is accentuated in a way comparable to Hector's breaking through the Achaeans' rampart (Hdt. 7.37; *Il.* 12.195-471). Demonstrating Xerxes' blindness to the educated audience, these Homeric associations prefigure an unhappy outcome for the campaign against Hellas.

32. Strasburger 1972: 11-17. The following examples may be noted: *Il.* 9.189; *Od.* 8.73; Hes. *Theog.* 100 (text and translation: Evelyn-White 1914). Herodotus

ἀξιόλογα (Thuc. 1.1; Hdt. 1.177), deeds worthy to be remembered, τὰ ἔργα μέγιστα in particular, that is the most important events (Thuc. 1.23.1), as the subject of a historical account should outshine the subjects of previous authors. According to Herodotus (7.20), none of history's earlier wars, not even the Trojan war, can outdo Xerxes' campaign, whereas Thucydides (1.1-23) prolixly informs us that there have only been three *erga megista* prior to his own time: the Peloponnesian war, the Persian war and the Trojan war. Of these the Persian war outdid the Trojan war, and the Peleponnesian war the Persian war with regard to extent and use of power. To the Greek historians, these three wars were all definitely historical.[33]

To a certain extent, the historian and the poet can be said to have a method of presentation in common.[34] Being stringently composed literary works, the *Iliad* and the *Odyssey* rather than Hecataeus' geographical and ethnographical lists influenced Herodotus' form (Lateiner 1989: 214). As in the works of Herodotus, the *aetiological account* dominates in the *Iliad*. The entire sequence of events is set going by the aetiological catchword 'wrath', that is the wrath of Achilles (1.1). The poet develops a chain of events, proceeding with three additional links: the strife of the kings, the wrath of Apollo and the plague, Agamemnon's offence against Apollo's priest Chryses, recounted in retrograde in *Il.* 1.1-12. Thereupon, the first book elaborates upon these four aetiological stages, whereby Achilles' conversation with

writes in order that ἔργα μεγάλα τε καὶ θωμαστά should not be forgotten (proem), that is become ἀκλεᾶ. This does not always refer to actions, but to monuments as well (Raubitschek 1939), that is human achievements in general. According to Gould (1989: 48-49), Herodotus expresses his debt to the epic narrative tradition as well as his own continuation of the same tradition. 'Herodotus supplied for the recent past what epic had done for the distant past: commemoration of outstanding human achievements' (Lateiner 1989: 51). Nagy (1987: 181) draws attention to the fact that in Pindar, λόγιοι and ἀοιδαί have parallel functions, both maintaining a man's κλέος, and that the actions of both may be termed ἀπόδειξις, 'public display'. Thus Nagy (p. 175) argues for the existence of a prose tradition, in which Herodotus is an outstanding example parallel to the poetic tradition.

33. As to the ancient Greeks' own view of their early history, see also Raubitschek 1989 and Pohlenz 1937: 103-104: 'Die "sogenannte" Heroengeschichte ist der ältere Teil der Menschheitsgeschichte'. Müller (1984: 338) likewise points to the era of the heroes as the oldest phase of Greek history.

34. Cf. Strasburger 1972: 38: 'in Wirklichkeit ist die Geschichtsschreibung es selbst, die in der Nachfolge Homers die Funktion des geschichtlichen Epos übernimmt'.

Thetis supplies the first and hitherto missing link in the chain of events: the capture of Chryses' daughter, the beginning of the various misfortunes (12-412). Strasburger rightly calls this 'a most clear and genuine historical exposition' (Strasburger 1972: 24-25). In his account of all the relevant factions, points of view, nations, and classes, Homer demonstrates a marked leaning towards *objectivity*,[35] a trait that is likewise found in Herodotus.[36] *Chronology* is also important here. The *Iliad* takes place within a timespan of approximately 50 days. Digressions, consisting of the participants' accounts of events that took place prior to the start of the *Iliad*, remain side issues and are not permitted to disturb the main account's chronological progression. The chronological structure of the *Odyssey* is far more complicated, but no less stringent, when the accounts of Odysseus' ten-year-long peregrinations are subordinated to the account of Telemachus' search for his father. In the course of this complicated progression, the poet is even able to mention events from the latter part of the Trojan war, events which are not related in the *Iliad*, and he likewise includes accounts of various Greek heroes' future fortune. In the same way, by means of its many references to the entire course of events, the *Iliad* conveys the impression that its story is part of a greater context, that of the whole Trojan war from its outbreak, caused by the abduction of Helen, to the fall of Troy (Strasburger 1972: 25-27).

Herodotus can be regarded as a poet in the same way that Homer can be deemed an historian. Strasburger points to the use of *speeches* and the *technique of mimesis* as the two most important Homeric '*literarisch-formalen* Gestaltungsmitteln' in the historiographic context (Strasburger 1972: 38-40). The narrative is dramatized by the characters' speeches and dialogues. In this way, Herodotus achieves

35. Strasburger 1972: 25; likewise Gomme 1954: 42-47.
36. As to Herodotus' objectivity, see also Gomme 1954: 111-15. According to Lateiner (1989: 103), Herodotus' work expresses an unbiased endeavour to understand 'the dynamis of politics' unlike official, biased accounts of the past. Another example of Herodotus' objectivity is the fact that his characters on all sides are endowed with good as well as bad qualities (Lateiner 1989: 157). Note W. Booth's description of objectivity as a rhetoric device in fiction in Booth 1961: 67-86. Booth (p. 69) has an interesting quotation from the great Russian author A. Chekhov: 'The artist should be, not the judge of his characters and their conversations, but only an unbiassed witness' (Chekhov 1965: 58). This is remarkably similar to Herodotus' statement about his own writing in 7.152.3; see n. 55.

the same as Homer does with his speeches: a spiritual perception of the historic situation, often of universal validity. The Greeks explain their reasons for fighting, to name an example, by saying that they are fighting for their liberty. These explanations are offered in the form of speeches at particularly crucial moments. The differences between Greeks and barbarians are likewise emphasized, particularly in the last three books, where dialogues between Greek and Persian occur frequently. In the Persian empire itself, the Greeks allegedly held long conversations with satraps and even with the sovereign himself, during which oriental despotism was compared to Greek liberty.[37] Historiography has also borrowed the mimetic technique from poetry, the aim being a totally realistic imitation of life and a dramatic presentation of all the emotions present in any given situation, so that the reader, like the spectator in the theatre, is included in and experiences the tragic reality. To quote Lateiner (1989: 189): 'Herodotus, like Homer, looks at action from the actor's as well as the observer's point of view. His poetic, rhetorical, and historical skill produces a "dramatic" narrative.'

Both Herodotus and Homer deal with historic themes. Based on the historical facts about the Trojan war, facts that the poet and his readers were in agreement upon, Homer created his narrative by making use of the elements that were suited to his purpose. What he and his readers knew as history became the framework for a narrative about what *could have happened* (Gomme 1954: 2 and 5-12; Skafte Jensen 1992: 25). Herodotus too is, however, the poet of his plot (Gomme 1954: 76). Books 7–9 tell of the war between the Greeks and the barbarians, and the detailed account of the Persian empire in books 1–5 shows how that empire arose, and who this Asian power was. Herodotus introduces his 'philosophy of history' with king Croesus of Lydia. Fortune and wealth are unreliable entities, but power is even more dangerous on account of its tendency towards *hubris*. This is explained by the theory of divine *phthonos*, 'jealousy'. Gods and humans both belong to the natural order of things, but each group have their own sphere. Human beings should not attempt to step out of their sphere. On this interpretation, history is transformed from a local, temporal sphere into a classical description of the fate that attends a person or a people, guilty of the pride that leads to a fall.[38]

37. Bockisch 1984. Hdt. 7.135 furnishes an example.
38. Compare Achilles' speech to Priam in Homer, *Il*. 24.518-51.

With Cyrus' conquest of Croesus' kingdom of Lydia, we are inducted
into the Persian camp, and by way of many diversions we are brought
to the time of the Ionian revolt. From thence, the history of Hellas and
Asia merges into one story, that of the war. At times Herodotus gar-
nishes his account with philosophical observations. These are particularly in evidence during Xerxes' discussions with Artabanus (7.8-18)
and Demaratus (7.101-105). By writing in a poetic vein, Herodotus
creates an *eusýnopton*, an organic whole consisting of the history of
the Persian empire, and in addition a great part of the history of the
Greek states. Thus Herodotus' historical work makes him a poet.[39]

As Herodotus mentions both legendary (for example, the stories of
abduction of women (1.1-5)) and historical subjects (for example,
Xerxes' invasion of Hellas), it is worthwhile considering whether he
himself made any distinction between legend and history. There is no
linguistic evidence to suggest that he did make any such distinction.
Herodotus uses the words *logos/legein* of his stories without differen-
tiating between legend and history.[40] There are only two instances of
the use of the word *mythos*, and they are probably employed polemi-
cally against Hecataeus.[41] H. Strasburger is nevertheless of the opinion
that people had begun to interest themselves in the 'historic era' as
opposed to the 'mythic era' as early as the seventh century BCE
(Strasburger 1972: 37, including n. 121). According to Strasburger,
we can discover a distinction between *spatium mythicum* and *spatium
historicum* in the poems of both Homer and Hesiod, as well as in the
later historiographers' works, where the gods' direct intervention in
affairs on earth is confined to the heroic age, in other words the time
before the heroes' return from Troy (Strasburger 1972: 21-24). A.E.
Raubitschek, on the other hand, maintains that Herodotus interpolated
his account of the Persian wars into an existing historical tradition

39. Gomme 1954: 78-94. Erbse (1961: 257) also emphasizes the influence of
Homer on Herodotus' digressions. For Herodotus as a poet, see also Fehling 1989:
175-215.
40. Nickau 1990: 83; Immerwahr 1966: 14, including n. 34.
41. Nickau 1990: 84-87. The idea critized in 2.23 that the source of the Nile is to
be found in Oceanus corresponds to a Hecataeus fragment (no. 302; Jacoby 1923:
39-40). A similar interpretation may be applied to 2.45.1: Hecataeus belongs
amongst those Greeks who had no notion at all of the state of things in Egypt. By his
use of the word μῦθος, Herodotus plays on Hecataeus' mode of expression, according to Nickau, cf. fragment 1 (Jacoby 1923: 7-8): Ἑκαταῖος μιλήσιος ὧδε
μυθεῖται...

(Raubitschek 1989). Using Thucydides (1.1-23) and Herodotus himself (9.26.2-5) he concludes that it contained a rational account of the epic tradition. Herodotus himself associated his own era with that of the heroes: the genealogy of King Cleomenes of Sparta reached as far back as the heroic era (Hdt. 6.51-55), and 20 of the Spartan leader Leonidas' ancestors were descended from Heracles (7.204), who, we are told, lived nine hundred years before Herodotus (2.145.4). Herodotus presents the Persian wars as the greatest event of all time. In 7.20 he compares Xerxes' invasion with four earlier martial expeditions, two he has given an account of himself, Darius' punitive campaign against the Scythians (4.83-144) and the Scythians' earlier conquest of Asia (1.103-106), and thereupon he mentions the Trojan war and a raid prior to it. All four campaigns are regarded as historical.

Nevertheless, it is frequently held, on the basis of Hdt. 1.1-5, that Herodotus distinguished qualitatively between the time prior to and the time after the advent of the Mermnadian dynasty in Lydia early in the seventh century BCE. Particularly the transition from the stories of the abduction of women to the Croesus-prologue in Hdt 1.5.3[42] is held to express Herodotus' conception of the difference between *spatium myticum* and *spatium historicum*.[43] However, Herodotus makes a critical evaluation of the Trojan war elsewhere (2.113-20) although it must be deemed an event which belonged to *spatium myticum* (Nickau 1990: 91-92). According to K. Nickau, Herodotus could have had at least two other reasons for refraining from choosing between the various stories of the abduction of women. Firstly, these legends gloss over the crux of the matter, the fact that Greek liberty was violated (1.6.2-3). Secondly, they presuppose that Hellenes and barbarians were two opposing units from the start of time (1.4.4). Against this, Herodotus' works have the opposition evolved during the course of history (Nickau 1990: 91-96). Another argument adduced in favour of Herodotus' alleged distinction is found in Hdt. 3.122.2 where Poly-crates is described in relation to King Minos as the first Hellene in the

42. 'About these matters, I will not say whether this has happened in this way or in another way, but having pointed out the man whom I myself know to have been the first to commence unjust acts against the Greeks, I will proceed further into the story...'

43. Pohlenz 1937: 7; Immerwahr 1966: 18; Bockisch 1984: 491; Lateiner 1989: 101.

so-called Human Age to have had mastery of the sea.[44] But here it is of importance that Herodotus treats the matter with slight ambivalence marked by the use of the word λεγομένη, 'so-called' (Pohlenz 1937: 104, n. 1). The historicity of Minos is evident in the history of the Carians, 1.171. Herodotus' basic principle of recounting what has been told is as much in evidence in recent history (for example, 7.152.3) as in the 'legends' (for example, 2.123.1). Methodologically speaking, the distant and the recent past are in no way incommensurable (Nickau 1990: 96-97).

These deliberations have to do with the question of Herodotus' self-knowledge. This is naturally of importance when we consider to how large an extent we can understand Herodotus to be either a poet or an historian. An historian must respect the reality of the affairs he recounts, whereas the poet may decide for himself what actually constitutes reality. 'History is recuperation; poetry is construction' (Rosenmeyer 1982: 245-46; cf. Thompson 1992: 376). However, if one distinguishes, as T.G. Rosenmeyer does, between a poet and an historian in this way, the difficulty arises that a rhapsodist, too, was bound by what he himself and his audience held to be 'reality'. The rhapsodist's knowledge was the truth, and therefore history, due to the fact that the Muses themselves had in their omniscience given the poet his knowledge.[45] A possible difference between a poet's self-knowledge and that of Herodotus could be deemed to be that Herodotus points to himself as an historian through his use of 'asides'. An instance of these asides may be found in 1.95, where he takes it upon himself to relate the only one of four versions of Cyrus' history that

44. '...τῆς δὲ ἀνθρωπηίης λεγομένης γενεῆς Πολυκράτης πρῶτος...; LSJ 342 s.v. γενεά 2: '...γ. ἀνθρωπηΐη the historical, opp. to the mythical, *age*...'; Lateiner 1989: 253 n. 38: 'Herodotus puts Minos in the Heroic, not the historical epoch'. This is presumably also what Mandell and Freedman (1993: 163) are referring to in the erroneous statement that 'Herodotus explicitly distinguishes between Minos and Polycrates in the midst of his Egyptian λόγος and he concomitantly differentiates between the prehistoric and the historic eras.' Huber (1965a: 1) finds his argument in Herodotus' proem where it is said that Herodotus will deal with deeds of men, τὰ γενόμενα ἐξ ἀνθρώπων.

45. Strasburger 1972: 20-24; cf. *Il.* 2.484-86; 2.761; 14.508; *Od.* 1.1-10; 8.487-91; Hes. *Theog.* 27-28; 36-52. Lateiner (1989: 55) emphasizes 'the essential and unavoidable fact that the events that he wished to preserve had occurred in the past', but modern distinctions between 'real' and 'fictive' events should not influence our understanding of Herodotus' or the rhapsodist's self-knowledge.

hasn't been 'improved upon'. Another is found in 2.99 and 2.123, where he puts forth his autoptic principle. As these remarks are very largely responsible for the view of Herodotus as a 'modern' historian and ethnographer,[46] it is important to elucidate whether Herodotus actually followed his own principles. Did Herodotus compile information in a manner radically different to that used by Homer? If Herodotus' method did differ from Homer's, we may say that even if their manner of presentation resembled each others, there would still be a significant difference between the poet and Herodotus.

The Question of Herodotus' Sources
Herodotus' many source-citations give some indication of his efforts as a collector of data. The citations give rise to at least two general problems. Firstly, they attribute narratives that are obviously the product of Greek (Ionian) thought to non-Greeks. Secondly, Herodotus claims to have heard in widely separated places stories that neatly dovetail together (Fehling 1989: 1). Traditionally, it has been maintained that Herodotus unconsciously gave wrong sources (Fehling 1989: 1-9), but D. Fehling (1971; 1989) has put forward the argument that Herodotus' 'citations' are literary devices, in other words deliberate fictions, and that their use follows simple literary rules.[47] Even when Herodotus claims to base his statements on personal inspection, Fehling holds it to be fictitious in the majority of cases (Fehling 1989: 168-70). '[T]here is possibly not a single passage, certainly none concerned with anywhere outside Greece, that we can treat as evidence that Herodotus went to a particular place' (Fehling 1989: 240-41). It is interesting that Fehling himself finds this literary device unremarkable and therefore places Herodotus in a literary tradition that, starting with the cultures of the ancient Near East, covers the Greek epos, the earliest Greek prose, Herodotus himself, the works of his Greek

46. Lateiner 1989: 218: 'In some respects, Herodotus conforms to modern notions'.

47. Fehling 1989: 9-11. Fehling's approach is not entirely new but highly inspired by Sayce (1883: xiii-xxxiii) and, especially, Panofsky (1885). Unfortunately, Jacoby 1913, perhaps the most influential work on Herodotus ever written, flatly snubbed Panofsky (col. 403): 'Der Versuch von Panofsky... alle Zitate (mit wenigen willkürlichen Ausnahmen) auf Schriftquellen zurückzuführen, verdient die ihm immer noch zu teil werdende Erwähnung eigentlich nicht.' In consequence, only a very few scholars have taken Panofsky seriously.

and Latin successors, and the Middle Ages.[48]

According to Fehling, Herodotus' source-citations are always tailored to the contents reported. As a general rule, he cites the source which would be the most obvious one, provided that the events in question actually had occurred in accordance with his narrative. Such source-citations may refer to inhabitants of the geographical areas occuring in the various tales. The main problem in this practice is that many of the stories containing source-citations are legendary and therefore factually 'wrong'. A narrative of this kind did not necessarily originate from the geographic locality where it was said to have taken place. The Babylonians probably never heard of the Tower of Babel or the Egyptians of Joseph and Potiphar's wife. An example of this technique can be found in Hdt. 8.38-39 where the author apparently has heard that the Persians who succeeded in fleeing from the battle at Delphi had said that two giants came to the assistance of the Delphians. The inhabitants of Delphi said that the giants were the local heroes Phylacus and Autonous. Herodotus' account presumes the miraculous event to have taken place and to have been observed and related by two independent witnesses, which, naturally, is nonsense. There can be only one primary source, but the fact that Herodotus refers to two makes sense within the narrative's own universe, where the Persians obviously could not have known the identity of the giants. The contents of the story have been apportioned to two complementary sources.[49]

> Fehling's reading of this story has caused some debate, but as far as I can see, his interpretation of the text is in no way weakened by the fact that Herodotus inserted the words ὡς ἐγὼ πυνθάνομαι, 'as I have heard' (8.38), as a comment to the barbarians' statement.[50] D. Lateiner has pointed out that Herodotus' referring to his own work as ἱστορίης ἀπόδεξις, 'a presentation of research' (proem), means his 'own creative

48. Fehling (1989: 154-74) gives a long list of literary parallels to Herodotus' use of source fiction.

49. Fehling 1989: 12-16. Other examples of this technique are the story of the death of Hamilcar, 7.166-67 (pp. 16-17), the abduction of women, 1.1-5 (pp. 50-57), the history of Egypt according to the priests, 2.99-142 (pp. 71-77), and the story of Aristeas who apparently died at Proconnessus at the same time as he was seen on his way to Cyzicus; seven years after his death he turned up again at Proconnessus, 4.14 (p. 21).

50. The opposite being maintained by Cobet 1974: 739-40; Marincola 1987: 28-29.

shaping of... what he has discovered' (Lateiner 1989: 50). Herodotus was fully aware of the fact that he had not recounted the events themselves but had presented a synoptic summary of them (Lateiner 1989: 7-10). Herodotus' πυνθάνομαι can be taken as a step between the events recounted, which here is the alleged fact that the barbarians had told the story, and the author's account of this, ἡ ἀπόδεξις.

According to this presentation, the barbarians had seemingly told 'someone' of the event, this person subsequently telling Herodotus the story stating his source to be the barbarians. The Delphians then added their information concerning the identity of the heroes. J. Cobet and J. Marincola point to Herodotus' use of mimetics (Cobet 1974: 739-40; Marincola 1987: 28-29). Herodotus told the story from both the Persian and the Delphic point of view, as if he had been present on both sides at the same time: 'the barbarians said that...'; 'The Delphians said...'. By πυνθάνομαι Herodotus merely shows that the story is one he had been told, without indicating that it was told him in the very words that he uses in retelling it. Thus Cobet and Marincola hold that Herodotus is not indicating two sources. One consequence of this 'single source hypothesis' is that Herodotus' πυνθάνομαι is an implied reference to the Delphian source in 39.1.[51] If we are to accept this interpretation, however, it is actually the Delphians who made use of mimetics, so that the method of presentation we otherwise attribute to Herodotus suddenly becomes that of his informants. The idea of Herodotus' mimetic presentation actually supports Fehling's theory of fictitious sources, as the mimetics belong to the source, viz. that the story about the heroes came from the Persians, fleeing from them, and that the Delphians added information that only they possessed to the account. Either Herodotus' presentation is due to his informants, it being they, not Herodotus, who employed mimetics, or else the informants themselves are a product of Herodotus' mimetics.

Apart from such complementary source-citations, Herodotus also dovetails sources. For example, in 2.104-105 Herodotus makes the Colchians and the Egyptians the same people, as both have negroid features, speak the same language, and live in the same manner.[52] The

---

51. Cf. Marincola 1987: 28: 'The usual explanation, that the story comes from the Delphians, can be maintained.'

52. Fehling 1989: 17. It does not help to suggest with Cobet (1974: 739) that μελάγχροές εἰσι καὶ οὐλότριχες (2.104.2) merely means that the Egyptians and the Colchians were darker hued and had less straight hair than the average Greek. 'To describe the average Egyptian in these terms is peculiar, to say the least, and for Herodotus' Colchians the description could not be more wide of the mark. If there ever was a tribe of that name in the Caucasus the only way it could have deviated from the normal Mediterranean type would have been in the direction of northern influences' (Fehling 1989: 18).

one source for these absurd facts is said to be Herodotus himself, who having noticed the negroid features of these two peoples makes enquiries among both and finds his assumption of a kinship confirmed. Later, this assumption is strengthened by the fact that four peoples state that they learned the practice of circumcision from the Egyptians and the Colchians. The only peoples practising circumcision from time immemorial are the Ethiopians, the Egyptians, and the Colchians. Apart from Herodotus himself, no less than six independent sources give a consistent, but impossible picture of the relationship between the Egyptians and the Colchians.[53]

Herodotus frequently attributes Ionian geological hypotheses, pseudohistory, or mythography to the persons in his narratives or epichoric sources. The myths of the abduction of women are a good example of this latter usage (1.1-5). The starting point is the abduction of Helen, from which the remaining narratives spring as a re-working of Homeric material. Herodotus' source-citations to these very Greek stories are absurd. He obviously considered very carefully which character in the story knew what, and fitted his sources to the narrative whose content is determined by the differences between Persians and Greeks.[54]

The principle of citing the obvious source is basic to Herodotus' source-citations, though the link between citation and story is never stated explicitly. The few exceptions, found by Fehling, can all be explained as following one of two other rules: regard for credibility and regard for party bias (Fehling 1989: 88-108). Thus every single source-citation follows three simple rules: 1) As a basic rule, Herodotus always cites the obvious source, in other words, the source which on the basis of the contents of the piece of information concerned would be its most probable and obvious witness. 2) One exception to this rule is caused by Herodotus' desire to protect his own credibility. The more unlikely a narrative is, the more Herodotus distances himself from it by quoting other, alternative sources and

---

53. Fehling 1989: 17-20. Another instance of dovetailed sources being fiction is the founding of Oracles in Libya and Dodona from Egyptian Thebes, Hdt. 2.54-57; Fehling 1989: 65-70. Dovetailed sources may be provided with fictitious 'Beweissstücke' ('Proofs') such as the bones said to be those of winged, Arabian serpents, 2.75. Fehling 1989: 21-30 and 77-86.

54. Fehling 1989: 49-70, including a number of examples of Greek mythical material attributed to non-Hellenic sources.

indirect information. A narrative told with Herodotus himself as its primary source never goes beyond the bounds of credibility. It is on account of this same consideration that the author states his important λέγω τὰ λεγόμενα, 'I tell what is told'.[55] 3) The other exception to the basic rule is that no information is imputed to a given source if the information concerned appears disadvantageous in relation to the part that the people in question occupy in the narrative.[56] That two parties each tell their own different, self-favouring version of a story is a phenomenon that belongs to this type of source-citation.[57]

With regard to approximately 60 of Herodotus' source-citations, even the hypercritical Fehling is forced to admit a possible concurrence with 'what really happened'. This does not seem, however, to have influenced Herodotus' selection of sources, as it is possible to explain them all on literary grounds found in the respective narratives. Nor are the authors quoted by Herodotus sources in the strict sense of the word but well-known utterances, stored in Herodotus' memory and corrected or stated to be authoritative (Fehling 1989: 143-54). Herodotus filled out the few facts known to him and supplemented them from his memory's store of details, thus making a flexible, lively presentation, into which he included everything he knew. This was not a method of researching the Persian war, but a way of recounting it in the same way as Homer had recounted the Trojan War. Herodotus intended to write something new, and the complex form of his opus was fully intentional. All the same, the gradual growth of the opus in Herodotus' head gave room for experiments and modifications resulting in accidentally linked connections

---

55. Hdt. 7.152.3: ἐγὼ δὲ ὀφείλω λέγειν τὰ λεγόμενα, πείθεσθαί γε μὲν οὐ παντάπασιν ὀφείλω 'for myself, though it be my business to set down that which is told me, to believe it is none at all of my business' (Godley's translation: Godley 1922: III, 463).

56. Examples of this are Hdt. 2.2 and 2.45, where the Greeks are chosen as a substitute source, as it would not be seemly having the Egyptians tell such stories about themselves. As to Hdt. 3.14, the Egyptians are, on the other hand, the appropriate source. In Hdt. 3.30 and 32, the Persians tell nothing that is disadvantageous to themselves and the Egyptians and the Greeks are cited instead.

57. Examples are Hdt. 1.70; 3.1-2; 3.47. In Hdt. 5.85-87, the Athenian and the Aeginetan/Argivian versions tally to a large extent, any differences being due to the regard for party bias. It is naturally a fiction to state that memories from three different geographic localities fit together so well. Source-citations with regard for party bias may also be found in legendary accounts: 1.171; 4.45; 6.54.

between the various parts, while other parts were dropped from the narrative during its final draft, for example the promised history of Assyria (Hdt. 1.184; Fehling 1989: 247-52).

The reception accorded to Fehling's hypotheses by the learned world has, to put it mildly, been cold. D. Lateiner is a good representative of this, when he calls Fehling's points of view 'extreme' as well as 'eccentric' (Lateiner 1989: 230 n. 9; 260 n. 47), although he does admit that Fehling's approach to Herodotus is 'severe but not baseless' (Lateiner 1989: 247 n. 18). This ambivalence is repeated when Fehling's book is designated both 'a corrective to Herodotolatric excesses' and 'a perverse contribution to historiography' (Lateiner 1989: 259-60 n. 47). Fehling's idea, however, that Herodotus in no way based his narratives on personal inspection seems to be borne out by O.K. Armayor, who has shown both the archaeological impossibility of Herodotus' avowed inspection and that his descriptions of the world outside Hellas depend upon Greek, particularly Ionian, tradition. Armayor's works cover Herodotus' descriptions of Egypt, the Black Sea, and the areas surrounding it, Thrace, Colchis, the interior of Asia minor and the Levant (Armayor 1978a, 1978b, 1978c, 1980, 1985). R. Rollinger (1993), too, expresses similar scepticism regarding Herodotus' presumed journeys to Babylon. One of Armayor's examples is Herodotus' journeys in Egypt. Amongst other objections, Armayor wonders how Herodotus came into contact with the Egyptian priests (2.143), this being about as probable as a modern tourist's being shown round Notre Dame by the archbishop of Paris, to quote Armayor's fitting comparison.[58] Even if Herodotus did meet the Egyptian priests, it surprizes Armayor that these should have told Herodotus Greek stories concerning the Phrygians as the oldest people on earth (2.2-3), Proteus, Menelaus, Helen, Paris, and the Trojan war (2.112-15), the Pythagorean teaching on metempsychosis (2.123), and the Greek oracles of Leto in Buto in Egypt (2.83, 2.133, 2.152, and 2.155-56). In spite of A.B. Lloyd's references to Greek ideas 'implanted in Egypt by Greeks', Greek material being intermingled with the priests' own folklore, Herodotus' leading questions, and Manetho, writing approximately a hundred and fifty years after Herodotus (Lloyd 1975: I, 89-113), 'we have no Egyptian evidence of

58. Armayor 1978c: 63-65. Earlier, How and Wells (1928: I, 413-14) denied that Herodotus spoke to the Egyptian priests, whereas Lloyd (1975: I, 94) has no doubt that Herodotus did meet them.

Greek ideas implanted in pre-Ptolemaic Egypt, nor a single pre-Ptolemaic Egyptian document to prove that Egyptian literary tradition was ever affected by the Greeks before the Macedonian conquest' (Armayor 1978c: 65). Lloyd, too, is forced to admit that 'from the historical point of view some things in Herodotus' account are profoundly disturbing' (Lloyd 1975: I, 94). Herodotus' sacerdotal traditions are not Egyptian stories about Greeks, but Greek stories about Egyptians. Though we cannot entirely rule out the possibility of Herodotus having been in Egypt, it must be said that his narrative bears little witness to it.[59]

Armayor's demonstration of the impossible and at times the absurd in Herodotus' so-called eye-witness accounts has been countered in rather spirited terms by W.K. Pritchett (1982), who maintains Herodotus' reliability whenever it can be verified archaeologically. Thus it is possible for Pritchett to point to a weakness in both Fehling and Armayor, namely that their discounting of Herodotus is more often based on canons of probability than upon archaeological evidence.[60]

Fehling's greatest service consists of his having proved the literary rules that Herodotus' source-citations follow without exception.[61] Fehling's thesis that Herodotus did not state his own conceptions (Cobet 1974: 742) but was fully aware of his fictitious use of sources is somewhat more dubious. As an alternative to Fehling's idea of

59. Armayor (1978c: 69-70) gives many instances of poorly founded descriptions of conditions in Egypt.

60. Pritchett 1982: 285. Pritchett makes an interesting comparison between Herodotus' putative journeys and Sir Walter Raleigh's journeying in South America in 1595 (pp. 281-85). Raleigh, too, tells tall stories based on personal inspection and epichoric sources. 'Herodotos and Raleigh grounded their belief in the existence of strange peoples and customs upon the testimony of the *epikhorioi*, as told through interpreters. Statements about what they saw with their own eyes have proved to be reliable. But both had seen so many marvels, as measured by the standards of their own civilizations, that they were prepared to accept others on hearsay. The proper approach to Books I–V.27 of Herodotos is to study them in the context of the works of other voyagers to unexplored lands.' My own suggestion would be to compare Herodotus with quite another type of traveller, such as, for instance, Freiherr von Münchhausen! More recently, Pritchett has devoted an entire volume to the refutation of Fehling and other presumptuous sceptics (Pritchett 1993). Unfortunately, the book was drawn to my attention too late to be mentioned comprehensively here. But see the review by R. Thomas (Thomas 1996).

61. Thus Marincola 1987: 27-32, including n. 3.

source-fictions, J. Cobet epitomizes the prevalent scholarship on Herodotus in our century[62] that explains Herodotus' objectively seen incorrect information by suggesting that he had spoken, not with natives, but with expatriate Greeks, or it may be that Herodotus had placed leading questions, thus causing his informants to agree with his pre-formed opinions on the state of things. Maybe Herodotus merely, naively, took old wives' tales at their face-value; it is also possible to regard the errors as being due to Herodotus' interpreters' transforming what was actually said into Greek conceptions. Finally, it is suggested that the information collected by Herodotus has been altered in his re-telling of it (Cobet 1974: 741-43). By virtue of such explanations used to rescue Herodotus from accusations of having 'lied',[63] the author is transformed into a naive and credulous traveller who unfortunately misunderstood everything he was told or saw and actually only worked on images fostered by his own imagination.[64] Against these views, Fehling depicts an intelligent narrator who used

62. Jacoby (1913) serves as a dividing line between the nineteenth century's more critical approach to Herodotus and our own century's less sceptical view of his reliability, though Jacoby does acknowledge the fact that 'Herodot ist reich an Motiven, deren historischen Wert wir vielfach bezweifeln, deren kompositionelle Bedeutung aber den denkenden Künstler beweist' (col. 487). For the history of scholarship before Jacoby, Myres (1953: 20-28) may be consulted. Among the many representatives of the 'Jacobian' school that still dominates Herodotean scholarship, the following may be mentioned: Pohlenz 1937; Momigliano 1958; Burn 1962; Hignett 1963; von Fritz 1967; Lloyd 1975–1988; Evans 1982; Waters 1985; Gould 1989; Lateiner 1989 and Evans 1991.

63. See the summary of scholarship in Fehling 1989: 1-9. Grene (1961) demonstrates that Herodotus' dramatic narration was inspired by contemporary theatre, but nevertheless he maintains that Herodotus is a reliable historian, whose trustworthiness is not shaken by the fact that he had been misinformed by his sources (p. 477). Lloyd's slightly huffy comments upon Heidel's opinion that Herodotus could not possibly have quoted Egyptian priests (W.A. Heidel: 'Hecataeus and the Egyptian Priests in Herodotus, Book II' [American Academy of Arts and Sciences: Memoirs, 18.2; Boston, 1935], *non vidi*), is characteristic: 'In other words, Herodotus is a barefaced liar!' (Lloyd 1975: I, 94 n. 26).

64. Cf. Evans (1991: 89-146), who, using modern anthropological method combined with the traditional picture of Herodotus, attempts to form an opinion on the oral tradition that may have been available to Herodotus as well as an opinion of Herodotus as an inquirer. Evans believes that Herodotus usually confronted informants with his own Greek notions, which he was able to make them confirm. On other occasions he misunderstood the answers he received, transforming them so that they accorded with Greek tradition.

extremely sophisticated means in writing a complex, playful, and 'deceptive' literary masterpiece.

To sum up: The picture of himself as a critical collector of data that Herodotus presents to his implied reader is a fiction. Fehling compares Herodotus' source-fictions with the epic invocation of the Muse that renders the singer an authority and at the same time fends off any questions about his sources of information (Fehling 1989: 157). Herodotus wrote the 'truth', a truth, however, that is not essentially different to Homer's 'truth' as told by Odysseus disguised as a beggar (*Od.* 14.191-359), or Odysseus' source-citation regarding Helios' conversation with Zeus (*Od.* 12.389-90; Strasburger 1972: 21).

Real Author and Dramatized Narrator
S. Mandell and D.N. Freedman (1993: 1-80) make an interesting distinction between the implied narrator and the real author in Herodotus. They have borrowed this exegetical idea from American theory of literature, the so-called Analytic Criticism or New Criticism (pp. 9-19). The 'I' who is telling the story is not the same person as the real author. Their only connection consists of the fact that the implied narrator has been invented by the real author. The person acting as an historian in Herodotus is not Herodotus the real author but his implied narrator, whom he calls by his own name (p. 15). He is the principal character in Herodotus and acts as if he were an historian working with oral data. He 'treats and reports the products of the real author's imagination and/or speculation as if they were facts' (pp. 12-13). By means of this literary character, 'the real author is eminently successful in presenting his work of historical fiction under the guise of autobiography' (p. 73).

However, it appears that according to Mandell and Freedman, not only is Herodotus' implied narrator an historian, he is a tragedian as well: 'The "tragic" model...is the perception of the implied narrator' (pp. 56-57), and increasing the confusion it is emphasized that the real author is a writer of 'historical, theologically oriented fiction' (p. 33). Mandell and Freedman's terminological confusion is extremely puzzling, and the puzzlement is magnified when, in spite of an apposite warning that the real author cannot be inferred from the implied narrator (Mandell and Freedman 1993: 15), this very thing is done by the statement that the real author was a serious historian who chose to write a piece of fiction and therefore deliberately distorted his data in order to be able to render a vivid picture of the principal character of this literary work, the implied narrator whom he called by his own name.[65]

In fact, Mandell and Freedman are aware of their terminological confusion. It is explicitly stated that 'we are not...interested in the difference between the implied author and the implied narrator', and hence, both are identified with 'the "I" who is telling the story' (p. 13 n. 17). This is a fatal flaw in their exegesis. A distinction between the implied author and the implied narrator seems absolutely necessary. W. Booth defines the implied author as an official version of the real author, resulting from the process of writing. An author with several works behind him has created an equivalent number of implied versions of himself. According to Booth, the implied author should not be confused with the speaker or the 'I' of the work concerned, as this 'I' is also created by the implied author (Booth 1961: 67-77). 'The "implied author" chooses, consciously or unconsciously, what we read; we infer him as an ideal, literary, created version of the real man; he is the sum of his own choices' (pp. 74-75). 'Even the novel in which no narrator is dramatized creates an implicit picture of an author who stands behind the scenes, whether as stage manager, as puppeteer, or as an indifferent God' (p. 151). Most tales are, in fact, presented as passing through the consciousness of a teller, whether an 'I' or a 'he', and these narrators are dramatized to a varying extent (pp. 151-53). Booth emphasizes that 'In any reading experience there is an implied dialogue among author, narrator, the other characters, and the reader' (Booth 1961: 155).

Using Booth's terminology, I think it is obvious that the dramatized narrator in Herodotus, the 'I', is an historian, whereas the implied

65. Mandell and Freedman 1993: 78: 'Knowing that traditional information secured orally *must be tainted*, the real author may have refashioned good material to make it appear flawed so as to give it the character of oral data. If so, it was to support and authenticate his pretense that his implied narrator had really received this material aurally. The real author also used false or perhaps merely flawed and inaccurate data to support the implied narrator's literary posture as a traveler and recorder or rememberer of orally related information... The implied narrator is neither careless nor a liar. The real author, however, may tell untruths because he is writing fiction rather than scientific or any other form of history. It follows that the real author may possibly have used far better and by far more written sources than the implied narrator acknowledges. If so, the real author altered some reports and fabricated others so as to illustrate his implied narrator's "historical" concepts.'

author is a tragedian.[66] In Herodotus, the dramatized narrator is by no means implied. On the contrary, he is introduced almost grandiosely in the very opening words of the work: Ἡροδότου Ἁλικαρνησσέος ἱστορίης ἀπόδεξις ἥδε, 'This [is] the setting forth of the research of Herodotus the Halicarnassian'. One of the reasons why Herodotus is experienced as great literature may very well be the dialectical relationship between the implied author and the dramatized narrator.

Mandell and Freedman seem to use the concept of the implied narrator in Herodotus for making a distance to the real author. Like so many other scholars in the past, their endeavours appear aimed at saving Herodotus from accusations of having lied. Based on Herodotus' dramatized narrator, his 'I', they create a fanciful image of a 'modern' historiographer with sound data at his disposal, data that the real author deliberately distorted in favour of a fictional account. In this way, the dramatized narrator and the real author are confused. Moreover, appointing Herodotus' dramatized narrator as the principal character renders a false picture of Herodotus' work. I do not think that Herodotus' aim was to present himself (or his implied narrator) to the reader. Rather, he intended to describe his world.

Herodotus the Tragedian

Herodotus and the Attic Tragedy

In point of language and structure, Herodotus' work has been profoundly influenced by the Attic tragedy.[67] According to M. Pohlenz, Herodotus had learned from the tragedians, not only to tell a story, but to interpret it as well (Pohlenz 1937: 213-14). As far as I am aware, H. Fohl's book from 1913 is still the standard work on this matter. Fohl attempted to show there to be many traces of the Attic tragedy, including actual borrowings from it, in the narratives of Herodotus.[68] It is, however, difficult to demonstrate a linguistic

66. This is not meant to be an exhaustive characterization of the implied author in Herodotus. Booth's concept of the implied author is all-embracing (Booth 1961: 73): 'It includes, in short, the intuitive apprehension of a completed artistic whole.'

67. Fohl (1913) and many subsequent scholars, among whom we may mention Huber (1965a) who has greatly inspired Lateiner (1989), tend to belittle the tragic influence on Herodotus: 'Dabei steht natürlich ohne weiteres fest, daß die Entlehnungen aus der Tragödie in der Hauptsache nur formeller Art sind', (Fohl 1913: 5).

68. Fohl (1913) deals with the following narratives: Gyges and Candaules (Hdt.

influence in the fashion that W. Aly (1969: 277-86), W. Schmid
(1934: 569 n. 7), and Fohl himself attempted, as the language we
regard as specifically tragic may be 'a poeticism common to several
genres, or indeed a usage common to several levels of diction'
(Chiasson 1982: 157). Notwithstanding this, C. Chiasson does find an
accumulation of linguistic, tragical 'borrowings' in the account of
Xerxes' decision to invade Hellas (Hdt. 7.8-18).[69] The cumulative
effect of these specifically tragic echoes emphasizes the similarity
between Xerxes' fate and that of the personages in dramatic tragedy
who make difficult decisions in consultation with the gods, only to
provoke their wrath and suffer the unavoidable consequences.

A number of resemblances regarding style, content, and language
exist between Herodotus and Sophocles.[70] Likewise, there seems to
have been an acquaintanceship between them, as Sophocles wrote a
poem to Herodotus of which the dedication is preserved in Plutarch.[71]
In many ways, they seem to have had the same outlook upon life, for
instance both give important women large parts,[72] and both believed
firmly in oracles. Dreams, oracles and prophecies are frequent in
Herodotus, and tragic motifs are likewise found when, for instance,
human flesh is served for dinner (Hdt. 1.119) or an animal fosters a
human child (1.122). Moreover, we find artificially touching scenes,

1.8-13), Croesus (1.28-91), Atys and Adrastus (1.34-45), Cyrus (1.107-122;
1.205-214), Periander and Lycophron (3.50-53), Polycrates (3.40-43; 3.120-25),
Xerxes (books 7–9). Thus we find the tragic narratives mainly in book 1 and 7–9,
though book 3 has two important exceptions from this rule. According to Chiasson
(1982: 156 n. 1), Fohl's book is 'The only detailed treatment'.

69. Chiasson 1982: 157-60. The words θεήλατος πυρόω, σκῆπτρα, ἐπαίρω
and the metaphor δούλιον ζυγόν (7.8. γ3, cf. Aescylus' *Persai* 50) are, according
to Chiasson, tragic echoes intended to colour the reader's perception of Xerxes'
character and situation. For ἐπαίρω, see, too, Avery 1979.

70. See the lists in How and Wells 1928: I, 7; Schmid 1934: 318 and 569-70;
Fohl 1913: 1-2, including n. 5. Text and translation of Sophocles: Storr 1912–13.

71. *An seni resp.*, 785B (text and translation: Fowler 1936) = testimonium 163 in
Snell *et al.* 1977: IV, 87: τουτὶ δ' ὁμολογουμένως Σοφοκλέους ἐστὶ
τοὐπιγραμμάτιον· ᾠδὴν Ἡροδότῳ τεῦξεν Σοφοκλῆς ἐτέων ὢν πέντ' ἐπὶ
πεντήκοντα; cf. Pohlenz 1937: 185-86. According to Jacoby, there is no reason to
doubt the authenticity of the epigram. We cannot, however, be entirely certain as
regards which Herodotus the dedication was made to. Herodotus was an unusual
name in Athens but quite common in Ionia and on the islands; Jacoby 1913: col. 233.

72. Compare Sophocles' *Antigone* and *Electra* with Herodotus' Semiramis,
Nitocris (Hdt. 1.184-87), and Artemisia (7.99; 8.87): Schmid 1934: 318 n. 4.

such as the exposure of the little Cyrus and later his return (1.107-122), Xerxes' weeping at the height of his good fortune (7.45), an oxymoron worthy of Sophocles,[73] the Persians' foreknowledge of the impending disaster (9.16), and the scene of Psammenitus (3.14). 'Here the story escalates into a *dramatikon* like the phenomenon the author had met in the Attic theatre' (Schmid 1934: 569-70). It is not only technicalities that were influenced by tragedy. Tragedy permeated Herodotus' entire work, the conclusion of which, the Persian war in book 7–9, is a dramatic picture of Xerxes' fortune and sad end, created by means that we recognize from the ancient Attic tragedy.[74]

A salient point of the connection between Herodotus and Sophocles is their conception of virtue, *areté*, as F. Egermann has demonstrated. The great tragic figures in Sophocles, Antigone or Electra to name two examples, are motivated by pure ideals, even though this motivation brings them misfortune. In Herodotus, Leonidas and the seer Megistias (7.217-24) are examples of the same kind. The same attitude is apparent in Herodotus' evaluation of the Athenians' brave and unselfish attitude to the dangers and difficulties caused by the Persian invasion (8.140-44; 9.4-6). Both Sophocles and Herodotus contrast the individual, governed by *areté*, with the world surrounding such individuals. Generally speaking, those who concern themselves with *areté* are regarded as foolish, because *areté* collides with what is practical or useful. They are advised to be 'sensible' by some near friend or relation who is himself threatened by the course of action decided upon by the virtuous individual.[75] Xerxes is an obvious contrast. Unlike the brave Athenians and Leonidas he fears danger (Hdt. 8.97; 8.100; 8.102; 8.103). Whereas the Athenians' great *areté* saves them, Xerxes' lack of it sets the seal on the Persian disaster. Faced with a fate they already know, people are either small and willing to conform or tragic and great. In order to become a tragic figure, a person has to be active. A passive attitude does not lead to greatness. Only

73. For a comprehensive list of oxymora in Herodotus, see Schmid 1934: 653 n. 3.

74. Schmid 1934: 570; Fohl 1913: 79-84; Aly 1969: 277-86 and Jacoby 1913: col. 488 give many examples of resemblances to Sophocles. Furthermore, Aly finds reminiscences of Aeschylus in Xerxes' dialogues with Mardonius and Artabanus at the start of book 7.

75. Herodotus gives Alexander as an example (8.140 and 143). Sophocles has the dialogues between Jocasta and Oedipus (*Oedipus Rex* 1054-72) and between Neoptolemus and Philoctetes (*Philoctetes* 1314-1407).

those who meet their fate with greatness (*areté*), who are constant in the face of danger, become truly tragic (Egermann 1965).

Here I have indicated a few of the main features of the general influence of the Attic tragedy upon Herodotus. A possible, specific example is the Gyges drama of which we possess a papyrus fragment from Oxyrhynchus. It is uncertain whether this play should be dated prior to or after Herodotus, so it is not possible to ascertain any influence in either direction.[76] An indubitable example is furnished by Aeschylus' tragedy *Persae*[77] which depicts an historical event that has a prominent place in Herodotus: the Battle of Salamis. In order to elucidate Herodotus' manner of tragic composition, I intend to compare these two works.

The many resemblances between Herodotus' account of the Persian war and Aeschylus' tragedy on Xerxes' defeat at Salamis, written in 472 BCE are well known.[78] Although it cannot be denied that Herodotus also made use of other sources,[79] he is obviously close to Aeschylus in his attitude to what was at stake during the Persian war and in his religious–moral interpretation of the outcome of the battle. Here I wish particularly to indicate six themes that were important to both Aeschylus and Herodotus: 1) *The dichotomous struggle*, 2) *the war seen as Persian* nomos, 3) *the theme of liberty*, 4) *Persian* hubris, 5) *the regulation of fate*, and 6) *the wheel of fortune*.

According to Aeschylus (*Pers.* 56–64), all Asia was united under Persia before Xerxes' campaign. The Persians had been given the barbarians' land, whilst the Greeks had been given Hellas (181-187). It was the will of Zeus that one ruler should rule all Asia (762-764).

---

76. Pap. Oxy. 2382 = fragment 664 in Snell *et al.* 1981: II, 248-51. See Lesky 1977: 224; Snell 1973. Raubitschek (1955) ascribes the fragment to Ion of Chios, and Raubitschek (1957) pleads Herodotus' dependence on this or on a similar tragedy; cf. Aly 1969: 34. Stahl (1968: 385 n. 1) gives a comprehensive bibliography.

77. Text and translation: Weir Smyth 1922.

78. For a brief introduction to *Persae*, see Lesky 1958: 86-90. Cf. Fehling 1989: 11: 'In earlier Greek literature the work that is closest to Herodotus in the rules it follows is Aeschylus' *Persae*.' On the verbal similarities between these works, see Hauvette 1894: 125-27; Pohlenz 1937: 116, 121, 124; Chiasson 1982: 156-57 n. 4.

79. As an example, one might compare the list of Xerxes' notables, Aesch. 21-58, and the Persian 'casualty lists', Aesch. 302-30 and 955-1001, with the personal names in Herodotus' catalogue of the Persian army, Hdt. 7.61-100. Fohl (1913: 71 n. 173) rejects the thought of Herodotus' having used Aeschylus' account.

Thus the strife is *dichotomous*.[80] The forces of a united Asia fight under the Persian overlord against Hellas which represents Europe.[81] In Herodotus, too, it is Asia's united forces[82] that fight against Hellas. Hellas is virtually synonymous with Europe[83] and, according to the implied author's conception, the path to the rest of the world. The Persian lands' borders, would, if the invasion of Hellas had proved successful, have reached as far as Zeus' very heaven (Hdt. 7.8γ). When advocating (7.8α) the war, Xerxes alludes to the *nomos* ('law' or 'custom') he has inherited from his predecessors. By virtue of this *nomos*, he intends to extend the might of the Persians as fully as his predecessors had done in their time. This *nomos* is given by the gods and must be obeyed unconditionally. Aeschylus operates with a similar motivation for the war in saying that fate (*Moira*) had enjoined victorious warfare upon the Persians since the days of old (*Pers.* 93-106) and that Xerxes intended to augment the wealth he had inherited from his father (753-58).

The theme of liberty is important in the works of both Aeschylus and Herodotus. We find it when Aeschylus tells of Atossa's dream about the barbarian woman who puts up with her chains, whereas the Dorian woman breaks hers (*Pers.* 181-99), in the statement about the Greeks having brought Darius' magnificent army to ruin although they have no 'shepherd', being neither slaves nor vassals (241-44), in the Greek battle-cry at Salamis (402-405),[84] and when the Persians bewail the fact that after the Persian might has been broken, people will no longer guard their tongues (591-97). In Herodotus, we also find frequent instances of the theme of liberty. To the dubious Xerxes,

80. Huber (1965b: 40, including n. 57) emphasizes Aeschylus' influence on Herodotus with regard to his view of the world.

81. Atossa's dream, *Pers.* 181-99, may be read as a dichotomous view of the world, there being Hellas and Asia.

82. Hdt. 7.9; cf. likewise the detailed account of the mobilizing of the Persian army and its advance upon Hellas, including the careful enumeration of the various forces, 7.19-100 and 7.184-87.

83. Hdt. 7.5.3; cf. likewise Onomacritus' collection of oracles which mention an army advancing upon Europe from Asia, 7.6.4. According to 7.8.2, Xerxes counted upon conquering a country that certainly was not smaller than that already in his possesion.

84. ὦ παῖδες Ἑλλήνων ἴτε,/ἐλευθεροῦτε πατρίδ᾽ ἐλευθεροῦτε δὲ/παῖδας, γυναῖκας θεῶν τε πατρῴων ἕδη,/θήκας τε προγόνων· νῦν ὑπὲρ πάντων ἀγών.

Demaratus from Sparta emphasizes the general Hellenic, and specifically Lacedaemonian love of liberty (Hdt. 7.101-105). That Hellas' liberty is jeopardized by the Persian war is maintained by the Hellenic ambassadors to Gelon, tyrant in Syracuse (7.157), and that the gods concur in this interpretation, is shown by the oracle of Bacis (8.77). The Greek love of liberty is contrasted with the despotism of the Persians whenever occasion presents itself. Two Spartan heralds lecture the Persians when they, in answer to the statesman Hydarnes' advice concerning voluntary subjection to Xerxes, reply that Hydarnes, being a slave, knows nothing of liberty. Had he done so, he would have advised the Spartans to use all possible methods in fighting for their liberty (7.135-36). Finally, it should be said that the contrast between sovereignty and slavery constitutes an *inclusio* encompassing Herodotus' entire history work. To quote D. Lateiner: 'the choice posed in the Epilogue [9.122] for the Persians between freedom and hardship on the one hand and slavery and luxury on the other, returns to the theme of freedom and to the "first initiator of unjust acts (1.5.3) committed against the Greeks", the distant origin of a long and connected series of wars' (Lateiner 1989: 48).

Another feature common to Aeschylus and Herodotus is the question to which the Persians' ignominious defeat gives rise, namely what constituted their *hubris*? Herodotus, at this point, frequently refers to the idea of a dynamic equilibrium, that is 'evening things out'.[85] One is guilty of *hubris* when one disturbs the equilibrium of the world. Herodotus' and Aeschylus' dichotomous division of the world is an expression of the equilibrium that Xerxes' attempt at bringing both halves under his rule threatens to disturb. His one thousand two hundred and seven ships against Hellas' three hundred and eighty[86] and the million-strong army from all of Asia against Hellas' army numbering thousands are striking examples of the lack of equilibrium.

---

85. Hdt. 6.11.3:...θεῶν τὰ ἴσα νεμόντων...; in 8.13, a storm, caused by the will of the gods, diminishes the Persian fleet, reducing it to the same size as the Hellenic fleet. Lateiner (1989: 194-95) indicates that many political actions create equilibrium (the Greeks and Persians, 1.1-5; Darius' reasons for invading Scythia and Hellas, 4.1.1; 5.105.2; 6.101.3; likewise Xerxes' reasons for invading Hellas, 7.8α.2; 7.8β.2; 7.11.4). 'Evening things out' is obviously Herodotus' most significant analogy, whether the mode of expression is divine forethought, human revenge, or judicial penalty.

86. Hdt. 7.184; 8.82. Aeschylus (337-47) gives 1.207 Persian ships against 310 Greek.

Xerxes' uncle Artabanus had actually warned him against this lack of equilibrium, but to no avail (Hdt. 7.10ε). Artabanus was proved right; Aeschylus agrees on this interpretation of the outcome of the battle, when he makes his messenger say that the Persian defeat is due to a *daimon*'s having poured an unequally measured fate over the warring factions.[87] When Xerxes, with the help of a deity, dares bridge the Hellespont (*Pers.* 65-72; 718-26), he demonstrates his belief that he, although mortal, can rule over all the gods (744-50). Acting in a fool's paradise, out of juvenile rashness Xerxes accomplishes a disaster which was predetermined by the gods, but which might have been deferred. 'When someone exerts himself, God assists (him)', Aeschylus points out.[88] Xerxes is unable to see through the *phthonos* (jealousy) of the gods, so the Greeks win a fantastic victory (353-432). In Herodotus, too, the Persians' crossing of the Hellespont and the building of Xerxes' bridge are the main events that constitute *hubris* (Hdt. 7.33-36; 7.54-57): Separate lands and continents should not be conjoined or in any other way allowed to mingle.[89] The account of the Persian defeat ends symbolically with the sacrifice by the Greeks of the torn ropes that for a short and fateful time joined Europe and Asia (Hdt. 9.121).

The Persian martial ambition should not, on the other hand, be regarded in itself as constituting *hubris*. Herodotus states that the Persians were successful as long as they kept within the divinely appointed borders.[90] Cyrus conquered Lydia (1.46-94), the Hellenic coastal areas of Asia Minor (1.141-76), and Babylon (1.178-200), but

---

87. *Pers.* 345-46:... δαίμων τις κατέφθειρε στρατόν/τάλαντα βρίσας οὐκ ἰσορρόπῳ τύχῃ.

88. *Pers.* 742: ἀλλ' ὅταν σπεύδῃ τις αὐτός, χὠ θεὸς συνάπτεται.

89. Lateiner 1989: 128; cf. Immerwahr 1966: 44: 'the proem calls attention to Persia's hubris in seeking world dominion by stating that the Persians themselves considered Asia to be theirs, but Europe to be separate. The unity of the work consists partly in the emphasis on the disregard shown by the Persian kings, in their Western attacks, of this native doctrine, which is recalled at the end of the *Histories* [Hdt. 1.4.4 = 9.116.3].' After the Greek victory in the Battle at Salamis, Themistocles' speech, besides mocking Xerxes the scoundrel, emphasizes this metaphysical aspect (8.109.3): τάδε γὰρ οὐκ ἡμεῖς κατεργασάμεθα, ἀλλὰ θεοί τε καὶ ἥρωες, οἱ ἐφθόνησαν ἄνδρα ἕνα τῆς τε 'Ασίης καὶ τῆς Εὐρώπης βασιλεῦσαι...

90. Cf. Lateiner 1989: 126-44: 'Limit, Propriety, and Transgression: A Structuring Concept in the *Histories*'.

when he attempted the conquest of the Massagetes who dwelled east of the Araxes where the sun rises (1.201; 1.204), the consequences were disastrous, Cyrus himself being killed in battle (1.201-14). Cambyses extended Persian rule to include Egypt (3.1-16), but the Phoenician lack of aid forced him to give up his attempted campaign against the Carthaginians (3.19), then to break off his advance upon the Ethiopians, due to his not having taken into account the fact that Ethiopia lies at the farthest ends of the earth (3.25.1), so his supplies failed and his army was actually forced to practise cannibalism as a result (3.17-25). Finally, the soldiers he sent against the Ammonians vanished without trace (3.26), and thus his planned campaign against these three peoples was brought to nought. Darius conquered Samos and put down a Babylonian revolt (3.139-60), and his governor in Egypt conquered the Hellenic Barce in Libya (4.145-67; 4.200-205). However, Darius, too, bit off more than he could chew. His campaign against the Scythians, a nomadic people, became a hunt against people who continually moved from place to place. There was, thus, nothing to conquer, and nobody to make into slaves (4.46). Portents having indicated an approaching catastrophe, Darius, his task unaccomplished, made an about-turn before disaster finally struck, leaving Megabazus, followed by Otanes, to subjugate as much of Europe as possible (4.83-144; 5.1-2; 5.26-27). In revenge for the Athenian support of an Ionian uprising (5.28–6.42), Darius despatched Mardonius, but after having conquered the island of Thasos and Macedonia, he and his army were forced to return home (6.43-45), and the following year, a new army suffered an ignominious defeat at Marathon (6.46-117). Darius achieved no more, being succeeded by Xerxes at this point. His renowned campaign against Hellas and his subsequent painful defeat by the Greeks constitute the subject of the last three books of Herodotus' opus.

A pattern may be observed in this series of Persian conquests and defeats. As long as the Persian king himself remained within his own territory, Asia with Egypt,[91] and neither moved to Europe nor to the outer ends of the earth,[92] he succeeded in his conquests. He became, however, guilty of *hubris* if he left his own territory, although he might well and actually did succeed in sending others to conquer

91. Africa, Phoenicia, the Syrian Palestine, and Arabia made up the one peninsula of Asia, and Asia Minor the other (Hdt. 4.38-42).
92. Hdt. (3. 98-117) gives a description of the rims of the earth.

places outside his territory. Aeschylus and Herodotus agree that Darius had vassals on either side of the Hellespont, although, after his Scythian disaster (on which Aeschylus is silent), he himself never left Asia.[93] The four Persian kings tried to abolish the divinely appointed borders of the Persian kingdom, each in his own direction: Cyrus towards the east, Cambyses towards the south, Darius towards the north, and Xerxes towards the west. Herodotus' 'tetralogy' expresses the same ideas as Aeschylus' tragedy. The Persians have divine sanction for their wars, and are victorious, as long as the king of Persia remains within his own boundaries, on the continent of Asia, and refrains from invading the other continent, Europe. Each of these continents, regarded as the two halves of the world, is bounded by the outer edge of the world, which in turn has a common boundary with Zeus' heaven. The boundaries between earth and heaven are likewise out of bounds to humans. Thus it may be said that Herodotus wrote his work within the same tradition as did Aeschylus.

This continuity is also demonstrated by Herodotus' detailed description of Aeschylus' world.[94] Where Aeschylus merely states that Xerxes intended uniting the entire world under his sovereignty, Herodotus describes the world more fully, historically, ethnographically and geographically.[95] The Persians, according to Aeschylus, flooded Hellas with soldiers (87–92), thus leaving Asia depopulated (718). Herodotus describes this in greater detail. Apart from giving the names, as Aeschylus had done, of a few of the important lords, he says that the army consisted of five million two hundred and eighty-

---

93. *Pers.* 871–77; according to Aeschylus, Darius never crossed the river Halys, *Pers.* 865. It may be argued that the defeat at Marathon was not caused by the Persians' having committed *hubris* by beginning this campaign, which Darius did not take part in himself, but that their *hubris* consisted of their theft of a statue of Apollo (Hdt. 6.118). The Persian defeat at Plataea, which took place after Xerxes had returned home leaving Mardonius and an army in Hellas, was anticipated and accounted for in a similar manner by the Athenians (8.143-44). The Athenians fought for their liberty, fully confident that the gods and the heroes would assist them, as the Persians had burned down their temples and statues. Aeschylus supports this explanation (*Pers.* 807–22).

94. Cf. Regenbogen 1930b: 95: Throughout his *historíe*, Herodotus, being Ionian, supports the metaphysical interpretation of the Persian wars put forward by Aeschylus.

95. Lateiner 1989: 152: 'The function of Herodotus's lengthy ethnography is to give historical meaning to the dichotomy "Greek versus Barbarian".'

three thousand two hundred and twenty men, excluding women, eunuchs and animals (7.186-87)! Aeschylus' interpretation of Xerxes' building of the bridge of the Hellespont may also be mentioned. Xerxes thought he could acquire mastery of the divine river Bosporus by means of slaves' chains (745–46). Xerxes, according to Herodotus, actually carried out this idea in practice by punishing the disobedient Hellespont with three hundred lashes and by sinking a pair of slaves' chains in its depths (7.35). These actions, which Aeschylus described as being due to the fact that Xerxes thought he could govern the gods (*Pers*. 749–50), give rise in Herodotus to the anecdote that a man from the Hellespont takes Xerxes for Zeus himself, the ruler of the gods (7.56.2).

As we have seen, Herodotus and Aeschylus have a common interest in *the regulation of fate*. In the Persian war, the gods strove on behalf of the Hellenes.[96] The gods cause Xerxes to commit *hubris*. Aeschylus states that it was with the help of a god that Xerxes threw his bridge across the Hellespont, but that the deity had also disturbed his judgment, thus leading him to begin upon the project (724–25; 107-10). In Herodotus, the earliest part of the account of Xerxes' campaign shows the god to be responsible for Xerxes' *hubris* (7.5-18), although Xerxes also acts hubristically on his own account. Aeschylus is deliberately and explicitly synergistic, as Zeus certainly had commanded the king to fulfill some ancient oracles, but Xerxes brought about his predestined misfortune through his juvenile haughtiness. Thus, when human beings overreach themselves, the god co-operates with them. By his ignorance and youthful crassness, Xerxes is himself responsible for the ensuing catastrophe (739–52). In the same way, the whole of Xerxes' behaviour may be said to be shown by Herodotus as synergistic. This is especially so regarding the punishment of the Hellespont (Hdt. 7.35). This synergistic tendency is, however, not as evident in Herodotus as in Aeschylus.[97] Herodotus and Aeschylus are agreed upon the fact that Xerxes was unable to avoid his fate of committing

96. As examples of this, see *Pers*. 345–46; 353–54; 454–55; 472–73; 532–36; Hdt. 7.139; 7.188-89; 8.13; 8.35-39; 9.16; 9.61-62. In addition, Herodotus has a number of oracles and portents as to the result of the war: 7.37-38; 7.140-44; 7.219; 8.64-65; 8.77; 8.114; 9.19; 9.36-37; 9.64.

97. But see Hdt 2.120.5: important misdeeds are severely punished by the gods; another instance of this is Arcesilaus who ignored an oracle and thereby was struck down by the fate that had been predetermined for him (4.163-64).

hubris by advancing upon Hellas and attempting to unite two separate continents, thereby making himself the equal of the gods.[98] An added offence was the fact that he depopulated Asia in his attempt to conquer Hellas.

According to Aeschylus, the Persian defeat is surprising. The inconsistent gods (*Pers.* 107–10) brought about the unexpected ruin of the Persians (1005–1007). Thus fortune changes (852–908). This is yet another theme which we also find in Herodotus: *the wheel of fortune.*[99] Herodotus concerns himself both with large and small towns, as towns that formerly were great have become small, and the opposite has also been known to occur (Hdt. 1.5.3-4). The fall of Croesus is explained by his being a descendant (five generations removed) of Gyges, but Gyges' *hubris* was in a way not his fault but rather caused by Candaules. The latter's *hubris* is explained, if explanation it is, by the fact that it had been decided that he should suffer a harsh fate.[100] This applies, too, to the other tragic figures in Herodotus: Astyages (1.107-130), Psammenitus (3.14), and perhaps Polycrates in particular (3.39-43 and 120-28).[101]

98. Aeschylus' statement that Zeus had commanded Xerxes to fulfill a number of oracles (739–40) agrees with Herodotus' account. Examples, in Herodotus, of oracles that are fulfilled during the Persian war are Onomacritus' (unspecified) collection, 7.6, and 7.140-41; 7.220; 8.20; 8.77; 8.96 and 9.43.

99. Hdt. 1.207.2:... κύκλος τῶν ἀνθρωπηίων ἐστὶ πρηγμάτων...

100. Hdt. 1.8. A similar motivation is made for the otherwise fortunate Egyptian King Apries' mistake, when, instead of consolidating his own power, he sent an army to what was a pre-evident defeat, 2.161. Other examples are: Scyles (4.79); Miltiades and the priestess Timo (6.134); Artaynte, Xerxes' mistress and daughter-in-law (9.109).

101. Cf. particularly 3.43.1 and, in another connection, Orchomenus' speech to Thersandrus: no one can avoid that which is to happen according to the will of a god (9.16). Other examples of the unpredictable wheel of fortune are the following: The will of fate determined Egypt's being visited by misfortune for a hundred and fifty years and the fact that the rulers who had understood fate's intentions and brought about Egypt's misfortunes were successfull when at the same time the good and just ruler was unsuccessfull (2.133); oracles told the Ethiopian Sabacus that he would rule Egypt for precisely fifty years (2.39); a divine will determined the success of the seven Persians' revolt against the magi (3.77); a happy inspiration from above leads the outlawed Syloson from Samos to give Darius a cloak whilst Darius is still unknown—thus, it is later possible for Syloson to persuade Darius to conquer his fatherland (3.139-40); a portent announces the impending doom of Babylon (3.153-54).

As has been seen, S. Mandell's and D.N. Freedman's statement that 'Herodotus' treatment of *res divinae* is no different than that of Aeschylus or Sophocles' (1993: 155), although slightly optimistic, is not entirely unfounded. Nevertheless, D. Lateiner maintains that Herodotus is by temperament a modern historian, who could just as well have lived in our times.[102] Consequently, he has to explain why Herodotus did not actually write like a modern historian, a problem solved by resorting to an idea of consideration for a somewhat backward audience: 'For his audience, such *tisis* was a more convenient and familiar way of linking events than the original historiographical analysis of cause that Herodotus invented'.[103] Explanations such as 'divine vengeance' were of symbolic importance tó Herodotus' god-fearing audience, but always allow for and co-exist peacefully with other, non-theological causes. In the same way that Anaximander speaks of *dike* ('justice') and *tisis* ('retribution') in nature and explains the physical universe in moral and forensic terms, the Ionian historian talks of *tisis* in history. '*Tisis* can effect its purposes without recourse to any *deus ex machina*' (Lateiner 1989: 203-204).

As a consequence of these attempts at playing down the metaphysical aspects of Herodotus' historical work, scholars such as Lateiner and J.A.S. Evans seek to 'demythologize' the concept of *nomos*. The Persians under Cyrus chose this *nomos* voluntarily,[104] but by Xerxes' time it had become an expression of the Persian nature (Evans 1991: 39). The continual growth of the Persian empire constituted a tradition that the Persian king was bound by (Lateiner 1989: 210; Evans 1991: 39-40). Lateiner reads Herodotus' concept of *nomos* as a political presentation of despotic behaviour. Xerxes' freedom of choice is, certainly, shown as limited metaphysically by fate and by his tragical

102. Lateiner 1989: 218. 'In some respects, Herodotus conforms to modern notions.'

103. Lateiner 1989: 141. Lateiner practically brushes aside Herodotus' metaphysical ideas saying that historians in general 'unify their narratives with particular words, themes, symbols, metaphors, seemingly peripheral subjects, and recurrent metaphysical ideas' (pp. 111-12). Compare Mandell and Freedman's criticism of 'scholars who take the...myths and legends in Herodotus' *History*, particularly those that contain representations of the gods acting in history, as charming literary enhancements that should not be construed seriously', (Mandell and Freedman 1993: 1-3).

104. Hdt. 1.125-26 and 9.122. When faced with a choice, the Persians prefer the role of rulers to that of subjects (Evans 1991: 26-27).

predestination, but of greater importance, according to Lateiner, was his rank and Persian *nomos*, in which no shadow of international justice can be found. '*Nomos* requires no explanation, because for Xerxes it is one' (Lateiner 1989: 181; Hdt. 7.8.1-2), Hellas being the logical goal for the continued Persian expansion required by Persia's imperialistic *nomos*.

In Hdt. 7.1-19, we find both a secular and a theological explanation for Xerxes' decision to attack the Hellenes, but the secular one suffices for Lateiner, as the text shows a completely satisfactory set of human motives, both psychologically and strategically speaking. Xerxes' 'Homeric' dream dramatizes the opus, but is 'redundant as explanation of an event destined to happen (7.17.2) for other, more verifiable, historical reasons' (Lateiner 1989: 204-205). However, in Aeschylus both the 'human' and the 'divine' motives recur as well as an explicitly synergistic statement, ideas that Herodotus may well have taken over. It may well be that *the reader* of the twentieth century CE would prefer the secular motives to the metaphysical ones, but the fact that they are presented side by side does not necessarily point to a qualitative difference. Here we may equally well plead for Aeschylus' synergism and for a continuation of the Ionian rational tendency. Homer is also echoed, as Artabanus' doubts about his dream are reminiscent of Nestor in the *Iliad* (2.79-83). The decisive factor in the *Iliad* was that the dream forced Agamemnon to act (2.1-47), and it is possible to state that Xerxes was similarly influenced by *his* dream.

It is obvious that Herodotus does not talk of metaphysical causes on all and every occasion and that other causes, both political and strategic, play an important part. Viewed apart, both the secular and the metaphysical explanation are fully adequate reasons for the campaign (Lateiner 1989: 204-205). Lateiner sees the secular explanation as the dominant factor, O. Regenbogen, on the other hand, views it as insufficient. Herodotus 'knows every pragmatic motive that modern historians usually insist upon...but this is not important to him, it is not sufficient to satisfy his asking for causal relations...Another kind of knowledge and cognition is more essential to him and closer to the meaning of things'.[105] It is possible to assert that the metaphysical

105. Regenbogen 1930b: 89. Thus I do not agree with G. von Rad's correction of Regenbogen. Asserting that Thucydides and Herodotus are not much different, he insists that 'Sowohl bei Herodot wie bei Thukydides ist ausschließlich der geschichtsimmanente Mensch der Gegenstand der Geschichtsschreibung' (von Rad

causes create the background for the secular. Lateiner rightly emphasizes that 'Croesus prefigures Xerxes in many respects',[106] and if this
is true, the metaphysical element will be felt to be dominant. The fact
that Herodotus gives both explanations does not mean that he necessarily preferred one to the other. Both were apparently necessary,
even if Lateiner doubts this. To say that Xerxes' dream was
'redundant as explanation of an event destined to happen...for other,
more verifiable, historical reasons', may best be described as an insult
to an author of genius.

The Herodotean Tragedy
Now it should be evident why Herodotus' work has been rightly characterized as 'a prose tragic epic' (Mandell and Freedman 1993: 69 and
75). In the following, I shall attempt to delineate the 'herodotean
tragedy' more fully, using the two herodotean *logoi* in which the
tragic presentation is most significant and most noticeable: the history
of Croesus and that of Xerxes.

Croesus
The history of Croesus, Hdt. 1.6-94,[107] may be divided into two sections: The first part comprises the account of the Mermnadian dynasty
(1.7-29) until the time of Croesus and the pinnacle of his fortune. This
latter point, when Solon arrives (1.29), marks the beginning of the
second part, Croesus' fall.[108]
    The narrative of Gyges and Candaules (1.8-13) which forms the
first of a series of *novelle* ('short stories') in Herodotus' work (Stahl
1968: 385) is, as Herodotus tells it, a tragedy. The action evolves from
Candaules' infatuation.[109] At the very beginning of the episode,

1944: 7, referring to Regenbogen 1933: 17).
    106. Lateiner 1989: 196; cf. Hellmann 1934: 33-34 n. 1: 'früher erzählte
Geschichten beitragen in ihrer paradigmatischen Verbindlichkeit oder Situationsähn-
lichkeit zur Erkläung der späteren...'
    107. Herodotus himself indicates this part of his opus to be a unit:...τὸν δὲ οἶδα
αὐτὸς πρῶτον ὑπάρξαντα ἀδίκων ἔργων ἐς τοὺς ῞Ελληνας, τοῦτον
σημήνας προβήσομαι ἐς τὸ πρόσω τοῦ λόγου...1.5.3; κατὰ μὲν δὴ τὴν
Κροίσου τε ἀρχὴν καὶ ᾽Ιωνίης τὴν πρώτην καταστροφὴν ἔσχε
οὕτω...1.92.1;...Λυδοὶ μὲν δὴ ὑπὸ Πέρσῃσι ἐδεδούλωντο, 1.94.7.
    108. Immerwahr 1966: 86; for the subdivision of the history of Croesus, see *ibid.*,
pp. 81-88.
    109. Fohl 1913: 6-20. Fohl emphasizes (p. 6), as does Stahl (1968: 385), the

Herodotus hints at the ending by his χρῆν γὰρ Κανδαύλῃ γενέσθαι κακῶς, 'Candaules necessarily fared ill' (1.8.2). The course of action and also the fall of Candaules are inevitable. Candaules the Heraclid, king of the Lydians, wished to prove to his guardsman Gyges that his queen was the most beautiful woman on earth. In order to accomplish this, Gyges had to see her naked.[110] Gyges is alive to the consequences of this action and protests, using two gnomic pronouncements, the one, that a woman in taking off her tunic likewise lays aside her modesty, the other that one should make do with viewing one's own property (Raubitschek 1957). Gyges declares himself convinced of the truth of Candaules' statement and requires no further proof. The king is not amenable to common sense but places the protesting Gyges behind the door of the queen's bedchamber, thus enabling him to make his own observations. Candaules' wife discovers the peeping Tom, and on the following day she delivers her ultimatum: Either Gyges avenges her offended modesty by killing Candaules and usurping his royal power, or else Gyges himself must die. As, deaf to Gyges' protests, the queen insists, he respects her demands by choosing the first option, royal power and the queen thrown in for good measure, an outcome that the Delphic oracle confirms, stating, however, that the Heraclidae will, five generations later, be revenged upon the descendants of Gyges. Candaules brings about his own ruin and his best friend is forced to administer the punishment for the king's *hubris*. The passive Gyges is flung into the stream of events until he faces the ultimate dilemma, and instead of a tragic and heroic death, he prefers, in a very human fashion, to call down guilt upon himself (Stahl 1968: 399, 385-86). In other words, Gyges is not the personification of *areté*. The episode lays the foundation of Croesus' tragedy, five generations later.

    Herodotus' account of the history of Gyges does not tally with the other versions in Greek literature (Hellman 1934: 31; Stahl 1968: 386). It is characteristic that Herodotus' Gyges has a passive part to play, and that Candaules' ruin is shown as 'a sequence of events that is ultimately determined by an impersonal constraint exerting its

importance of the fact that Herodotus' first novel-like episode was conceived as a tragedy.

    110. Candaules' bedazzlement has already been implied in the hubristic suggestion, but it is specifically characterized as such by the remark that the Lydians regarded being seen naked as extremely shameful (1.10.3).

influence on man'.[111] The narrative points to two important characteristics of divine retribution, *tisis*: *Tisis* is only concerned with the
action itself, with guilt viewed objectively. It is not important whether
Gyges himself was guilty. What is important is the fact that he committed a guilty act. *Tisis* is not only connected to one person's life, but
is in effect for a much longer period, here the course of five generations. F. Hellmann sees this as an important aspect of Herodotus' historical work. The individual is entangled in the historical context and
can be said to have been caught up in actions beyond his control. This
is indicated by the narrative's motto: 'Candaules necessarily fared ill'.
Croesus' fate was determined by Gyges' action. The actual theme of
the history of Croesus is to be found in Herodotus 1.13.2: 'the Pythian
priestess declared that the Heraclidae should have vengeance on Gyges'
posterity in the fifth generation' (translation from Godley 1926: I,
17). Here, as is usual in Herodotus, the ending of the story comes as
no surprise to the reader. Herodotus merely shows '*how* an obvious
outcome of the sequence of events is accomplished in history', and this
anticipation of events emphasizes the divine background for everything that happens (Hellmann 1934: 33-35).

The remainder of the first section of the Croesus-*logos* resembles
most nearly a chronicle, as it enumerates the rulers of the Mermnadic
dynasty, the dates of their reigns, and outstanding events until the time
of Croesus and his conquest of all of Asia Minor west of the Halys
(1.14-28). At this point, Croesus' power reaches its zenith, and
Herodotus pauses to predict Croesus' fate in the following section
(1.29-45; Immerwahr 1966: 83). Solon puts in an appearance and
states that no man should be deemed fortunate until his entire history

---

111. Hellman 1934: 31, referring to 1.8.2: χρῆν γὰρ Κανδαύλῃ γενέσθαι
κακῶς. Skafte Jensen (1992: 31) warns against exaggerating the 'fatalism' in Greek
epics and drama: 'That which looks like fate might be held to be tradition'. Fohl
(1913: 19-20) views the statement in 1.8.2 as a kind of prologue in which the reader
at an early juncture is informed of the end of the story. In Attic tragedy, when the
audience cannot be expected to be fully aware of the course of events in a drama, the
author can inform them in the prologue. That there is something more at work here is
indicated, however, by the use of a similar phrase, χρεὸν εἴη, when Onomacritus
reads his oracles concerning the crossing of the Hellespont by a Persian for Xerxes
(7.6.4). Granted, Onomacritus has been introduced as an unreliable seer, but as to
the Persians his unreliability is solely concerned with the choice of which oracles to
read, as he keeps silent regarding the oracles that disfavour the Persians. This in no
way affects the truth of the actual oracles.

is known (1.29-33). This sentiment is then illustrated by the tale of the death of Croesus' son Atys (1.34-45), and later by the account of the Persian king Cyrus' conquest of Lydia (cf. 1.86).

When Solon, the law-giver of Athens, paid Croesus a visit, the latter, having heard of the wise and famous man, proudly displayed his treasures, and asked whom of all the people Solon had met he would call the most fortunate. Herodotus does not beat about the bush here, but tells us what answer Croesus expected: 'this he asked expecting he [himself] to be [named] the most fortunate of men...' (1.30.3). As might have been expected, things turned out otherwise, as Solon mentions the Athenian Tellus who lived an ordinary and happy life, crowned by a hero's death in the defence of his home city. As the next most fortunate, Solon, upon Croesus' renewed question, names the Argives Cleobis and Biton, who, in answer to their mother's prayer to the goddess Hera, were given the ultimate gift: Death in the very sanctuary. Croesus thereupon demands an explanation, and Solon points to the uncertainty of human life: 'But whosoever continues to possess most, and thereafter ends his life happily, is as far as I am concerned...worthy of being called by that name...The gods have visited many people with good fortune, [and later] destroyed them' (1.32.9). The gods do not permit mortals to rise above the usual sphere of mortal beings with regard to either power, greatness, or good fortune. Human existence is constantly threatened by the irritable, jealous gods (Regenbogen 1930a: 115). This description of the uncertainty of human existence forms the basis of Herodotus' subsequent presentation, and later, on the Persian pyre, Croesus is forced to admit the universal truth of Solon's words (1.86.5).

The more immediate application of Solon's philosophy is found in the account of Atys and Adrastus (1.34-45). The beginning anticipates the sorrowful conclusion (1.34.1): 'After Solon had left, the god smote Croesus...because he had regarded himself as the most fortunate of mankind'. C.W. Fornara divides the story into six dramatic scenes;[112] 1) A dream warns Croesus that his son Atys will be struck

---

112. Fornara (1983: 171), adding the following remark about the ancient historiographers: 'they visualized episodes as if they formed the scenes of a play'. Hellmann (1934: 61-66) has a somewhat different division of the scenes. Lesky (1977) calls the stories of Atys and of Gyges the only ones in Herodotus where it is possible to see the contours of a scenario similar to that which is usual in Attic tragedy. However, Lesky denies that Herodotus used scenes from existing Attic tragedies as a

by a spear and die. The king takes his precautions by finding his son a
wife, keeping him at home away from warfare, and removing all
weapons from his vicinity (1.34). 2) A certain Adrastus comes to
Sardis seeking purification and protection, as he has inadvertently
killed his own brother (1.35). 3) Croesus agrees to help some Mysians
drive a fearsome wild boar from their fields (1.36-42). 4) Atys,
having succeeded in persuading Croesus that his dream had nothing to
do with hunting a boar, receives permission to hunt under Adrastus'
protection (1.36-42). 5) As might be expected from Herodotus' presentation, Atys is hit by accident by Adrastus (1.43). 6) Herodotus
points, in great detail, to both the connection between Croesus' dream
and Atys' fate ('hit by a spear, he [Atys] fulfilled the words of the
dream', 1.43.3), and to the tragic irony of the story. In his grief,
Croesus calls upon Zeus because he unwittingly received the murderer
of his son as a guest and because he, in the man he had chosen to be
his son's protector, found his worst enemy (1.44). The distraught
Adrastus begs Croesus to strike him down by the corpse, as Adrastus
has once more inadvertently killed a man and ruined the life of the
man who had purified him of his first killing. Croesus, however, takes
pity upon Adrastus, saying that he is not guilty. The god, who had
already warned Croesus, is. Adrastus then commits suicide upon Atys'
grave (1.44-45). As a tragic figure, Adrastus is the opposite of Gyges,
as he chooses death rather than a life burdened by guilt (Rieks 1975:
43).

The episode of Solon and the story of Atys express important elements of the world view behind the Croesus-*logos* and the remainder
of the work. To use F. Hellmann's terminology, the episode of Solon
is dominated by the theme of *teleuté*, the uncertainty of human existence and the fragility of good fortune, whereas the episode of Atys
shows the theme of *adynaton apohygeín*, the impossibility of prevent-
ing impending misfortune (Hellmann 1934: 36-37). Solon's experience
that each day brings something new and his conclusion that man is
sheer *symphoré*, 'coincidence' (1.32.4), is borne out by the story of
Atys, giving insight into the background for the cause of events: The
unavoidable will of the god. However, in opposition to Solon's jealous
and labile god,[113] divine *nemesis* unfolds after *hubris* has been committed (Hellmann 1934: 67). The story of Atys is a paradigmatic

model, but indicates a more general influence from Sophocles.
113. 1.32.1: τὸ θεῖον πᾶν ἐὸν φθονερόν τε καὶ ταραχῶδες.

expression of the fact that although a certain incident may appear con-
fusing, it nevertheless shows the working of the divine power towards
a predetermined goal. The entire sequence of events, divine action as
well as human reaction to it, serves to accomplish this goal. Preceding
the actual account of the fate of Croesus, the episode of Adrastus
shows this background of the story (Hellmann 1934: 60-61).

Cyrus' assumption of power wakens Croesus' desire of curbing the
Persian power. He asks the most reliable oracles' advice as to whether
he should go to war against the Persians, and whether he can expect to
retain the absolute power he thus hopes to acquire (1.46-56). He
interprets their answer in the affirmative when he is told that if he
makes war on the Persians, he will bring a great empire to nought
(1.53) but when a mule is made king of the Medes, he will do well to
flee (1.55). Since a mule can never rule men, Cyrus feels secure and
makes an alliance with the Spartans, the bravest among the Hellenes
(1.56-71). The account of Croesus' attack on Cyrus begins with a
proleptic section: Croesus has misunderstood the reply from the
oracle, and he is also warned by the wise Lydian Sandanis (1.71) of
the risk he is running by carrying out his attack upon the Persians.
Here Herodotus treats us to a number of digressions, first an account
of the geography of Asia Minor in the vicinity of the river Halys,
which forms the border between the Median and the Lydian kingdoms
(1.72). Next an account of the reasons for Croesus' attack on the Persians: He partly wanted to conquer new lands in addition to what
belonged to him, and partly desired revenge on Cyrus, who upon
coming to power had subjugated Croesus' brother-in-law, Astyages of
Media. An account of the making of Astyages' marriage with Croesus'
sister is likewise given at this juncture (1.73-75). After this,
Herodotus picks up the thread of his original discourse with a reference to Croesus' consulting the oracles and the ambiguous reply
(1.75). Thereupon the war begins: After two indecisive battles and a
fortnight's siege, Cyrus conquers Croesus' capital Sardis, and Croesus
himself is taken prisoner (1.75-86).

Cyrus has Croesus cast onto the pyre, but his curiosity is aroused,
and in answer to Cyrus' question, on the brink of disaster, Croesus has
to admit that Solon's prophecy was correct, thus bringing the story to
its tragic climax (Fohl 1913: 28-31). Forced thus to reflect upon
Solon's words on the uncertainty of fate, Cyrus orders that the pyre
be extinguished. This is only possible with divine assistance, which

proves that the gods are not inimical to Croesus. Nevertheless, Croesus accuses the gods of having encouraged him to make war, thus sealing his fate (1.86-87). With Cyrus' permission, he consults the Delphic oracle, and this time the Pythia refrains from speaking in riddles: Not even a god can escape the will of fate. Croesus has paid for the guilt of his forefather, five generations removed. The fact that Apollo befriended Cyrus is shown by the god's success in postponing the fall of Sardis three years after the date originally determined by fate. Quite apart from this, Croesus misled himself by misunderstanding the earlier oracles and by neglecting to consult the Delphic oracle an extra time (1.90-91).[114]

The *adynaton apophygeín* theme, the idea that human beings cannot avoid the fate that the gods have decided upon, dominates the entire story of Croesus. His precautions were carefully made, he discovered which oracle was most reliable, sought by gifts to incline it favourably towards himself, and thereafter sought its advice twice. This makes the Pythia's reproach that Croesus had not consulted the oracle in Delphi a third time sound a little sarcastic. He then sought information as to which of the Hellenes were the bravest and allied himself to them, as well as to the Egyptians and the Babylonians. This motif of the tragic hero taking every precaution against an impending disaster, which Hellmann calls the *elpís* theme, is strongly marked, but all Croesus' careful precautions prove vain.[115] Before everything went so dreadfully wrong, the scene with Sandanis (1.71), an example of the typical warning before the catastrophe, showed Croesus' blindness (Hellmann 1934: 69). At this point, the reader already knows that the god is responsible for Croesus' fate, and the incident with Atys has shown that it is impossible to avoid the plans the gods have made. The Sandanis scene is intended to demonstrate once more that the gods make those mad who approach a chain of events the gods have decided upon (1.71.1; Hellmann 1934: 112). The first instance of this phenomenon is Croesus' erroneous interpretation of the oracles. Sandanis' abortive warning is given as an example of the general rule stated much later in Herodotus' opus: 'that which happens [as a result] of the god's [decision], no man may hinder. Nobody believes the person who tells the truth, [about this]' (9.16.4). This scene is the first of a series

114. For a more detailed account of the closing scenes of the history of Croesus (1.86-94), see Hellman 1934: 103-111.
115. More about the *elpís* theme in Hellmann 1934: 73-77.

of warning-scenes interpolated immediately before plans that fail.[116] The main theme in many of these scenes[117] is that the ruler in question is warned against carrying out a conquest. The warning proves vain, due to the ruler's having been blinded by a god (Hellmann 1934: 79-98). This is yet another way of demonstrating the unavoidability of the course of history. Croesus' blindness is clearly seen too in his motivation for the campaign against the Persians (1.73): He intends to conquer new lands πρὸς τὴν ἑωυτοῦ μοῖραν, 'against his fate', and even holds himself to have been encouraged to do so by the oracles.

The course of history is thus unavoidable, both in the story of Croesus and in Herodotus' work in general. This fact may also be elucidated by the succession of the barbarian kings. We have already seen that in Lydia, the Mermnadae both came to power and lost it again due to the ruling of fate. Croesus' foe, the Persian king Cyrus, likewise came to power due to the working of fate. Croesus' maternal grandfather, Astyages, king of the Medes, had been warned of Cyrus' rise to power in two dreams (1.107-108). Wishing to prevent his dreams from being fulfilled, Astyages became tragically and ironically the means of bringing the prophesied events to pass (1.108-130). Cyrus' dynasty came to an abrupt close with his successor Cambyses, who dreamed that a certain Smerdis came to the throne. As Cambyses had a brother of this name, he obviated, as he thought, the threat. Thus he brought the magus Smerdis' uprising and usurpation of the throne to pass, thereby fulfilling his own dream (3.30, 3.61-64). The usurper was, in turn, thrown down, and Darius ascended the throne (3.66-88). He was fate's darling, as shown by the fact that Darius' rule was foretold Cyrus (1.209-210). Moreover, Darius' ascension was due to a false lot being cast, but the result was nevertheless confirmed by a portent (3.83-87).

There are indeed other of Herodotus' narratives that deserve the name of tragedy as well. In the story of Cyrus' birth and rise to power (1.107-130), we encounter Harpagus who even though he acts justly loses his only son in a cruel manner when the king of the Medes, Astyages, whom the gods have blinded (1.127), oversteps the limits of reasonable vengeance and subsequently loses his own power.

116. Hdt. 1.206-208, 3.21-25, 3.40-43, 3.123-26, 4.83, 4.134, 5.36, 7.8-11, 9.1, 9.16, 9.41, 9.82.
117. Hdt. 1.206-208, Cyrus and Tomyris; 3.21-25, Cambyses and the Ethiopians; 4.83, Artabanus and Darius; 7.8-11, Xerxes, Mardonius, and Artabanus.

In the story of Astyages, the king's attempts to avert an impending disaster actually accomplishes it. Likewise, Harpagus' attempts, or rather his wife's attempts, at avoiding a tragedy actually bring it down upon them. The tale of Cyrus' death (1.205-214) may also be termed a tragedy.[118] Other examples are the stories of Periander and Lycophron (3.50-53; Fohl 1913: 62-66; Gould 1989: 52-53) and of Polycrates' signet ring (3.39-43; 3.120-28; Fohl 1913: 66-68). Finally, we encounter individuals who manifest tragic characteristics, even though their stories are not developed into tragedies to the same extent as the above-mentioned examples.[119] The greatest and probably most important tragedy in Herodotus' historical work is, though, the account of Xerxes' campaign against Hellas which fills the final three books of the opus.[120]

Xerxes

Herodotus' various stories are separate entities, but they are at the same time part of a larger context in that the earlier stories of the same kind provide a background for the subsequent new episodes (Hellmann 1934: 98). Xerxes' campaign is explained (7.8β) partly as a revenge for the part played by Athens in the earlier Ionian revolt against Persian rule (5.28–6.42), during which the Athenians supported the Ionians by giving them 20 ships.[121] Xerxes' predecessor Darius had sworn to be revenged (5.105) and had sent his army under the command of his son-in-law Mardonius against Athens and Eretria. There were two reasons for advancing on Hellas: The desire for revenge and the desire to conquer as many Hellenic cities as possible.[122] This two-fold motivation for the war, revenge and lands, connects Mardonius' campaign with Croesus' motives for attacking the Persian kingdom. Apart from wishing to curb the growing Persian power before it waxed too great (1.46.1; 1.71.1), Croesus desired

118. For the stories of Cyrus viewed as tragedies, see Fohl 1913: 49-62; Redfield 1985: 112-13.

119. Mycerinus, 2.129-35; Psammenitus, 3.14; the wife of Intafrenes, 3.119; Artaynte, 9.109-113.

120. Rieks 1975: 42: 'Die umfassendste tragische Konzeption liegt... zweifellos den drei Schlußbüchern zugrunde.'

121. Hdt. 5.97.3:... αὗται δὲ αἱ νέες ἀρχὴ κακῶν ἐγένοντο Ἕλλησί τε καὶ βαρβάροισι.

122. In Hdt. 6.43.4–44.1, Athens and Eretria are merely excuses for the Persian campaign, the conquest of Hellas being the actual aim. See also 7.138.1.

more land than that which belonged to him, πρὸς τὴν ἑωυτοῦ μοῖραν, that is 'against his fate', and in addition, he wanted to revenge himself upon Cyrus who had brought about the downfall of Croesus' brother-in-law, the Median king Astyages. Seen against this background, Darius' twofold motive for attacking Hellas is sinister. Darius too desires land 'against his fate'.

Mardonius' campaign was only partially successful (6.43-45). Therefore Darius made another attempt, only to suffer a surprising defeat at Marathon (6.94-120). The last three years of his life were taken up with the preparations for a third campaign, and so the scene was set when the next Persian actor made his first appearance. Xerxes actually had no immediate wish of carrying out his father's plans, but it soon became apparent that he had no choice in the matter. First, the formerly unfortunate Mardonius who now hopes to become the governor of Hellas starts agitating (7.5). He goes on about vengeance, the king's prestige, and about how extremely splendid and fertile Europe is. Then, what might with a modern expression be called a Hellenic 'lobby' tries to convince the king with the aid of the seer Onomacritus. This latter produces those pronouncements of his oracle that show a Persian attack to be the will of fate. At the same time, however, he carefully avoids any oracle which hints that fate might not actually be disposed to favour the Persians (7.6).

Xerxes allows himself to be persuaded and explains his decision to his nobles (7.8-11) by referring to the custom (*nomos*) he has inherited and must abide by (7.8). Since the time of Cyrus, Persian power has continuously been augmented. 'Indeed a god wills it[123] and this is beneficial for our own various efforts'.[124] The Persians are governed by a benign god.[125] Xerxes wishes to show himself worthy of his illustrious ancestors by augmenting the power of Persia every bit as much

123. This idea, θεός τε οὕτω ἄγει, in itself, points to Xerxes as a tragic hero, cf. How and Wells 1928: II, 128-29. In the tragedy, these words express 'die fatalistische Ergebung in drohendes Mißgeschick und Verderben' (Fohl 1913: 69-70).

124. In this reading, the sentence ἀλλὰ θεός τε οὕτω ἄγει is understood as the grammatical subject of συμφέρεται ἐπὶ τὸ ἄμεινον, the participial construction αὐτοῖσι ἡμῖν πολλὰ ἐπέπουσι being the indirect object. Other readings are represented by Horneffer (1971: 438): 'Die Gottheit will es so, und alles, was wir unternehmen, gerät uns', and Godley (1922: III, 309): 'It is the will of heaven; and we ourselves win advantage by our many enterprises.' Translations like these tone down Xerxes' understanding of destiny as beneficial to Persia.

125. Cf. also Artabanus' conception of τὸ χρεόν (Hdt. 7.18). See further below.

as they did. By advancing upon Hellas, the Persians will win honour as well as a great, rich, and much more fertile land. They will also attain satisfaction for their ignominious defeat at Marathon and revenge on Athens. If they succeed in subjecting the Hellenes, Persia's borders will stretch to Zeus' heaven. This is where Persian rhetoric becomes hubristic. Xerxes is right in thinking that he, being a true king of Persia, has to augment the might of Persia, and that in doing so, he is acting in accordance with the will of fate. He is, however, wrong in believing that fate is favourably inclined towards him.[126] In his blindness, Xerxes is unable to see the actual, hubristic meaning of his kingdom's bordering upon Zeus' heaven by means of the conquest of Europe.

Artabanus, the king's uncle, warns him (7.10). In times past, he had warned Darius against the Scythian campaign (4.83) and his pessimism had been justified. The supremacy of Persia should actually restrain Xerxes from attacking, as in spite of this supremacy there is a possibility of defeat. The god strikes those mortals that stand out above others with his lightning in the same way as he sends his bolts down upon the tallest houses and trees. Likewise, a great army is frequently destroyed by a small one when the jealous god enters the fray. At first, Xerxes does not allow himself to be dissuaded (7.11), but he changes his mind later upon further consideration (7.12.1). Thus, in spite of a dream warning him not to change his mind, he announced that he would not, after all, attack Hellas. However, threatened by yet another dream the following night, he once more reconsiders the matter. Artabanus, having had a similar dream, warns him not to prevent that which necessarily must take place, *to chreon* (7.17.2). The gods seem to be determined upon the destruction of Hellas (7.12-18).

Artabanus, who is usually wise, demonstrates blindness too, when he here understands *to chreon* as the favour of fate. In the history of Croesus, Herodotus has earlier pointed this out as an erroneous understanding of the *chreon*, and Artabanus has learned from Persia's earlier history that one should be on guard against wishing for more

---

126. Evans (1991: 26) maintains that Xerxes' conviction that Persia's expansionistically inclined *nomos* has divine sanction is a symptom of Xerxes' blindness. On the contrary, both Xerxes' and Artabanus' dreams show that the king was right. Xerxes' blindness should rather be seen as consisting of his lack of understanding of the nature of the god or fate as being unfavourably inclined towards him. Cf. Aesch. *Pers.* 725.

than what one already has. Because of the Persians' unfortunate experience during Cyrus' campaign against the Massagetes (1.201-214) and
Cambyses' similar experience with the Ethiopians (3.20-25), he had
previously advised Xerxes to do nothing (7.18). Before his dream,
Artabanus was very well aware that the Persians, by attacking, would
commit *hubris* and incur the wrath of the god. Before the story of his
and Artabanus' dreams, Xerxes, given the choice between two courses
of action, the one incurring and the other impending *hubris*, had
chosen the former (7.16.2).[127] The outcome of the campaign shows
the malignancy of fate—Xerxes' downfall was predestined.[128]

After arming for four years, Xerxes moves to Sardis at the head of
the largest army Herodotus has ever heard of (7.19-31). This journey
and its continuation across the Hellespont into Hellas is marked by an
ominous dream and several obviously portentous omens, all of which
are either misunderstood or ignored.[129] At the ford of Abydos,
Xerxes reviews his troops, and at the sight of all the ships and soldiers
he rejoices,[130] but is seized, almost at once, by compassion at the
thought of the brevity of human life. Not one of all these people will
be alive a hundred years later. A philosophical discourse takes place
between Xerxes and Artabanus on the brevity and uncertainty of
human life and the jealousy of the god. No one is so happy that he
does not, at least once in his life, wish he were dead. 'When life

127. I have already mentioned the similarity between the false dream in Homer
(*Il.* 2.1-47) and Xerxes' dreams. Here I would add that Herodotus cunningly indicates the deceit of Xerxes' dream when the dream in 7.12 states that Xerxes has to
carry out the campaign because he had ordered the Persians to raise an army. No one
would be prepared to overlook his changing his mind. The Persians' reaction when
the king announces his decision in spite of the dream shows quite clearly, for the
reader at any rate, that the dream was false: κεχαρηκότες προσεκύνεον, 'they
were pleased and threw themselves down' (7.14). That a dream may at one and the
same time be divinely sent and deceptive is also to be seen in Homer.

128. Fohl (1913: 72-73) regards, along with the dreams, Xerxes' indecisiveness
to be a dramatic means of holding back the action. The other warnings during the
campaign that are unable to prevent the king's downfall have the same effect.

129. Dream: 7.19. Omens: 7.37, 7.42, 7.43, 7.57. Later on, too, the outcome of
the Persian–Hellenic confrontations is announced by omens, signs, and oracles:
7.113; 7.139; 7.140-44; 7.169-71; 7.178; 7.180; 7.219; 7.220; 8.20; 8.41; 8.53;
8.55; 8.64-65; 8.77; 8.84; 8.96; 8.114; 8.133; 8.137; 8.141; 9.19; 9.33-37; 9.41;
9.42-43; 9.61-62; 9.64; 9.91; 9.92; 9.93; 9.120.

130. 7.44-45. This is comparable to Cyrus, who rejoiced at the height of his
power.

becomes unbearable, death becomes the most desirable refuge for mankind. Once the god has allowed [us] to taste that life [is] sweet, he thereby shows that he is jealous' (7.46.4).[131] Artabanus, at this juncture, gives vent to his anxiety concerning the fate of the army and navy. There is no harbour big enough to shelter the entire navy in the event of a storm, and the enormous army risks famine, as it moves further and further into enemy country. Xerxes deprecates these objections and sends the overly cautious Artabanus home to Susa (7.44-53) before he and the army begin the crossing of the Hellespont by means of the specially-built bridge (7.54-56) and thus commence the subsequent march upon Hellas (7.57-100).

Upon arriving at Therme (7.105-130), Xerxes was met by the heralds he had sent in advance to demand the subjection of Hellas. Now they return with the answer to his demands. Herodotus interpolates a story about divine retribution in order to explain why Xerxes had sent no heralds to Athens and Sparta. The omission was due to the shameful treatment given in the past to the heralds whom Darius sent on the same business. When Sparta was smitten by divine wrath later, two heralds were sent to Xerxes, bearing the message that Xerxes might treat them as he pleased. The king refrained from revenge on this past occasion and sent the heralds home. He refused to overstep $τὰ$ $πάντων$ $ἀνθρώπων$ $νόμιμα$, 'the law of all people', which was what the Spartans had done. However, the sons of the Spartan heralds were smitten by divine retribution many years later (7.131-37). Here once again, Herodotus gives his reader an indication of which direction the story is taking. Croesus too, by attacking the Persians, had overstepped 'the law of all people' and set the events in motion that were to lead to Xerxes' campaign. Being the ruler of the Lydians, Xerxes is Croesus' successor. So, bearing that story in mind, we have good reason to suppose that the wrath of the god will also strike Xerxes.

The Athenians receive two answers from the oracle at Delphi. One of them hints that the Athenians will defeat the Persians in a battle at sea. The Persian and the Hellenic armies and fleets start manoeuvering, and at this juncture Herodotus holds a census of both the Persian and the Hellenic forces. Compared to the Persian millions, the number of Hellenes is practically microscopic. It is, however, some consolation that Xerxes is not a god, but only a mortal. No mortal exists who does not receive his portion of misfortune, and the greater he is, the

---

131. Comparison may be made to Solon's speech to Croesus.

greater his misfortune may be expected to be (7.202-207). The Greek army fights well in the narrow pass of Thermopylae, and it is not until Ephialtes of Malis betrays it that the Persians win (7.208-33). After this, we are told of the naval battles at Artemision during which the Persian fleet was greatly reduced by a storm sent by the god for the purpose of making the two warring parties more equal, a purpose likewise helped by the Hellenes' receiving reinforcements. After these two indecisive naval battles, the Hellenes retreat into central Hellas (8.1-23). Xerxes moves from Thermopylae to Boeotia which is friendly towards him (8.24-34), whilst the Athenians evacuate Attica so that Xerxes has to make do with taking an Athens devoid of people. The Hellenes' fleet gathers at Salamis where it prevails against the numerically greater Persian fleet (8.40-96).

During the entire course of these events, Xerxes' hubristic conduct exemplifies his blindness. First there are three examples of pride: the canal at Atos (7.22-24), his treatment of the rich Pythius (7.27-29), and the building of the bridge of the Hellespont with the subsequent punishment of the sea (7.19-36). In addition, there is the muster at Abydos where Xerxes, like Croesus before him, counts himself fortunate at the very pinnacle of his power. That Xerxes also weeps at this point, is due solely to the thought of the brevity of life which prevents him and his men from enjoying this happiness for ever (7.45-46). As he has done earlier (7.11), he here, referring to his supremacy, deprecates Artabanus' practical objections to the fortunate outcome of the campaign which Xerxes confidently expects. Artabanus is told he may return home if he is afraid of the campaign against Hellas. Thus the threat expressed in 7.11.1 becomes reality (7.47-52). At Sardis and again after the crossing of the Hellespont, Xerxes ignores two unambiguous omens pronouncing the unfortunate outcome of the campaign. Herodotus here includes, ironically, mention of Xerxes' refusal on an earlier occasion to overstep 'the law of all people'. This he is currently doing. Faced with conflicting advice, Xerxes consistently makes the wrong choice. Thus he decided upon the campaign after taking Mardonius' advice rather than Artabanus' (7.5-11). Later, he refuses good tactical advice from Demaratus of Sparta who is taking part in the campaign against Hellas, preferring to listen to his own brother Achaemenes (7.234-37). Later again, he disregards the wise female commander Artemisia's advice, taking instead that of his other naval

commanders (8.66-69[132]). Finally, Xerxes' disgraceful treatment of
the corpse of Leonidas should be mentioned (7.238), an act that classes
him with Cambyses, who is depicted in Herodotus' account as completely mad.[133]

Xerxes, like Croesus, is thrown down at the height of his power.
Herodotus' heavy emphasizing of Xerxes' colossal wealth and superi-
ority serves as a tragic background for his account of Xerxes' downfall.[134] Through his extensive preparations, Xerxes unwittingly
brought about his own ruin. It took him four years to raise an army
whose absurd size is described, firstly concisely (7.21), later in inor-
dinate detail. Rivers and lakes dry up when the army fetches drinking
water (7.108-109; 7.127), and the Hellenic cities forced to feed the
army are all but ruined (7.118-20). The army's marching order is
minutely described (7.40-41), its size being such that the crossing of
the Hellespont takes a full week (7.55-56). Xerxes musters his troops
at Doriskos, and at this point Herodotus lists all the peoples present
and states the infantry to be one million, seven hundred thousand men
strong (7.60-100). It is against this dramatic background that Xerxes
asks Demaratus whether the Hellenes, who only number a few thousands, will dare withstand the Persian millions. Demaratus is of the
opinion that they will and is later proved right (7.101-105).

After this, both the army and the fleet are augmented as the peoples
on the line of march are incorporated (7.115.2). In this way, Xerxes
finishes up at the head of an army numbering more than five million.
The fact that this unrealistically large military force[135] is, in the final
instance, of no use whatsoever to Xerxes, is due to the god who strikes
mortals down with lightning if they overreach themselves. This is
what Artabanus had already warned Xerxes about (7.10ε). Twice the
Persian fleet is reduced by a storm, thus making the opposing forces
more equal (7.188 and 8.13). Xerxes' downfall is seen to be caused by
a divine law that has already been defined in the history of Croesus

132. Artemisia's wisdom is stated in Hdt. 7.99.

133. Cambyses' desecration of the corpse of the Egyptian king Amasis being
regarded as an indication of his growing insanity, Hdt. 3.16, cf. 3.38.1: Πανταχῇ
ὦν μοι δῆλα ἐστὶ ὅτι ἐμάνη μεγάλως ὁ Καμβύσης.

134. Thus Fohl (1913: 69), who points to Aeschylus' *Agamemnon* by way of
comparison.

135. See the discussion of Herodotus' figures in How and Wells 1928: II, 363-
69.

(1.207.2): [ὁ] κύκλος τῶν ἀνθρωπηίων πρηγμάτων, the wheel which, in turning, does not permit the same people to be fortunate all the time, or as Solon said 'the god has visited many with good fortune, then destroyed them utterly' (1.32.9). Apart from Artabanus' warning, this divine law may be found in the course of Artabanus' and Xerxes' conversation where Artabanus reminds him of the uncertainty of life (7.46). It may likewise be found in the edifying message of the Hellenes to their allies: Every mortal is given his portion of misfortune, the greater he is, the greater his misfortune also will be (7.203.2).

Commencing his miserable retreat (8.113-20), Xerxes leaves Mardonius on the latter's own suggestion to subject Hellas and gives him three hundred thousand choice troops for the purpose (8.97-107). Acting upon an oracle, the Spartans demand reparation of Xerxes for the death of Leonidas. This demand makes Xerxes, unwittingly and tragically, foretell the defeat of Mardonius at Plataea: 'then this man Mardonius will give them the reparation they deserve' (8.114). In Boeotia on his way to Athens, Mardonius ignores the Thebans' suggestion that he should make Boeotia his headquarters, making do instead with bribing the leading men in the Hellenic cities. He takes Athens, which turns out to be an empty city, the population having crossed to Salamis. At a feast in Boeotia, a Persian foretells the Persian defeat. It is not possible to prevent what the gods have ordained, because no one believes the man who knows what is going to happen. Although they have a presentiment of the forthcoming defeat, many Persians are forced all the same to obey orders, thus flying in the face of their perfectly correct intuition (9.1-18).

Having been defeated by the numerically inferior Hellenes at Erythrai in Boeotia, Mardonius is advised by the respected general Artabazos to win the Hellenes by bribery, rather than to risk yet another battle. Once again, Mardonius ignores good advice. In the face of the omens, he starts the battle of Plataea which the Hellenes win with the assistance of the goddess Hera. Mardonius is killed, thus offering the Spartans reparation for the slaying of Leonidas. Practically the entire Persian army is mown down, whereas the Hellenes' losses are quite small (9.19-75). At the same time that the Persian army suffers defeat at Plataea, the fleet suffers a no less annihilating defeat at Mycale in Ionia. After Mycale, the Hellenes sailed to the Hellespont in order to break the bridges whilst the sad remnant of the

Persian army makes its way to Sardis (9.90-107). The Hellenes can then, after another few diversions, return to their homes. Herodotus concludes his account with the laconic statement: 'And in that year nothing further was done' (9.114-21).

As has been seen, events are foretold by means of dreams, omens, and portents, and by proleptic dialogues as well. During the first council of the Persian notables (7.8-11), the subsequent course of events may be glimpsed in Artabanus' speech, when he attempts to warn Xerxes of the possibility of defeat. He notes that, as it has often been the case that a large army was defeated by a small one, Xerxes should remain at home, if he is absolutely determined upon attacking Hellas, sending Mardonius instead with an army. Artabanus is afraid that the Hellenes will win over the Persian fleet and subsequently destroy the bridge at the Hellespont whereby the Persian troops on land will be lost. Artabanus foretells great losses, if Xerxes leaves Persia, as well as the death of Mardonius in either the territory of the Athenians or of the Lacedaemonians. The Hellenes actually do defeat the Persian fleet. That they do not also destroy the bridge of the Hellespont is solely due to a storm's having done so before they arrive there (8.117; 9.114). After Xerxes' defeat, Mardonius takes over the command of a smaller army, and the king returns home (8.100-119). Mardonius, too, falls as predicted (at Plataea, 9.63).[136] In a later speech, Artabanus discusses the uncertainty of life. With regard to the present campaign, Artabanus mentions that the colossal fleet will be unable to find shelter in the event of a storm and that the equally large army risks facing famine the further it advances into Hellas (7.46-50). The campaign ends with Xerxes' downfall, the fleet is twice diminished due to storms, and the army suffers starvation, although not until its retreat. The prophecies of Demaratus are perhaps less imposing, but he does actually foretell that the Hellenes will fight bravely against the much larger Persian force, a statement that sounds ominous, both on its own and in combination with the other prophecies (7.101-105; 7.209). Before Salamis, Xerxes asks Artemisia's advice.

136. In addition, Artabanus' statement that the god strikes the tallest houses and the tallest trees with his bolts and that he causes a big army fright and panic with his lightning and thunder (7.10ε), according to Fohl (1913: 71), deliberately refers to (7.42), where thunder and lightning diminish the Persian army, furthermore (8.12), where a heavy storm reduces the fleet, and, finally, (8.37), where flashes of lightning fall down from heaven upon the barbarians at Athena Pronaia's shrine at Delphi.

She is against a battle, as Xerxes risks defeat, and she fears the defeat of the fleet will also mean the defeat of the army (8.68), which is what happens. Finally, there is Xerxes' unwitting prophecy of Mardonius' defeat (8.114; 9.63-64).

An important feature of these prolepses is seen in the story of the feast in Boeotia during Mardonius' campaign. Even if one knows what the gods intend, one cannot prevent it (9.16). Though the various people with whom Xerxes and Mardonius[137] discuss forthcoming events have their doubts about the future, both the king and the general remain blind to the implications. This blindness is likewise seen when Xerxes ignores omens which could easily have been read correctly. As with Croesus: τὴν πεπρωμένην μοῖραν ἀδύνατά ἐστι ἀποφυγεῖν καὶ θεῷ, 'it is not possible even for a god to flee from a fate that has already been decided' (1.91.1).

Xerxes' threat that Artabanus may stay at home with the women whilst Xerxes conquers Hellas (7.11) may be regarded as a tragic irony. After flying from Hellas, Xerxes becomes involved in an ignominious intrigue in the harem (9.108-113; Fohl 1913: 71-72). Had it not been for this intrigue, the king's misfortune would have consisted only of his defeat, and his luck would have changed when he returned home. He is, after all, still the ruler in Susa, the result of his campaign was not as poor as all that. He did achieve one goal, revenge upon Athens which he fired.[138] To quote Fohl: 'The fact that the king is now entangled in women's disgraceful intrigues at home supplies the picture of his misfortune with a telling, dark background, as he has himself...designated it as a most ignominious thing to stay at home with the women' (Fohl 1913: 78-79). It is, however, doubtful whether the lasting misfortune that Xerxes could be expected to suffer after the account of his ignominious defeat in Hellas can be said to consist of the intrigue in the harem, although Fohl is certainly right in that it may be regarded as tragic irony on account of the ridicule the king is made to suffer. Xerxes' final misfortune is not recounted in Herodotus who, after a digression to the time of Cyrus, concludes his

---

137. After Xerxes' defeat, Mardonius, too, appears as a tragic figure. He has no option but death on the field if he is to retain his honour (8.100). He too has been blinded, thus ignoring good advice (9.2-3, 9.41), not to mention disregarding the omens that prophesied a defeat at Plataea (9.37, 9.41). His campaign and defeat are obviously determined by fate, as the discussion at the feast shows (9.16).

138. Cf. Artemisia's advice, Hdt. 8.102.

account with the events of 479 BCE (9.114-22). That the murder of Xerxes in 465 BCE (Frye 1984: 127) is not included by Herodotus, even although it may be inferred from the gods' hostile attitude to him, may be seen as comparable to the fact that Achilles' approaching death is foretold in the *Iliad* (18.95-96) without this poem's giving the account of the actual incident.

The Herodotean Tragedy

In Herodotus, historiography no longer merely consists of a compilation of facts, arranged either in chronological order or after other principles. From now on it also deals with cause and effect.[139] The first five books of Herodotus' opus are intended to show in detail the differences between Greeks and barbarians under the Achaemenids, as well as explaining what exactly created these differences, and how a small and disunited people could withstand the combined military power of the whole of Asia (Lateiner 1989: 157). Aetiology is of major importance in Herodotus' work.[140] This causality is expressed in metaphysical and tragical categories, strongly inspired by Aeschylus. The Persian wars were fought between Europe and Asia, the Persians having divine sanction for their subjugation of Asia. The Persian king, by crossing from Asia to Europe, disturbed the equilibrium of the world and committed *hubris. Hubris*, which is due to the gods' deception, is, however, unavoidable. Herodotus adopts Aeschylus' picture of the world, but describes it in far more detail. *Hubris* as committed by the Persians is seen by Herodotus as part of a far greater historical pattern, during which the four Achaemenian kings attempted to extend the Persian kingdom, each in his own direction. Herodotus describes how these endeavours called down divine *nemesis*.[141]

The history of Croesus invokes all the metaphysical themes dominant throughout Herodotus' opus. The account commences with the tragedy of Gyges and Candaules, where Gyges' choice results in a

---

139. Bockisch 1984: 488-89; Momigliano 1978: 4. According to Momigliano (1972), classical historiography deals mainly with describing and explaining *change*.

140. Lateiner (1989: 196-205) gives five 'systems of explanation' employed by Herodotus: the immoral and divine jealousy, *phthonos*; the amoral fate, *moira*; references to the gods' intervention in history; *tisis*, representing the dynamic equilibrium of history; and finally, the rational, political analysis.

141. Darius, however, had turned back before *nemesis* took effect as portended.

curse upon the family, bringing about Croesus' fall after five generations. The reason for the hubristic action that Candaules forced upon Gyges is stated simply as *chren*, 'it was necessary'. Solon, visiting Croesus, demonstrates the principle of *teleuté,* the uncertainty, changeability, and unpredictability of life. The tragedy of Atys and Adrastus that looks irrational in the perspective of this life reflects historical continuity when the god works towards a certain goal over several generations. The death of Croesus' son Atys becomes understandable when it is seen as *nemesis* occasioned by the fact that Croesus regarded himself as fortunate. Events in this story are set in motion by a sinister dream that Croesus tries to prevent from coming true, an example of the *elpís*-theme. However, neither his presentiment nor all his precautions can prevent what must happen—this represents the *adynaton apophygeín* theme. Apollo tries to prevent Croesus' downfall, but it transpires that not even a god can prevent what fate has ordained, although he may be able to delay it. Croesus takes all possible precautions before the campaign against the Persians, but they are all proved vain. He misunderstands the oracles and ignores the advice Sandanis gives him. This is, to use a Homeric expression (*Il.* 19.86-96), an example of *áte*, the bewilderment or infatuation caused by blindness or delusion sent by the gods when some predetermined incident is about to occur. The same *áte* makes Croesus motivate his attack on the Persians by the desire for land πρὸς τὴν ἑωυτοῦ μοῖραν, 'against his fate'.

Political arguments and a somewhat discriminating choice of oracles persuade Xerxes to attack Hellas. The fact that fate was inimical to Xerxes is concealed from him. When he reconsiders matters, due to Artabanus' warning, a dream forces him to continue the war rather than avoiding *to chreon*, 'what is going to happen'. Artabanus' warning with which Xerxes complies, unlike the other similar scenes in the opus, may be regarded as an instance of *adynaton apophygeín* as well. Both Xerxes and his adviser Artabanus demonstrate their blindness when they believe so whole-heartedly that the gods are favourably inclined towards the Persians. During the campaign, Xerxes ignores omens and sensible advice, and his behaviour is hubristic in other ways as well. During the war, the gods restore the disrupted equilibrium of the military forces. These themes which we have already seen in the story of Croesus are found here in the historical account of the Persian war. The same may be said of such ideas as the brevity and uncertainty of life and the jealousy of the gods. The greater a king is, the more misfortune he may expect. The *elpís* motive which is strongly defined in the story of Croesus becomes even more marked here, when, in the course of his campaign, Xerxes uses every conceivable measure to ensure his military supremacy. But as with Croesus, it is all in vain. Here too, as with Croesus, we are explicitly told that no one can prevent what must happen even if he possesses an intuition about forthcoming events. Humans are the helpless victims of fate.

The ultimate reason for the Persian war lies in the inscrutable, divine will. When Candaules became infatuated by the beauty of his wife, a chain of historical events was started that was to continue for several hundred years and to culminate in the ignominious defeat of the Persians. The first person to violate the Hellenes' liberty was, as far as Herodotus knew, the Lydian king Croesus (1.5.3). It is with him that Herodotus commences his main history. Croesus conquers practically all of Asia Minor west of the Halys (1.28). That this territory is actually his, according to Herodotus' conception of the world, is shown by one of the reasons stated for Croesus' attack on the Persians, namely that he wished for land πρὸς τὴν ἑωυτοῦ μοῖραν, 'against his fate' (1.73). This expression is used of neither Croesus' earlier conquests nor those of his ancestors which all lay west of the Halys. On the face of things, this seems to be a contradiction of the idea that all Asia belonged, according to the workings of fate, to the Persian king Cyrus.[142] The events concerning Croesus are, however, the start of the realization of Cyrus' pan-Asian rule which had been ordained by fate. Croesus' downfall is explained by the curse that Gyges' action had called down upon his family (1.13; 1.91). However, Gyges' action was caused by Candaules' *hubris* (1.11). As the reason for Candaules' *hubris* is only explained by a *chren*, 'it was necessary' (1.8.2), Croesus' destiny must be said to be ordained by fate. It was fate that made Croesus wish to extend his territory 'against his fate', and in this way Cyrus' pre-ordained fate as ruler of all Asia was brought to pass.[143] It

142. Two dreams portended to Cyrus' grandfather, the Median king Astyages, that Cyrus was to be king and that he should rule the whole of Asia (1.107-108). The same thought lies behind the warning of Tomyris, queen of the Massagetes, that Cyrus should not cross the river Araxes (1.206.1).

143. According to 1.130.3, Cyrus became lord of all Asia by subduing Croesus. It is only after this statement that Cyrus' actual conquering that continent is recounted (1.141-200).

is, however, easier to start a process than to stop it. The Persian war machine rumbles on, both under Cyrus and his successors Cambyses and Darius. They extend the Persian borders towards the extreme ends of the earth in the east, south, and north respectively, whilst Xerxes moves into Europe which is dominated by Hellas. The subjugation of Hellas was to give access to the far west. By Xerxes' time the pattern was fixed (Redfield 1985: 113). The experience garnered in the first six books of Herodotus' opus is summed up by Artabanus in his speech to Xerxes: One is feeding *hubris* when one endeavours to obtain more than what one already possesses (7.16). Artabanus has formerly seen a great power forced to subject itself to a lesser, examples being Cyrus' campaign against the Massagetes, Cambyses' campaign against the Ethiopians, and Darius' campaign against the Scythians. Artabanus advises Xerxes to remain at peace. Xerxes, having listened to Artabanus, cancels the planned campaign, but just as he is prepared to learn from history and stop the 'machinery', he is shown in a dream that the historical pattern of Persian conquests beyond the divinely appointed boundaries is ordained by fate, and therefore it is not within Xerxes' power to stop it (7.12, 7.14, 7.17-18). Croesus' provoking of the Persian war machinery was preordained, and therefore the Persians were able to conquer the territory that was predestined to belong to them. But the Persians' exceeding their borders, their *hubris*, which is also initiated by Croesus' provocation, is likewise ordained by fate.

The Herodotean tragedy can be characterized as follows: One commits *hubris* by overstepping one's given borders. These can be either physical or moral. The kingdoms of Persia and Lydia have their physical borders, and overstepping them cost their kings their lives. Moral limits can be universal, or individual. One is expected to respect both 'the law of all people' (7.136) and other peoples' customs and usages, 'for custom is lord of all' (3.38). One should also take care not to overreach oneself and thus approach the divine sphere, for when this happens, the divine *phthonos* (jealousy) comes into play and evens things out again (7.10), or the wheel of fate turns (1.207.2). Tragedy occurs when a divinely sent bewilderment, *áte*, causes the victim to overstep boundaries and thereby commit *hubris*. The *nemesis* of the god then strikes, *nemesis* being the principle of evening out.

Reparation is made for the overstepping of boundaries,[144] an act which itself was caused by the god. *Nemesis* may even, as with Croesus, be the result of an ancestor's actions.[145] Those who grow too great on account of what seems to be a fortunate fate and are in danger of approaching the divine state, either due to great happiness (7.46), wealth, or power (7.10), are smitten by misfortune that gives the mortal concerned a more fitting mixture of good and evil[146] or arranges greater equality between two enemies.[147] With regard to the last-named possibility, the reduction of an *agan* ('too much'; Regenbogen 1930b: 87), Herodotus uses the expressions 'divine jealousy' or the 'wheel of fate', according to whether the perspective is divine[148] or mortal.[149] One of the main features of Herodotus' opus is that it demonstrates that this pattern has incessantly decided the course of history. This message is proclaimed clearly in important passages of the work, but is not repeated *in absurdum*. In the wording of O. Regenbogen, Herodotus is not a preacher, but a story-teller.[150]

144. Examples: Candaules oversteps a moral limit (1.8); Croesus receives ambiguous oracles which he interprets to mean he should attack the Persians (1.73, 1.75, 1.87) thus overstepping physical boundaries; Cambyses' insanity is delineated in great detail (2.27-38). The best example is perhaps Xerxes' two and Artabanus' single dream by which the king is forced to attack Hellas, thus committing *hubris* (7.12-18). Artabanus' speech makes it very clear that this is *hubris* (7.16), even though Artabanus at the same time is misled into thinking that it is not (7.18).

145. Cf. likewise Croesus' son Atys who died because Croesus regarded himself as fortunate (1.34-45).

146. The story of Polycrates shows that too much luck can be a sign that fate is inimical, as the greater one's luck, the greater misfortune one must expect due to the jealousy of the gods. Polycrates' friend Amasis warns him of this, and Polycrates tries to avert disaster by causing loss to himself. He throws his ring into the sea, but this does not work. Fate is not to be placated and ungraciously returns the ring, then arranges the pre-ordained catastrophe (3.39-43; 3.120-25).

147. Twice the hellenic fight against a superior force is motivated by θεὼν τὰ ἶσα νεμόντων (6.11, 6.109), and twice the Persian fleet is reduced by a storm (7.188, 8.12-13).

148. 3.40.2: τὸ θεῖον...ἔστι φθονερόν.

149. 1.207.2: μάθε ὡς κύκλος τῶν ἀνθρωπηίων ἐστὶ πρηγμάτων; 7.10ε: ὁθεὸς φθονήσας.

150. Regenbogen 1930b: 82: 'an entscheidenden Wendepunkten [erschließen] sich diese Hintergründe mit einer Klarheit.'

Herodotus' Opus as a Piece of Corporate Historiography

According to J. Mejer, the fact that Herodotus attempts to describe the history of *all* the Greeks constitutes the actual novelty in his opus (Mejer 1985: 203). Herodotus' opus is a corporate history. With the history of the Persian wars as its backbone, it tells the history of the Hellenes from the earliest times until the defeat of Xerxes in Hellas in 479 BCE. Herodotus uses familiar Greek traditions so that his history agrees with facts that his readers, generally speaking, regarded as the truth about the Hellenic past. He likewise demonstrates the reasons that enabled liberty-loving Hellas, which was weak, to conquer the despotic and powerful Persian kingdom.

Using this description, both J. Huizinga's definition of 'history' as well as J. Van Seters' views that history must basically be national may be applied to Herodotus. Huizinga defines history as 'the intellectual form in which a civilization renders account to itself of its past' (Huizinga 1936: 9). Being an intellectual form, history may neither be mythical, nor fictitious.[151] A civilization, by which a group governed by the same *Weltanschauung* is meant, renders itself an account of those events of its own history that it regards as important, and that are of a teleological nature.[152] History is first and foremost a literary form, but makes use of a presumed knowledge of events that have taken place. Van Seters makes a distinction between historiography, regarded as any text that gives ancient historical events, and history, and he understands Huizinga's 'civilization' as a nation or a people. Thus Van Seters is able to list five criteria that must be followed in a historiographic text if it is to be deemed history (Van Seters 1983: 1-5): 1) 'History writing is a specific form of tradition in its own right' and not merely an accidental accumulation of traditional material. 2) 'History writing is not primarily the accurate reporting of past events. It also considers the reason for recalling the past and the significance given to past events.' 3) 'History writing examines the causes of present conditions and circumstances.' 4) It is 'national or corporate in character', and 5) it is 'part of the literary tradition and

---

151. Huizinga 1936: 8: 'Mythical and fictitious representations of the past... for us they are not history.'

152. Huizinga 1936: 6: 'Civilization has meaning only as a process of adaptation to an end; it is a teleological concept, as history is an explicitly purposive knowing.'

plays a significant role in the corporate tradition of the people'.

The Greek word *historía* has a two-fold meaning: 'inquiry' or 'knowledge so obtained' and a 'written account of one's inquiries, narrative, history' (LSJ: 842), the latter being a literary form. Where Huizinga and Van Seters emphasize the literary form, T.L. Thompson solely acknowledges the intention of 'historicity' as a criterion of history writing: 'the truth of the events recounted'.[153] The 'classical Greek genre of historiography…[is] a specific literary genre relating to critical descriptions and evaluations of past reality and events, in contrast to more fictional varieties of prose' (Thompson 1992: 372-73). Following this definition, the earliest Greek historian must be Hecataeus with the next indubitable possibility being Thucydides. Herodotus is, as we have seen, inadmissible[154] in spite of the fact that he, in his introduction, explicitly describes his opus as *historíes apódexis*, 'a presentation of research'.

I have indicated the resemblance between Herodotus and fiction such as the epic tradition and the Greek tragedy above. There are, however, marked differences between Homer and Herodotus, including the self-evident fact that Homer wrote poetry and Herodotus prose. These differences, however, do *not* occur in either the contents of the works, in their stringency with regard to truth, or in the agreement to be found on what we today define as historic events. If one should wish to define the differences, Van Seters' view of history as a literary form is of importance. Homer could be said neither to belong in Van Seters second nor third category. Homer was purely concerned with the distant past, whereas Herodotus concludes his work in the recent past, which he discusses on a causal basis.[155] In much the same way, Thompson (1992: 373, 389-90) may be correct in saying that the

153. Thompson 1992: 372-83. It is not important whether the historiographer actually succeeded in this effort—only his intention is at stake here (*ibid.*, p. 389 n. 64).

154. This is also the opinion of Thompson 1992: 373 and 389-90.

155. These examples are of course not the entire difference between the two authors. Mandell and Freedman (1993: 170) point out that '[t]he Homeric works are not national epics; and each of them is about half the length of either Herodotus' History or Primary History'. By the term 'Primary History', Mandell and Freedman allude to the sequence Genesis–2 Kings in the Hebrew bible.

Hittite annals of Ḫattušili I[156] and Muršili II[157] and the Neo-Babylonian Chronicle Series[158] reflect a historiographic interest marked by factuality which Herodotus often, but not always, has difficulty in living up to. I am, all the same, inclined to agree with Van Seters that these texts from the ancient Near East containing lists of facts do not give the *experience* of history in the same way as the often unreliable Herodotus.

156. Text and translation: Imparati and Saporetti 1965.
157. Text and translation: Götze 1933.
158. Text and translation: Grayson 1975b: 69-124.

Chapter 3

THE DEUTERONOMISTIC HISTORICAL WORK

A Summary of Research[1]

In the early nineteenth century, W.M.L. de Wette attempted to show that Deuteronomy has its own distinctive style and that it was written later than the other four books of the Pentateuch (de Wette 1805; cf. Rogerson 1992: 39-42). In his famous *Lehrbuch der historisch-kritischen Einleitung in die Bibel Alten und Neuen Testaments*, he postulates an 'obvious affinity' between Deuteronomy and the book of Joshua (de Wette 1817: 193), and in later editions of this work, he finds this 'Deuteronomistic' affinity in the books of Judges and Samuel as well.[2] J. Wellhausen differentiated between sources and redaction in the books of Judges, Samuel, and Kings so that the sources, chronologically speaking, belonged more or less to the era they described, whereas he ascribed the editorial process to the period of the Babylonian exile.[3] This redaction is mainly to be seen in the chronological framework, the way in which events are connected from the cultic point of view, and in 'homiletic' remarks inserted into the sources. Since Wellhausen, many scholars have attempted to make distinctions between various strata of sources, but even after a hundred years' research there is still no consensus on the subject. This is especially true of research on Kings. Since A. Kuenen (1890), a great number of scholars have pleaded for a twofold redaction of the Deuteronomistic tradition and have regarded the version in the books of Kings that has come down to us as a revised edition of a pre-exilic history of the monarchy, the revision having been carried out during

1. Mayes 1983: 1-21; Weippert 1985; O'Brien 1989: 3-23.
2. For example, see the seventh edition (de Wette 1852); the book of Joshua: pp. 195, 210-13; the book of Judges: pp. 218-19; the books of Samuel: p. 228.
3. Wellhausen 1905: 223-93; Wellhausen 1889: 213-301. Cf. Weippert 1985: 224.

the exile (Long 1984: 14; Weippert 1985: 225). This and similar redaction-critical approaches have given rise to a veritable deluge of scholarly works intended to demonstrate the composite nature of the redaction of the Deuteronomistic historical work.[4] Each of the many suggestions is fully plausible, but they are also mutually incompatible. Taken as a whole, they, to quote H. Weippert's apposite description, make up, at best, a patchwork quilt rather than a hypothesis (Weippert 1985: 226).

M. Noth (1943) propounded the hypothesis that Deuteronomy, Joshua, Judges, Samuel, and Kings originally were a literary entity, a 'Deuteronomistic historical work' written a few decades after the catastrophe of 586 BCE in the form of an aetiology on the destruction of the temple and the state. As an indication that the work was written by a single person, Noth stated that language,[5] chronology[6] and ideology are consistent throughout the whole work. Noth regards many passages as later additions, but basically the work owes its existence to one person who during the exile gathered the various traditional beliefs on Israel's history from many sources and combined them in one account under the aspect of ideas reflected in Deuteronomy. The central Jerusalem cultus is repeatedly emphasized, and history shows forth divine justice. The heroes, those who adhere to Yahweh, are rewarded, while villains are punished. The literary unity is achieved by epitomizing digressions in the narrative (Josh. 12; Judg. 2.11–3.6; 2 Kgs 17.7-23), grand speeches by leaders at pivotal moments (Josh. 1.2-9; Josh. 23.2-16; 1 Sam. 12; 1 Kgs 8.14-61[7]) and a schematic

---

4.	Weippert (1985: 225-26) gives a number of instances.

5.	Detailed studies have later been made by Weinfeld 1972: 320-65; Hoffmann 1980: 327-66.

6.	This is, however, by no means unproblematic. See Mayes 1983: 4-6.

7.	2 Sam. 7 containing Nathan's prophecy could, perhaps, be included, but this is uncertain. Noth (1943: 64) denies its being Deuteronomistic, while von Rad (1947) and his followers (see the list in Weippert 1985: 219) regards Nathan's prophecy as the commencement of the Deuteronomistic theme of the eternal promise to the house of David which is repeated throughout 1 and 2 Kgs; see von Rad 1947: 193-95. Weippert (above) rightly points out that one's conception of 2 Sam. 7 depends upon whether the Deuteronomistic work is regarded as being inclined for or against the monarchy. If 2 Sam. 7 is, as Weippert calls it, a 'Stützpfeiler der dtr Geschichtsdarstellung', the tendency is for the monarchy, whereas the Deuteronomistic influence in 2 Sam. 7 is minimal, if one pleads a disinclination towards the monarchy in the work as such.

chronology of 480 years running from Moses to the building of Solomon's temple (1 Kgs 6.1). The book of Joshua depicts the conquest of the land as a success due to the people's obedience to Yahweh fulfilling the blessings in Deut. 28.1-14. The books of Judges, Samuel and Kings in turn depict the disastrous consequences of disobedience in accordance with the curses of Deut. 28.15-68. The misfortunes culminate in the Babylonian exile, a tragedy caused, according to Noth's Deuteronomist, by the faithlessness of the kings towards Yahweh (Noth 1943: 3-27). The nearest parallels to the Deuteronomistic historical work is, according to Noth, the Hellenistic and Roman historiographers who using unnamed sources wrote, not of their own time, but of a more or less distant past.[8]

Noth's thesis that Deuteronomy and the former prophets constitute a literary unit is still highly respected,[9] whereas the questions of date, authorship, and purpose are the subject of debate. Here mention will be made of some of the important points of view in this debate. S.L. McKenzie (1991: 5-19) has classed them in two main groups: 1) ideas of a single, exilic author, and 2) redactional theories.

According to H.-D. Hoffmann (1980), the Deuteronomistic work is an Israelite cultic history with a leitmotif that may be termed *cultus semper reformandus*. An exilic or post-exilic author created the work mainly from oral tradition, but with regard to both contents and form he took a great liberty in making his own reconstruction of the course of events. There is very little in the work that disagrees with its uniformity and which must therefore be ascribed to another author.[10] Hoffmann examines all the texts that mention cult-localities, cult-personnel, rituals, cultic objects, and gods, and he concludes that Moses is the prototype for all subsequent cultic reformers in the Deuteronomistic work (p. 313). From Moses' time to that of Joshua, the cultic reforms are developed into a programme which in reality

8.   Noth 1943: 11-12. Noth's observations indicate a date of writing far nearer to the start of the Common Era than Noth himself seems aware of. Long (1984: 29) likewise dates the Deuteronomistic work '[a]t least a century earlier than Herodotus', even although Herodotus provides the model for the paratactic composition of the Deuteronomistic work that Long (pp. 19-30) advances.

9.   McKenzie 1991: 3. O'Brien (1989: 3) practically canonizes Noth and calls his work 'a standard feature of scholarly understanding of the composition of the historical books'. Of important dissidents, von Rad (1957: 344), Fohrer (1965: 210-212), and Westermann (1994) should be mentioned.

10.   2 Kgs 17.34-41 (Hoffmann 1980: 139) and 2 Kgs 16.10-18 (p. 144).

belongs to the postexilic theology and its struggle for pure belief in Yahweh, Josiah's reform being the model for the Israelites' new start after the exile (Hoffman 1980: 319-20). According to Noth, the Deuteronomist mainly complemented his sources by adding ordinary generalizations, but Hoffmann attributes texts containing a wealth of details to this author as well. They serve to give the accounts historical local colour and to underline their credibility (p. 315).

Hoffman's provocative thesis has not, naturally, remained uncontested. H. Weippert remarks that the accounts of the cult are asymmetrically placed in the work and regards this as the greatest weakness in Hoffmann's exposition. Some texts are mere references whereas others are comprehensive. There is too a total lack of accounts of the cult with regard to many kings of Judah and of Israel, while among the judges only Gideon can be regarded as a reformer of the cult (Weippert 1985: 222-23; Hoffmann 1980: 272-92). M.A. O'Brien complains that 'Hoffmann is hard put to convince the reader that...[the cultic reform] is the dominant theme of Deuteronomy, Joshua, Judges and Samuel' (O'Brien 1989: 16). It is, however, possible to understand why the Deuteronomist treated the pre-monarchic era differently from the monarchic, if we follow J. Van Seters' correction to Hoffmann:

> While the record of the monarchy in Kings focuses on evaluating the progress of people and their kings from the time of Solomon until the end, this appraisal does not make sense without the story of the rise of the monarchy, the enunciation of the divine promise to David, and the establishment of the true cult center in Jerusalem under Solomon. The author must first set out these constitutional elements of the Israelite state by which all the 'reforms' must be judged (Van Seters 1983: 320).

A.D.H. Mayes has difficulty in imagining the society in which the Deuteronomistic work, as presented by Hoffmann, could have been conceived:

> It is surely inconceivable that the exilic or early post-exilic periods would present a suitable context for a presentation of Israel which emphasized that no matter how good the individual might be the end of the nation could only be destruction... Josiah cannot act as an example for the deuteronomist's audience, if it requires just one Manasseh to bring about perdition (Mayes 1983: 13-14).

However, a similar example may be found in the Attic tragedy where the hero meets his unavoidable fate, irrespective of how he attempts to thwart it. Herodotus, as we have seen, uses tragedy historiographically and it is possible to understand the Deuteronomistic work in the same way. By doing so, Mayes' observation is no longer an objection against regarding the Deuteronomistic work as a unified one. Quite another point is that the tragical ornamentation of the course of history in the Deuteronomistic work points, in itself, to a later date than Hoffmann assumes. It is probable that this style of writing was influenced by the Hellenistic culture, as it is in Hellas that the nearest parallels may be found.[11]

J. Van Seters (1983) assumes that an exilic author has collected disparate material and arranged it paratactically in a great work, intended to teach Israel about its own past. The author may have been acting under the influence of the dissolution of the nation caused by the exile. He takes certain liberties with his sources. He was the first to shape them into a continuous historical account, acting here more as an author than as a redactor. The nearest parallel to his work is found in Greek historiography, especially Herodotus, whereas the Babylonian Chronicle Series is the nearest parallel to the 'official' (but unfortunately quite hypothetical) sources quoted in the Deuteronomistic work. The Deuteronomistic historian is, Van Seters says, 'the first known historian in Western civilization truly to deserve this designation' (p. 362). Quoting R. Polzin's fitting characterization (1989: 14), Van Seters attempts to establish 'what belongs to Dtr's history (much more than previously thought), what predates it (much less than originally maintained), and what was later added to it (much more than anyone had realized)'. Several lengthy passages are, according to Van Seters, postdeuteronomistic additions, the most remarkable of these being the Court History of David (2 Sam. 2.8–4.12; 2 Sam. 9–20; 1 Kgs 1–2).

Van Seters' conception of the Deuteronomistic work as a unified, paratactically conceived work seems strange to many interpreters accustomed to redaction-historical and literary-critical approaches. This is so, even though Van Seters himself writes within a continuation of a historical-critical tradition, when he, in spite of his own recommendation to make comparative studies of Herodotus and the Old Testament,[12] concentrates in his own study of the Deuteronomistic

11. Van Seters (1983), but in spite of these similarities he still holds the exilic period to be correct.
12. Van Seters 1983: 39: 'On the basis of narrative style and technique alone the

work on putting forward yet another suggestion as to its genesis (Van Seters 1983: 209-353; cf. Polzin 1989: 13-14). S.L. McKenzie's remark that Van Seters is unable to explain 'the literary unevenness or the presence of what appear to be pre-exilic themes' (McKenzie 1991: 17) evidently shows that he has missed Van Seters' point. Paratactic writing results very easily in a narrative that strikes the modern reader as uneven. Van Seters' best example of this is Herodotus, whose work certainly owes its existence to one author. It is unclear what McKenzie actually means by pre-exilic themes. The Deuteronomistic work is an account of the history of Israel until the exile—the work thus consists in its entirety of pre-exilic themes! If by pre-exilic themes McKenzie means the reform of Josiah, which is prominently placed in the Deuteronomistic work, then it is possible to advance Hoffmann's argument that the reform of Josiah is a model for the future. It is thus easy to explain the presence of a pre-exilic theme in exilic or postexilic historiography.

B.O. Long, who is in definite agreement with Van Seters, concisely refutes those who argue for multiple redactions in the Deuteronomistic work (Long 1984: 15-19). In his commentary on 1 Kings, he characterizes such ideas as 'based on little more than modern cultural preferences and literary tastes' (Long 1984: 18). Like Van Seters, Long regards Herodotus' paratactic narration, as demonstrated by H. Immerwahr (1966), as the model for the Deuteronomistic work. In the same way as Herodotus, the Deuteronomist constructed his work of 'individual items of varied lengths placed in series'.[13] '1–2 Kings, and the Dtr history, were composed by one person and remain essentially a unified work' although one cannot disregard the possibility of 'a few interpolations here and there...(for example, 2 Kgs 17.34-41)' (Long 1984: 21).

B. Peckham follows his own peculiar path regarding the origin of the Deuteronomistic work.[14] The author is 'Dtr²' (Peckham 1985: 73) who used a number of complete, literary works which he dovetailed and reworked systematically (Peckham 1985: 21-68). His oldest source is the Yahwist (J), followed by a historical work by 'Dtr¹' who knew,

Old Testament and Herodotus share a great deal in common and ought to be studied together.'

13. Long (1984: 19; pp. 19-30) gives a review of the paratactic effects in 1 and 2 Kgs.

14. Peckham 1985. See his schematic outline, pp. 96-140.

quoted and interpretated J. A third, 'priestly' author (P) re-wrote J as an alternative and corrective to Dtr[1], while the Elohist supplemented J and P and likewise corrected Dtr[1] (pp. 1-19). According to Peckham, '[t]he Dtr[2] history is a comprehensive and systematic revision of the sources' in the form of 'a running commentary' (p. 21). Finally, 'Ps' added the legal texts in Lev. 1.1–7.38; 11.46–27.34 (pp. 69-71). In this way, the entire history from Genesis to 2 Kings acquired its present form.[15]

Hypotheses maintaining a composite, deuteronomistic editorial process may, as H. Weippert suggests, be grouped under three headings (Weippert 1985: 218 and 228-29): 'Layer models', 'block models', and 'combined models'. H.W. Wolff (1961) doubted Noth's thesis that the Deuteronomistic work was intended to demonstrate that the fate of Israel and of Judah was the result of divine judgment (Noth 1943: 109). Wolff felt that so monumental a work covering seven hundred years' history could not have been written with only this one purpose. It would, after all, have been possible to express the sentiment more concisely and therefore more clearly. The nadir of Israel's history does not lead to destruction in the Deuteronomistic work but to the repentance of the people, and new divine endeavours regularly save the people of Israel from danger. Thus the Deuteronomistic work preaches repentance.[16] Another Deuteronomistic hand adds that human endeavours are not at stake here. Repentance is less a human action than a result of divine judgment.[17] Carrying Wolff's idea of 'another hand' further, a number of scholars understand Noth's Deuteronomistic work, not as the work of a single author but as the result of a joint enterprise,[18] reconstructing its formation as having taken place in several stages.[19] Thus the influential 'Smend school'[20]

15. For a number of literary-critical objections to Peckham's idea of two Deuteronomistic historical works, consult O'Brien 1989: 18-20.

16. Judg. 2.16; 1 Sam. 7.3; 1 Sam. 12.19; 1 Kgs 8.47; 2 Kgs 17.13; 2 Kgs 23.24-25. Wolff 1961: 178-84.

17. Deut. 4.29-31; Deut. 30.1-10. Wolff 1961: 184.

18. Nicholson (1967) and Weinfeld (1972) assume the existence of a deuteromomistic 'school' or group of tradents from whose efforts, during the time from the destruction of the Northern kingdom until the exile, the Deuteronomistic work gradually grows.

19. Weippert (1985: 230-31) gives many examples.

20. O'Brien (1989: 7-8 n. 22) gives a comprehensive list of studies following the Smend school.

talks of a *Grundschrift* written by 'DtrH' ('H' for *Historiker*) shortly after the destruction of Jerusalem, this original account being supplemented and formed by 'DtrP', who contributed the stories of the Prophets and placed history in a scheme of prophecies and fulfillments. Finally, 'DtrN' commented upon both redactions from a nomistic point of view. All three layers belong to the period immediately following the destruction of the temple (580–560 BCE).[21] R. Smend himself points out a major weakness in the hypothesis: 'The deuteronomistic historiographers are close to each other as to intentions. Each of the later ones use a wording already in existence. They all turn out to be disciples of their predecessors—therefore it is often very difficult to tell them apart'.[22]

One of the first to criticize Noth was G. von Rad (1947) who regarded 2 Samuel 7, Nathan's promise, as the start of the eternal promise to David, which is reiterated throughout the books of Kings, thus making a contrast to the historical pessimism Noth otherwise found in the Deuteronomistic work. This opinion set the ball rolling in the second of Weippert's two groups, the 'block models'. The foremost among these today is the 'Cross school'. F.M. Cross (1973) regards the DtrH as consisting of two editorial blocks: The deuteronomistic one dating from the time of Josiah, and the exilic one from approximately 550 BCE. Jeroboam's sin and Nathan's prophecy

---

21. Smend (1971) determines a number of passages in the books of Joshua and Judges as nomistic additions to a *Grundschrift*. These additions do not regard the conquest as entirely over, its consummation being dependent upon obedience to the law. Dietrich 1972 finds three separate strata in Kings, the two Smend operates with, and 'DtrP'. He ascribes them all to approximately 580–560 BCE. Veijola (1975, 1977) pursues Dietrich's three strata in the books of Samuel and states them to have each their own picture of David. DtrH, being friendly towards the monarchy, regards David as Yahweh's faithful servant, who is rewarded by becoming the forefather of an everlasting dynasty. DtrP views David as the prototype of the guilty and sinful human being. DtrN tries to reconcile this contradiction between DtrH and DtrP. He shares DtrP's critical attitude to the monarchy, but at the same time hopes, as DtrH does, that the house of David will continue to rule. Smend (1978) combines his own starting-point from 1971 with Dietrich and Veijola in a combined model for the formation of the entire deuteronomistic work.

22. Smend 1978: 124. See also Koch's critism of Dietrich: 'Welcher Zuverlässigkeit kann der Aussonderung einer Schicht DtrP zukommen, wenn dort "fast alle Wendungen ... in Quellen vorgeprägt waren" [Dietrich 1972: 100], während doch solche Spracheigentümlichkeiten den einzigen sicheren Schlüssel zur Aussonderung redaktioneller Überarbeitung darstellen?' (Koch 1981: 116 n. 10).

concerning the house of David are prominent in the deuteronomistic account of the monarchy. These two themes merge with the account of Josiah's reform (2 Kgs 22.1–23.25). Josiah is the ideal king who shows himself to be the worthy recipient of the divine promise to David (2 Sam. 7) as well as being the reformer who by destroying the shrine in Bethel does away with the sin of Jeroboam. DtrH is thus propaganda and programme for Josiah's reform. A third theme, the impending destruction of the Davidic dynasty, should be attributed to a later redaction[23] as should the present ending of DtrH, 2 Kgs 23.26–25.30. This blames Manasseh for the exile and describes the ending of the kingdom of Judah laconically and without the theological reflections that are usually characteristic of the deuteronomist. Where the deuteronomistic block is characterized by the optimism of its time, the exilic block is correspondingly pessimistic, being the history of a decline. The exilic editorial additions to DtrH can be recognized as they attach conditions to the promise to David, presuppose the exile, or address the exiles in order to lead them to repentance.[24]

Quite a lot of scholars find the idea of an editorial rupture after Josiah convincing. H. Weippert reaches the same conclusion on the basis of an examination of the evaluations of the kings of Judah and Israel (Weippert 1972). R.D. Nelson emphasizes 'the rubber-stamp character' of the regnal formulae of the last four kings of Judah when compared with those of the earlier kings (Nelson 1981: 36-41). Generally speaking, the exilic author's contributions may be termed abridgements and summaries. Another example of this may be found in 2 Kgs 25.22-26 which is simply an abstract of Jer. 40.7–41.8 (p. 86). Nelson's exilic author is mainly concerned with the fact that the people have not listened to the voice of Yahweh, while Nelson's deuteronomist like that of Cross emphasizes the unconditional duration of the Davidic dynasty. The exilic redactor condemns all four of the kings he mentions in the same manner, and the sin of Manasseh weighs far more heavily than Josiah's repentance—the judgment upon Judah is unavoidable. Like Cross, Nelson regards DtrH as royal

23. 2 Kgs 21.2-15. The prophecy of Hulda (2 Kgs 22.15-20) was altered to fit in with this later redaction. Likewise Deut. 4.27-31; Deut 28.36-37; 28.63-68; Deut. 29.27; Deut. 30.1-20; Josh. 23.11-16; 1 Sam. 12.25; 1 Kgs 2.4; 1 Kgs 6.11-13; 1 Kgs 8.25b; 8.46-53; 1 Kgs 9.4-9; 2 Kgs 17.19; 2 Kgs 20.17-18.

24. McKenzie's categories which are deduced from Cross' list of passages ascribed to his exilic redactor (McKenzie 1991: 7, including n. 11).

propaganda from the time of Josiah, whereas the exilic redactor created an aetiology on the divine judgment.[25] R.E. Friedman (1980, 1981) is likewise an advocate of Cross' editorial rupture in 2 Kgs 23.26, after which the themes of the cult on the hill-tops, David the ideal king, and the pattern of prophecy and its fulfilment cease. 2 Kings 23.26 is the beginning of the history of the decline, while 2 Kgs 23.25 is the conclusion of the history of the prosperous period. According to Friedmann, 'Dtr[1]' wrote a work about great men in the history of Israel. The felicitous conclusion of this history is told in 2 Kgs 23.25, where Josiah is described as the inimitable king, faithful to both the law and Yahweh, in terms that are reminiscent of the description of Moses in Deut. 34.10. 'Dtr[2]', on the other hand, wrote a popular history, thereby rather upsetting things for the Davidic dynasty. Friedman finds it unlikely that Dtr[2] would have written the account of the pardoning of Jehoiachin, 2 Kgs 25.27-30, so this must be a later addition.

The above-mentioned scholars of the 'Cross school'[26] are typical examples of a tendency towards ascribing an increasing amount of material to the exilic redactor, whom all characterize as taciturn. This includes material in the parts of the work dealing with older times (Weippert 1985: 242-43). Thus his eloquence in 2 Kgs 17.7-20; 17.34b-40 is remarkable.[27] On the other hand, the 'Smend school' has another problem, namely that different strata resemble each other linguistically and ideologically, and chronologically they are close to each other as well. These factors often make it difficult to differentiate easily between the individual strata. A third solution is put forward by the 'combined models' (Weippert 1985: 245) which presuppose both the editorial rupture after Josiah of the 'Cross school' and the strata of the 'Smend school'. A.D.H. Mayes (1983) suggests the existence of the pre-exilic 'dtr historian' whose work concluded with 2 Kgs 23.4-20 and 2 Kgs 23.25. He identifies this person with Smend's DtrH and Cross' deuteronomist. Apart from the Dtr historian, Mayes has a 'dtr editor' of whom he finds traces throughout the work, and whom he credits with having brought the work up to date until the exile by

25. Nelson 1981: 121-23. For some weaknesses in Nelson's distinctions, see Weippert 1985: 239-41.
26. O'Brien (1989: 11 n. 33) gives a comprehensive list of studies following the Cross school.
27. Nelson (1981: 43, 55-65) ascribes this passage to the exilic redactor.

adding 2 Kgs 23.26–25.30. The Dtr editor is, according to Mayes, the same as Smend's DtrN and Cross' exilic redactor. In Deuteronomy, Joshua, and Judges, Mayes finds a third editorial layer dealing with the Levites, rites and Shechem, as well as occasional priestly additions. Much of the material contained in DtrH was, however, to be found at a pre-deuteronomistic editorial level.

In continuation of the Cross school, M.A. O'Brien (1989) sees the original DtrH as a history of the leaders of Israel from Moses to Josiah, who was a contemporary of the deuteronomist. The deuteronomist divided the course of history into three parts: the period of Israel under Moses and Joshua, the period from the judges to the monarchy, and the period of Israel under the prophets and kings. The deuteronomist used comprehensive sources for each of these periods, but he reworked them so that they agreed with his theology. Moses made the deuteronomistic law into a normative programme for Israel's existence in the land. This programme was fully realized under Solomon (1 Kgs 8.56) but became corrupted due to Solomon's later faithlessness towards Yahweh (1 Kgs 11.1-7). The reform of Josiah led Judah back to the right path. O'Brien intends to establish the existence of at least six documents, which the deuteronomistic author has edited, dovetailed, and generally brought into line with his own theology. Later this work was extended during three exilic editorial layers.[28] This tendency towards splitting the deuteronomistic historical work up into more and more layers obviously makes it increasingly unlikely that anyone except the scholar who originally identified the many layers should ever be able to recognize them.

B.O. Long advocates cautiousness when evaluating the different hypotheses put forward as an explanation of the formation of DtrH. He rightly emphasizes that 'Decisions essentially turn on a subjective judgment: the degree to which one is satisfied that a given hypothesis explains the literary facts. Are the differences in the books of Joshua through Kings best explained by differences in the sources utilized by an author–editor(s)? Or are these differences best accounted for by

28. O'Brien 1989: 288-92. In that respect, R. Stahl is the equal of O'Brien. According to McKenzie (1991: 18), Stahl advances no fewer than nine (!) deuteronomistic editorial layers: 'Aspekte der Geschichte deuteronomistischer Theologie. Zur Traditionsgeschichte der Terminologie und zur Redaktionsgeschichte der Redekomposition' (Dissertation; Jena, 1982 [*non vidi*]).

envisioning a series of independent editions?' (Long 1984: 15). Long
is not content to leave it at that, but finds that one may well doubt
hypotheses that maintain a composite deuteronomistic editorial process. Like Weippert (1985: 226), Long indicates the ambiguity of the
material as well as the fact that the different hypotheses are irreconcilable in spite of their individual plausibility. 'The literary facts
prove intractable to the usual methods which deny redundancy,
digression, or multiple viewpoints to an ancient author' (Long 1984:
16).

S.L. McKenzie has actually no particular objections to Long's and
Van Seters' placing of the DtrH in the period of the exile. His own
observations about 'the distinctiveness of the 2 Kings account following Josiah's death and the associations between Josiah and the earlier
DH can be accommodated within the model of an exilic history work
as envisioned by Van Seters and Long' (McKenzie 1991: 133), but
'[t]here is nothing in the historiographic model of composition advo-
cated by Van Seters and Long that *demands* an exilic date' (p. 134; my
italics). In other words, the choice of the time of Josiah is just as
likely a date as the exilic period, substantiated by the idea of paratactic
composition. However, the fact that 'Cross' initial postulation placed
the bulk of the DH at the time of Josiah' (p. 134) seems to be a con-
clusive piece of evidence to McKenzie. It is, nevertheless, possible for
Long to maintain the exact opposite: 'there is no *necessary* reason to
accept the multiple-redaction approaches to 1–2 Kings (and the Dtr
History)' (Long 1984: 21).

It is characteristic for the different endeavours at distinguishing
sources that they aim at removing all the tensions and contradictions
in the text by splitting it up into various sources that have been linked
together by editorial comments. These hypothetical sources are presumed originally to have been without the tensions and contradictions
we find in the Hebrew Bible. Thus it is presupposed that texts which
were originally readable have been garbled in the course of time.
Obvious weaknesses in the many endeavours at explaining the text in
this manner are the complete lack of consensus and the fact that *all* the
sources mentioned are hypothetical. There is no other reason for
insisting upon their existence than the fact that advocates of these
hypotheses refuse to make do with the extant text of the DtrH but
prefer to work on hypothetical texts. Of course, the Old Testament
historian did not create his work *ex nihilo*. We may assume that he did

indeed have sources for his history. The problem is that when we attempt to consider what these sources actually were, we have absolutely nothing except our own imagination to go on. Every new scholar working on a historical-critical basis ends up with his own particular result, which usually proves irreconcilable with that of anyone else.

Ancient Near Eastern Historiography in the Prehellenistic Period

Like Herodotus, the Deuteronomistic historical work expresses its own, peculiar metaphysical truths. By way of introduction to the further discussion of the Deuteronomistic work, it is useful to make a brief summary of ancient Near Eastern historiography. This will demonstrate that the Deuteronomistic historical work is unparalleled in Near Eastern literature of the pre-hellenistic period.[29]

Hittite historiographic texts from the Old Hittite Kingdom to the end of the Empire (c. 1650–1200 BCE)[30] are principally concerned with the acts of kings.[31] In the Hittite annals, the great king justifies himself in a general way through his own or his ancestors' great deeds, such as military campaigns, building or cultic activities.[32] The

29. In this survey, Sumerian literature will be excluded.

30. The earliest historiographic record, that of Anitta of Kuššar (text and translation: Neu 1974: 10-15) being about a century older—see Van Seters 1983: 105-107. The chronology follows Gurney (1981)—see his 'Table of Hittite Kings', *ibid.*, p. 218. It should be mentioned that after the decline of the Hittite Empire, Hittite culture had what Gurney terms 'a strange afterglow' lasting for no less than five centuries in the form of a large number of independent petty 'Neo-Hittite' kingdoms in Syria and the Taurus area; see Gurney 1981: 41-47.

31. The sixteenth-century Ammuna Chronicle also gives details of the activities of the king's lieutenants. Van Seters 1983: 108; Hoffner 1980: 305-306. Laroche 1971: 5 no. 18.

32. Van Seters 1983: 107-113. The oldest annals are from the time of Ḫattušili I (seventeenth century); Hoffner 1980: 293-99. It seems likely that Ḫattušili intended his annals to establish his right to be called a great king, as he compared himself to the legendary Sargon (KBo X 1 Rs. 20; KBo X 2 III 32) and designated his opus 'D[UB] LÙ-na-an-na-aš ŠA¹Ḫa-at-t[u-š]i-l[i', 'The tablet of the manly deeds of Ḫattušili' (KBo X 2 IV)–a king is only a king, if he commits manly deeds. Text and translation: Imparati and Sapporetti 1965. Three great annals exist from the time of Muršili II (fourteenth century): The 'Ten Year Annals' about the first ten years of the king's reign, 'The Detailed Annals' about the first twenty years, and 'The deeds of Šuppiluliuma I', an account by Muršili II of his father's deeds; Hoffner 1980:

past was also used in a more specific way to justify a king politically if he had usurped the right to the throne[33] or in some other way offended against custom,[34] to admonish his subjects,[35] to glorify the king[36] and to justify particular cultic initiatives.[37] From the fourteenth century onwards, there are historical prologues to state treaties[38] in which the circumstances leading to the present relationship between the Hittite king and the vassal state in question are mentioned. In Van Seters' wording, '[t]he concern with the past is not so much one of causality, that is why a certain state became a vassal of the Hittites, but of precedent, that is why it should continue to be a vassal state' (Van Seters 1983: 117). Not all state treaties deal with vassal states. The treaty between Hattušili III and Pharaoh Ramses II[39] is, according to the prologue, a renewal of the relationship between these two countries established at the beginning of time by the great gods. There is no differentiation made here between history and myth.

The deeds of the king are likewise the main subject of the *Babylonian and Assyrian* historiographic texts, which usually either have a didactic tendency or are propaganda (Grayson 1980). They may be

311-15; Cancik 1976: 101-184. Texts and translations: Götze 1933 and Güterbock 1956. A late text mentions Tudḫaliya IV's and his son, Šuppiluliuma II's successful campaigns against Alašiya (Cyprus; thirteenth or twelfth century); Hoffner 1980: 286 and 317-18. Text and translation: Güterbock 1967.

33. Telepinu's Proclamation (approximately 1500 BCE); Van Seters 1983: 116-17; Hoffner 1980: 306-308; Liverani 1977. Text and translation: Sturtevant and Bechtel 1935: 175-93.

34. Ḫattušili I's Political Testament (seventeenth century); Van Seters 1983: 114; Hoffner 1980: 300-302. Text and translation: Sommer and Falkenstein 1938: 2-17.

35. Ḫattušili I's Political Testament; the Palace Chronicle from the time of his son, Muršili I (Van Seters 1983: 114-15; Laroche 1971: 3 no. 8); Telepinu's Proclamation (Van Seters 1983: 115-16).

36. The Story of the Siege of Uršu in the time of Ḫattušili I, extant in an Akkadian version, both glorifies the king and is didactic; Van Seters 1983: 115; Hoffner 1980: 299-300. Text and translation: Güterbock 1938: 113-38.

37. The apology of Ḫattušili III (thirteenth century); Van Seters 1983: 118-21; Hoffner 1980: 315-16. Text and translation: Sturtevant and Bechtel 1935: 64-83.

38. Šuppiluliuma I, Muršili II, Muwatalli, Ḫattušili III, Tudḫaliya IV, and Šuppiluliuma II; Van Seters 1983: 116-18; Hoffner 1980: 311; von Schuler 1964. As to the treaty of Šunaššura of Kizzuwatna and, probably, Šuppiluliuma I, see Liverani 1973b.

39. Translation of both the Hittite and the Egyptian version in Pritchard 1969: 199-203. On the relationship between Ḫattušili III and Ramses II, see Liverani 1990.

divided into three groups: royal inscriptions, chronographic texts and historical-literary texts. *The royal inscriptions* may be commemorative texts describing building activities, and in Assyria military campaigns as well. These inscriptions may include a delegation of authority to the king by the gods. From the beginning of the thirteenth century BCE, there are Assyrian annals dealing with the king's military campaigns and building activities. A great deal of the king's success is attributed to the gods. A small group of Assyrian texts, 'The letters to the god', were, seemingly, intended to be read ceremoniously after successful military campaigns (Oppenheim 1960). These 'letters' are stringent literary compositions, markedly dramatic, and showing great interest in the ways and customs of foreign lands. The genre bears certain resemblances to the following century's Ionian historiographic tradition and to Herodotus (Oppenheim 1960: 146). Of *the chronographic texts*,[40] the king lists seem, apart from their chronological purpose, to have been intended to establish the political position of given cities and to justify the right of certain dynasties to rule over other kings and cities.[41] The Babylonian Chronicle Series, covering the period from the reign of Nabû-našir (747–734 BCE)[42] to at least as late as the second year of Seleucus III (224 BCE), records military and political events with the king as the focus of attention.[43] They were presumably not intended as propaganda, as Babylonian defeats are included. Indeed, the texts look like reliable sources for the events mentioned. Other Mesopotamian chronicles present the king in the best possible light,[44] or serve other forms of propaganda.[45]

40. Grayson 1980: 171-81; Grayson 1975a: 1-67, 193-201.

41. Wilson 1977: 86-107; Grayson 1983. The oldest examples are the eighteenth-century Larsa King List and the nineteenth-century Ur-Isin King List. The longest is the Babylonian King List 'A' covering the period from the first dynasty (nineteenth–sixteenth century) until the seventh century, while the extant part of the list from Uruk covers the seventh to the third century. The Assyrian list maintains the succession of Assyrian kings from the oldest times until Šalmaneser V (726–722 BCE). The Mesopotamian chronology is that of Brinkman 1977.

42. In all probability, the first tablet of the series is extant. See 'Chronicle 1' 4.39 (Grayson 1975b: 87, 17).

43. Grayson 1980: 173-75; Grayson 1975b: 69-124 no. 1-13a.

44. The Esarhaddon Chronicle; Grayson 1980: 175-76.

45. The Weidner Chronicle covering the time span from the Early Dynastic period of Sumerian history (first half of the third century BCE) to at least the time of Šulgi (2094–2047 BCE) advances the claims of Marduk. In particular, the necessity of

Thus the insistence upon facts in the Babylonian Chronicle Series is unique. All the *historical-literary texts* are either didactic or propagandistic. Akkadian prophecy, which typically justifies an idea or institution, establishes its credibility by means of a *vaticinium ex eventu* (Grayson 1980: 182-85). Akkadian historical epics are poetical narrations of heroic royal deeds.[46] The many fragments of Babylonian epics (Grayson 1980: 186-187) depict the sovereignty of Marduk and the dreadful fate overtaking the Babylonian king who neglects his cult.

Egyptian historiography may be said to be represented by three groups of texts: king lists, royal inscriptions and political propaganda (Van Seters 1983: 131-181). A tradition of apparently historiographically motivated *king lists* are represented by the 'Palermo Stone' (twenty-fourth-century BCE)[47] and the 'Turin Canon' (sixteenth-century BCE).[48] The historian Manetho (third-century BCE) probably used a king list of this type.[49] Intending to demonstrate the ancientness of the kingdom, this historiographic tradition recounts its glorious deeds down through the ages.[50] That the country, according to the

providing fish for his temple, Esagil, is emphasized (Grayson 1980: 179-81; text and translation: Grayson 1975b: 145-51). The Assyrian 'Synchronistic History' telling of invasions of Assyria by the Babylonians from the time of Puzur-Aššur III (first half of the fifteenth century BCE) to that of Adad-nirari III (810–783 BCE) invents the notion of a specific boundary line between Assyria and Babylonia. Frequent Babylonian violations of fictitious border treaties have always ended in Assyrian victories (Grayson 1980: 181-82; text and translation: Grayson 1975b: 157-70).

46. Examples being the Sargon Epic (translation: Pritchard 1969: 119) and the Assyrian panegyric on Tukulti-Ninurta I (1243–1207 BCE); Grayson 1980: 185-86; Machinist 1978; Machinist 1976; Lambert 1957. Text and Translation: Machinist 1978: 60-139.

47. Gardiner 1961: 62-64; Van Seters 1983: 131-34. Description and translation: Breasted 1906: I, 51-72.

48. Redford 1986: 1-2: 'for Pharaonic times... the Turin Canon of Kings... is only the sole survivor of a long line of similar lists which must have been copied over many centuries'. Roccati 1986; Gardiner 1961: 47-48; Hayes 1970. Text: Gardiner 1959. Description: Redford 1986: 2-18.

49. Redford 1986: 203: 'one must conclude that... the tradition of a "running king-list", attested by TC, was not interrupted at the end of the New Kingdom, but continued unimpaired down to the Ptolemies'. Van Seters 1983: 135-38; Helck 1956. Text and Translation of Manetho: Waddell 1940.

50. Distinct from these historiographic king lists, we find many lists which had a particular cultic or political application; Redford 1986; Van Seters 1983: 137-38; Gardiner 1961: 48-50.

Turin list, was ruled in pre-dynastic times by gods and heroes shows, when compared to the Palermo stone from the Old Kingdom, a radical shift in historical perspective, as the Palermo stone has no mention of divine kings. Apparently, a distinction was made between myth and history in the Old Kingdom which is unique when compared with later historiography in Hatti, Mesopotamia and Egypt. As late as in Manetho, the tradition known from the Turin list is reflected in that the country from the oldest times was united under successive divine and heroic kings, whereby a divine genealogy is placed within historic times. *Royal inscriptions*, too, give the king a certain memorial. These usually have a dramatic content, created, for instance, by the use of direct speech. Two main types are found: Dedication and commemorative inscriptions (Van Seters 1983: 141-60). Dedication inscriptions enumerate the king's building activities, his cultic dispositions and, often, his military accomplishments. A discursive variety relates in minute detail all the circumstances of a building project or religious reform, usually very dramatically. Commemorative inscriptions are often dramatic and digressive, with the gods' choice of the king as a maintainer of justice prominently placed. Such texts are known from the end of the Second Intermediate Period (beginning of the sixteenth century BCE) onwards, and are usually found in connection with temples. Some of the most significant examples are Thutmose III's military accomplishments (fifteenth century BCE), recounted on several of his monuments. The most comprehensive are the annals engraved in the great temple of Amon-Ra at Karnak.[51] Another climax is to be found during the Third Intermediate Period, in the Piankhi Stela (eighth century BCE), a well-written and dramatic literary composition praising the pious and magnanimous king.[52] *Political propaganda* may be found in the form of texts that make use of the past to influence public opinion in politically unstable times, where, for instance, the male line of descent had been broken, or when an usurper seized the throne (Van Seters 1983: 172-81). Such texts

51. Description and translation: Breasted 1906: II, 163-217. This discursive annal style was continued by Thutmose III's successor, Amenhotep II, although the latter's stelae in Memphis and Karnak are mainly taken up with the king's personal exploits (translation: Pritchard 1969: 245-47). After this the writing of annals was discontinued; Van Seters 1983: 147-52.

52. Van Seters 1983: 157-60. Description and translation: Breasted 1906: IV, 406-444.

explain the king's place in the continuity of history by rewriting history. Frequent themes are the deity's choice of the monarch early in the life of the latter, the true king, who re-establishes the country after a chaotic period, the king as the guardian of shrines, or the pious king, described as the good shepherd of his people.

Few *prima manu* texts, or reliable copies thereof, are known from the *Syro-Palestinian* area before the Hellenistic period.[53] The notable exception is, of course, Ugarit, but there are practically no Ugaritic texts that can reasonably be described as historiographic (Van Seters 1983: 199-205). Among the few West Semitic historiographic texts, the history of Idrimi of Alalakh is remarkable.[54] It contains an account of the flight of Idrimi's ancestors from Aleppo to Emar, from whence Idrimi departs and after many voyages and adventures ascends the throne of Alalakh. In the course of his reign, he carries out a series of honourable deeds. The text is probably a legend, created by the scribe Šarruwa, who signed it. Presumably, Šarruwa lived two centuries after Idrimi's reign during the fifteenth century BCE. In the interests of propaganda, Šarruwa created a 'historical' portrait of the founder of the dynasty.[55] The statue of Idrimi represents a traditional, Western Asiatic genre: the memorial inscription. Other examples are Šuppiluliuma II's Hittite text and subsequent Hittite hieroglyphic texts,[56] Phoenician and Aramaic texts from Karatepe, Zinjirli, Byblos and Hamath, and the Meša-stela.[57] They relate the deeds and virtues of a divinely chosen king in the form of an autobiography intended to ensure the king's being remembered after his death.

There are, too, only a few historiographic texts from the *Persian*

53. Van Seters 1983: 188-208. For a discussion of the problems relating to the Tyrian 'annals' referred to by Josephus, see pp. 195-99. As to the Phoenician history by Philo of Byblos as we know it from Eusebius, see pp. 205-208, and Baumgarten 1981.

54. Van Seters 1983: 188-95; text and translation: Smith 1949: 14-23.

55. Sasson 1981. Liverani (1973a: 182-83) rightly underlines the fairy-tale pattern of this story.

56. For a short presentation of the Hittite hieroglyphic texts, see Hawkins 1982: 437-39. Texts and translations: Meriggi 1967, 1975.

57. Karatepe: Donner and Röllig 1962: I, 5-6 no. 26; Zinjirli: pp. 4-5 no. 24, and pp. 38-40 no. 214-16. Byblos: p. 2 no. 10; Hamath: p. 37 no. 202. Moab (the Meša-stela): p. 33 no. 181. According to Hawkins (1982: 437), the Aramaic and Phoenician inscriptions were modelled on the Hittite hieroglyphic genre. See also Miller 1974.

empire.[58] Three Akkadian texts, however, show the official view of the past after Cyrus II's conquest of the Neo-Babylonian empire.[59] This propaganda shows the defeated Nabonidus (555–539 BCE) and his government in the worst possible light to the conquered Babylonians. The dominant theme is one of restitution. Nabonidus, having permitted the empire to decline, was led by his demon (*šedu*) to commit cultic misdemeanours and to replace the gods of Babylon with others. This rouses Marduk's wrath, and the deity proclaims the just Cyrus ruler of the world. Helped thus by Marduk, he is greeted by the Babylonians as their saviour. Cyrus proclaims peace, reinstates the proper cult, stops the decline, abolishes the *corvée*, returns the foreign gods to their rightful homes, rebuilds the local temples, and allows the captured peoples of these cities to return. Similar propaganda regarding restitution had been used earlier by Neo-Babylonian rulers,[60] but it was perfected by the Persians (Thompson 1992: 348-51). The Achaemenian inscriptions in Persian show that Cyrus' successors continued this policy.[61] The imposing Behistun monument[62] is not only a memorial to Darius but also establishes and consolidates the usurper's

58. Meyer 1954: 3-13; Frye 1984: 87-88; Dandamaev and Lukonin 1989: 368-401. Note Momigliano 1990: 6: 'Persian history is still in the hands of Herodotus'.

59. The Nabonidus Chronicle: Grayson 1975b: 104-111. The Verse Account of Nabonidus: Smith 1924: 83-91. The Cyrus Cylinder: Weissbach 1911: 2-9.

60. Nebuchadnezer II's (604–562 BCE) Wadi-Brisa inscription (Pritchard 1969: 307); Nabonidus' Ḥarran stelas (Pritchard 1969: 560-63); Nabonidus' basalt stela in Istanbul (Pritchard 1969: 308-311). In comparison to the former policy of the Neo-Assyrian empire, it was a novelty to employ propaganda against a conquered people. Earlier on, it had been intended solely to gain the king the support of his domestic subjects or army; cf. Thompson 1992: 346-48.

61. On the Behistun monument (1.48-70; Kent 1953: 117-18 and 120), Darius I repeats Cyrus' propaganda, on this occasion with Gaumata as the foe who was cast down with Ahuramazda's help. Cosmos was brought into being, according to another inscription, when Ahuramazda bestowed the earth which was in commotion upon Darius: Naqš-i-Rustam a, 31-36 (Kent 1953: 137-38). In the so-called *daiva*-inscription at Persepolis, Darius' son Xerxes (486–465 BCE) tells of a rebellious land in his empire where he replaced false gods (*daiva*) with the worship of Ahuramazda and replaced other rotten things with healthy ones (Xerxes, Persepolis h, 35-46; Kent 1953: 151-52). The chronology is that of Frye 1984: 359. As to the Persian historiographical sources, I have used Kent 1953 as a representative selection of texts. For a collection of newer finds, see Mayrhofer 1978.

62. Hinz 1976: 9-13 and 21-25; Dandamaev and Lukonin 1989: 368-70; Balcer 1987. Text and translation: Kent 1953: 116-34.

power (Olmstead 1948: 107-118). He is the rightful king on account of his lineage and the choice of Ahuramazda (1.1-71). During the first year of his reign, the pious king puts down no fewer than 19 uprisings, a fact he recounts in detail (1.71–4.36). His success is due to his devotion to Ahuramazda and to just government (4.59-69; 4.36-39). Other similar historical presentations are not often found.[63] It is much more usual to find general remarks on the virtues of the Persian ruler: he has been placed as ruler of all the earth by Ahuramazda, whom nearly all the longer inscriptions praise in a doxology.[64] The ruler's deeds include vast construction-works, and, in the case of Darius I and Xerxes, the facts that they took great trouble to create peace everywhere and that their reigns were just and capable, are likewise counted among their achievements.[65] The king acts by virtue of Ahuramazda's blessing, and frequently blessings are invoked upon the king, the land, and the Persian people itself, the fulfilment of these blessings, however, being dependent upon the people's obedience to Ahuramazda and the king.[66]

63. Darius I, Susa f, 12-15 (Kent 1953: 142, 144); Xerxes, Persepolis f, 15-40 (p. 150). There are, apart from these, small historiographical remarks in connection with building projects, for example Darius, Suez c, 7-8 (p. 147): 'from Persia I seized Egypt'. Artaxerxes II has a history of the palace: Susa a, 3-4 (p. 154).

64. Darius I: Persepolis a (Kent 1953: 135); d, 1-11 (pp. 135-36); e, 1-18 (p. 136); h, 1-9 (pp. 136-37); Susa a, 1-3; b; c; d, 1-2 (p. 141); e, 1-30 (pp. 141-42); f, 1-21 (pp. 142-44); i (p. 144); j, 1-2 (pp. 144-45); k, 1-3 (p. 145); Suez c, 1-7 (p. 147); Naqš-i-Rustam a, 1-47 (pp. 137-38). Xerxes: Persepolis a, 1-10 (pp. 147-48); f, 1-36 (pp. 149-50); h, 1-28 (pp. 150-51). Artaxerxes I: Persepolis a, 1-16 (p. 153). Artaxerxes II: Hamadan c (p. 155).Artaxerxes III: Persepolis, 1-20 (p. 156).

65. Darius I: Persepolis a (Kent 1953: 135); Susa d (p. 141); e, 30-49 (pp. 141-42); f, 22-57 (pp. 142-44); Suez c, 7-12 (p. 147); Naqš-i-Rustam b, 5-45 (pp. 138-40); Suez c, 7-12 (p. 147). Xerxes: Persepolis a, 11-15 (p. 148); f, 36-40; g (p. 150); j; Susa a (p. 152); Van (pp. 152-53); Artaxerxes I: Persepolis a, 17-21 (p. 153). Darius II: Susa a; b (p. 154). Artaxerxes II: Susa a (p. 154); d (pp. 154-55). Artaxerxes III: Persepolis, 21-23 (p. 156).

66. Darius I: Persepolis d, 12-24 (Kent 1953: 135-36); e, 19-24 (p. 136); h, 9-10 (p. 137); Susa a, 4-5; d, 3 (p. 141); e, 49-52 (p. 142); f, 57-58 (pp. 143-44); i (p. 144); k, 4-5; l (p. 145); Naqš-i-Rustam a, 48-60 (pp. 137-38); b, 1-4.45-49 (pp. 138-40). Xerxes: Persepolis a, 15-20 (p. 148); f, 40-48; g (p. 150); h, 46-60 (pp. 151-52); Susa a (p. 152). Artaxerxes I: Persepolis a, 22-24 (p. 153); Darius II: Susa b, 4 (p. 154). Artaxerxes II: Susa a, 4-5 (p. 154); d, 3-4 (p. 155). Artaxerxes III: Persepolis, 24-26 (p. 156). For a thorough examination of the religious ideology

All of these ancient Near Eastern societies have formulated written testimony as to their views of the past. Everywhere we have seen history used as propaganda with the deeds of the king as the focal point. The Babylonian Chronicle Series is unique in having an unbiased interest in history, even though here, too, it is the kings and their armies we hear about. Here we find another novelty: The account of a nation's political and military fate is interwoven with a chronological account of the succession of the kings whose date of accession provides the means of dating various other events. The Chronicle Series starts in the eighth century BCE, but there is no proof of A.K. Grayson's contention that it also was written down from this time (Grayson 1975b: 11), as it is not possible to date any of the existing tablets earlier than the Persian era.[67]

Thus all of Israel's neighbours wrote about the past, even though, as a general rule, it was used to exercise an authority over institutions, customs, rights, and behaviour (Van Seters 1983: 357), rather than being an object of mere registration. However, there are no historiographic works similar to the historical works of the Old Testament or to Herodotus. These texts differ from the other categories mentioned on account of their length, and because they are intended to tell the history of an entire people or nation. They are also remarkable for depicting history as a process involving cause and effect, these being in turn responsible for the state of things at the end of the historical works (Van Seters 1983: 4-5): the Babylonian exile in the Deuteronomistic historical work and the fortunate conclusion of the Persian war in Herodotus.

Another important difference between the non-biblical works mentioned above and the historiography of the Old Testament is the role of the divine in history. All deities in the ancient Near East involve themselves to a certain extent in human affairs. B. Albrektson has pointed out that in Mesopotamia the gods were not only gods of nature but also had the power to intervene in events on earth and that they, in this way, resemble the God of the Old Testament (Albrektson 1967:

of the Achaemenian rulers, consult Ahn 1992.

67. Van Seters 1983: 82 n. 98. The colophon of Chronicle I (4.43; Grayson 1975: 87), which is the longest and most comprehensive text in the series (from the third year of Nabu-naṣir's reign until the first year of Šamaš-šuma-ukin's reign, that is 744–688 BCE), dates the tablet to the twenty-sixth year of Darius' reign, that is 547 BCE.

16-23). It is, according to Albrektson, common both in Mesopotamia and Israel to regard historical events as the result of the divine will (pp. 24-41), to deem the king to have been divinely chosen so that he may fulfill the same divine will (pp. 42-52), and to hold that the deity acts through history in order to achieve a given aim (pp. 68-97). In the Old Testament, the Yahwist as well as the author of the Deuteronomistic historical work, writes in accordance with, to quote Albrektson, 'the viewpoint of a result already arrived at'. The Yahwistic conception of history is a teleological one, *telos* being the empire of king David and king Solomon, whereas the Deuteronomistic historian writes from a dogmatic point of view, 'i.e. the view that history is the realization of the law of retribution' (pp. 82-83).

W.G. Lambert categorically denies that the idea of Yahweh working towards a given aim is a phenomenon that resembles anything known to Mesopotamian historiography: 'In ancient Mesopotamian texts there is nothing comparable' (Lambert 1970: 173). There human beings are created in order to serve the gods and to supply them with food and drink. At a certain point in history, all the good things of life and of civilization were granted to the human race by the gods. Thus Mesopotamian norms were of divine origin and were therefore to be honoured. This may be considered similar to Yahweh's endeavours to maintain his norms among the Israelites. The Old Testament god's intervention serves this purpose as well as being aimed at a fixed goal in history, whereas only the former is applicable to the Mesopotamian gods. Their intervention preserves status quo, if for instance, a nation or a city is punished for having neglected its god (Lambert 1970: 173-75; Lambert 1972: 70-72).

Lambert's contention that a dynamic, divine plan in history cannot be found in Mesopotamia is in turn contested by H.W.F. Saggs (1978: 64-92). Two versions of the divine plan in history may be found in the Old Testament: Yahweh's covenant or, as Saggs suggests, treaty, with Abraham and his seed, and Yahweh's covenant (or treaty) with David and his successors. God promised both the Israelite ethnic group and the dynasty of David lasting existence. Saggs finds similar ideas particularly in Neo-Assyrian texts where divine intervention is intended to secure the continued existence of the royal house, lead the Assyrian armies to victory over foreign lands, punish rebellion against Aššur, expand the borders of Assyria, and to demonstrate the might of Aššur over all of humanity. This divine plan is indicated by the national god Aššur's epithets. Assyrian hegemony is to be secured, and those that disturb the *pax assyrica* are to be destroyed (Saggs: 79-85). In this way, however, Saggs actually confirms Lambert's idea of the endeavours of the Mesopotamian gods to maintain the status quo, which in this case consists of a ruling dynasty and of Assyrian hegemony. Both Saggs and Lambert agree that these features are to be found in Israelite historiography. An example of this is the divine promise that the royal house will flourish, a promise that in Nathan's prophecy (2 Sam. 7) and in the Assyrian texts,[68] is not actually given until *after* the dynasty in question has come to power. However, Israelite historiography is also teleological. In texts such as Josh. 24.2-13 and the significant 'Dream of Abraham', Gen. 15.13-16, this teleology is expressed in the fact that the deity works throughout successive generations towards his goal of creating a people loyal to himself, and settling them in Canaan. The Mesopotamian gods, on the other hand, only maintain or perhaps restore a state that has already been created.

J. Licht has called the dream of Abraham '[t]he only type of Old Testament statement about divine intervention which cannot be matched by some quotation from ancient Mesopotamian literature'. Licht defines this type of Old Testament statement as 'contemplations of divine action through several generations' with von Rad's historical *credo* as an example. Apart from reacting to human behaviour, the God of Israel also pursues a 'long-term policy'.[69] If it is not in Israel's immediate neighbourhood that we find the same conception of history as that of the Old Testament, where the deity works throughout many generations in accordance with Licht's 'long-term policy', we can indicate Hellas instead, where the said characteristic is recognizable in Herodotus, among others.

The Deuteronomist as an Antiquarian

Like Herodotus, DtrH frequently offers more than one version of a given story. This may be seen in the three versions of how Saul became king in 1 Samuel 8–12. He is anointed in secret by Samuel in 10.1-16, next he is chosen publicly by lot at Mizpah, 10.17-25, and after the victory over the Ammonites, he is chosen again at Gilgal,

---

68. See Saggs' examples, pp. 81-85.
69. Licht 1983: 110-111; von Rad 1938: 11-16.

11.14-15. Where Herodotus offers his own opinion as to the course of a given sequence of events and specifically states his sources and any varying accounts, no similar treatment of the differing versions is given in the Old Testament, though it seems unlikely that the Old Testament authors or editors were unable to perceive the inconsistencies that are so glaringly obvious to modern scholars. Nevertheless, the differing accounts of Saul's king-making have been gathered together to form a sequence. The same may be said of the account of David's arrival at Saul's court. In one version, David is a musician employed to play when Yahweh's evil spirit troubles the king (1 Sam. 16.14-23). In another version, the young David was taken into the king's household after the successful fight with Goliath (1 Sam. 17). These two versions are connected by 1 Sam. 17.15, a verse that in turn contradicts the fact that Saul met David for the first time according to vv. 33-37 and 55-58 (Fokkelman 1986: 201-205).

This feature of Old Testament historiographic practice in which differing sources are compiled into a sequence, J. Licht (1983) compares with Herodotus and Plutarch. They frequently quote different accounts of the same event, giving as their source such statements as 'others tell this story:...'. D. Fehling's research on Herodotus' source references shows that the majority of his sources are probably fictitious (Fehling 1971, 1989), and thus the distance between the historians of the Old Testament and Herodotus becomes far less. Herodotus quotes different Greek versions of the events he relates, while the Old Testament historian quotes different Israelite versions. In accordance with his own literary context, Herodotus then invents sources to which he ascribes his different Greek versions, whereas the Old Testament historian compiles his versions in a continuous account. The only real difference is the lack of connecting comments in the manner of Herodotus in the Old Testament that justify the use of differing accounts.

However, the Old Testament occasionally does resemble Herodotus' practice with regard to source references. This phenomenon may be found in the two versions of Saul's death told in 1 Samuel 31 and 2 Samuel 1. The first of these relates that Saul committed suicide because his armour-bearer refused to obey Saul's order to strike him down. The second version tells that an Amalekite from Saul's army brings David the news of Saul's death which the Amalekite had brought about himself, acting on Saul's orders. The aim of the second version is obvious: the Amalekite hopes that by saying he has killed Saul, he will win David's favour, and at the same time he protects himself by saying that he acted on Saul's orders. In this way, the two differing versions of Saul's death are well accounted for. From the narrative's own point of view, it is possible to argue that the first version is true, and that the second one is a lie told by the Amalekite.

This example does not seem to be typical of the Old Testament narratives, where the reason for alternative or even irreconcilable accounts of the same event being given are often incomprehensible, or at least difficult to place within the historiographic progression.[70] According to the classic method of explanation propounded by J. Wellhausen (1889) and, with regard to the deuteronomistic historian, developed principally by L. Rost (1926) and M. Noth (1943), a number of original historical works and sources from the early monarchy onwards were edited, dovetailed, and later expanded in the course of various redactions. Each of them had its own interests to consider at the expense of a logical progression. This, however, has proved anachronistic. To the extent that the biblical traditions reflect history, Israel's formation as a people must be connected with an integration of the whole of Palestine and Transjordan. Judging by archaeological evidence, this happened no earlier than the Persian era (Thompson 1992: 315-16). Thus the Israelite, written tradition cannot have been initiated prior to this time either (p. 356 including n. 10), nor did it require many generations to reach its present form. Whenever a scribe copied a text, he actually created a new original, and the degree of agreement between this new text and the first one depended entirely upon the scribe's intentions and those of his superiors (Davies 1992: 100-101).

According to T.L. Thompson, the Old Testament texts 'reflect the antiquarian efforts of curiosity and preservation'. Historians 'critically distinguish and evaluate their sources. They "understand" history, and therefore at times slip into tendentious ideologies and theologies. The antiquarian on the other hand shows the more ecumenically pluralistic motivations of the librarian: classifying, associating, and arranging a cultural heritage that is both greater than the compiler or any single historiographical explanation' (Thompson 1992: 377). In the Hebrew Bible, the traditions in Genesis–2 Kings are externally structured as a

70. For a typology of variant traditions in the Pentateuch and the Former Prophets, see Thompson 1992: 359-65.

succession of great periods, but this only represents a secondary classification of the material. Indeed, disjunction is such a common phenomenon that 'in the larger blocks of tradition, narrative development has only the appearance of chronological progression' (pp. 377-78). The chronology resulting from the sequence of the individual literary units is entirely independent of the literary units themselves. As a text block, the tetrateuch–deuteronomistic tradition progresses as a sequence of great leaders: Adam, Cain, Noah, Abraham, Jacob, Joseph, Moses, Joshua, the judges, followed by Saul, David, Solomon and the subsequent kings. This heroic structure is secondary—it arranges, interprets and gives meaning to the narratives in the tradition (pp. 355-58). They have been collected and interpreted as a warning and as the basis for an idealized ethnicity in the future. The compiler has presented an ethnographic aetiology intended to create an Israelite *ethnos* from the various peoples who found themselves in Palestine after the disturbances caused by the Persians (pp. 382-83).[71]

Likewise, Herodotus has collected a number of disparate traditions and imposed his own structure on them. Fehling's statement that Herodotus used fictitious sources in order to tell as many stories as possible makes Herodotus an antiquarian as well. But the fact that both Herodotus and DtrH arrange material in the form of a causal and corporate chain of events is a new departure in the literature of antiquity. The reason for the Persian defeat in Hellas and for the Israelite exile respectively is explained, presumably as a model of the correct behaviour expected of the peoples involved in the future. Herodotus explains that it is worthwhile to fight for liberty, and that Hellas should not be divided, as it was during the Peloponnesian war during which Herodotus wrote his opus. In DtrH, it is specifically indicated that in order to remain in their own land, the Israelites ought to worship Yahweh in the correct manner and be just, justness being described as conduct in accordance with the divine law.

According to S. Mandell and D.N. Freedman (1993: 94), the Deuteronomist 'wanted his implied reader to perceive his implied narrator as an historian, and, consequently, deem his work historical'. Because they do not want to distinguish between an implied author and a number of dramatized narrators, they have to work with 'an

---

71. For a possible model for the formation of the Old Testament and its recording in writing from the sixth to the third century BCE, see Davies 1992: 94-133.

omniscient implied narrator' or 'the primary or overriding implied narrator', as well as a number of secondary implied narrators (pp. 129-31). However, the said distinction is much more simple as well as adequate. The implied author is not a *persona* in the text. He stands outside, all *personae* in the text are his creations. This applies to the many dramatized narrators in DtrH as well.

Mandell and Freedman rightly emphasize the Deuteronomist's concise plan for his account of the course of events. As regards everything that lies outside the scheme of its theology of history, the implied reader is referred to the sources that were apparently used for the deuteronomistic account. But Mandell and Freedman's insufficient terminology causes the same problems for the characterization of their implied narrator in DtrH as those that were pointed out in conjunction with their treatment of Herodotus: 'Both Israel's origins and its history are described by the overriding implied narrator of Primary History in accordance with the theological precepts that he wishes to be perceived by the implied auditor/reader...But this primary implied narrator is represented as an historian who believes that he is reporting valid historical data' (pp. 141-42). Thus the primary implied narrator is characterized as an historian as well as a theologian. Rather, W. Booth's terminology seems apposite: an implied author is behind DtrH, and the work is a result of his many choices. 'The "implied author" chooses, consciously or unconsciously, what we read; we infer him as an ideal, literary, created version of the real man; he is the sum of his own choices' (Booth 1961: 74-75). Mandell and Freedman's primary implied narrator is, being a *persona* in DtrH, almost schizophrenic, as he is both a critical historian and a theologian. An implied author in Booth's terminology is, on the other hand, not a literary *persona loquens*, a character in the work. He is behind and thereby outside a manifold and compound literary work with many dramatized narrators. He is an abstraction, the sum of the choices made when the work was drafted. If this work is complex and contradictory, this applies to the implied author as well.

Moreover, one must seriously doubt whether DtrH in fact purports to be critical historiography as insisted upon by Mandell and Freedman: 'he enhances his illusion of historicity by depicting his implied narrator as referring the reader "continually to the sources for everything which lies outside the scheme of its theology of history", thereby showing his real intent. Dtr wanted his implied reader to perceive his implied narrator as an historian and, consequently, deem his work historical' (Mandell and Freedman 1993: 94, quoting von Rad 1984: 205). J. Gray draws attention to the classification of Joshua, Judges, Samuel and Kings as the Former Prophets which 'emphasizes their character as primarily the theological interpretation of the history of Israel from the settlement of Israel in Palestine until the Exile' (Gray 1970: 1). Rather than historiography, DtrH might be characterized as a theological commentary to the course of history. The written sources referred to in Joshua, 2 Samuel, and Kings are disputed. Whereas Gray is fairly optimistic: 'It is not difficult to conjecture with a fair degree of probability the amount of the content of Kings drawn from these respective sources' (p. 6), D.B. Redford (1993: 330-32) entirely denies the very existence of the sources referred to in Kings.

In DtrH, two types of source citations can be distinguished. Josh. 10.13 and 2 Sam. 1.18 quote a certain ספר הישר, the book of Jashar, indicating that what is written in these two passages can be found in the book of Jashar as well. The second type of source citations are the ספרי דברי הימים, 'Annals' or 'Diurnal Deeds'. Thirty-three times, the reader of the books of Kings is confronted with a triadic citation formula consisting of the following elements:

1) ...דברי (כל) ויתר, '(all) the other events of...'
2) the king's name and several expressions of his achievements
3) הל(ו)א \ הם א(ו) \ הל(ו)א המה \ א(ו) הנם כת(ו)בים, 'they are recorded...' על ספר דברי הימים למלכי ישראל \ יהודה, '...in the annals of the kings of Israel/Judah'.

As will be seen, this is a stereotyped formula. The only variations occur in the middle link where specific events are rarely met with. As regards Israel, this is seen seven out of eighteen times,[72] whereas

72. 1 Kgs 14.19 refers to Jeroboam's war, probably the rebellions against Solomon, 11.26-40, and Rehoboam, 12.1-25. 1 Kgs 16.20 mentions Zimri's conspiracy which is also accounted for in 16.15-18. In 1 Kgs 22.39, Ahab is, apart from what has been previously narrated, credited with an ivory house and various cities. 2 Kgs 13.12 and 14.15 refer to Joash's war against Amaziah, reported in 14.8-14. Jeroboam II's conquest of Hamath and Damascus according to 2 Kgs 14.28 repeats the information stated in 14.25. Finally, Shallum's conspiracy in 2 Kgs 15.15 is also mentioned in 15.10. The remaining eleven references have no specific incidents: 1 Kgs 15.31; 16.5; 16.14; 16.27; 2 Kgs 1.18; 10.34; 13.8; 15.11; 15.21; 15.26; 15.31.

Judah has only four mentionings of specific events out of fifteen occurrences of the citation formula.[73] Out of a total of thirty-three instances, specific events capable of rendering probable the existence of sources such as 'the Annals of the Kings of Israel' are referred to eleven times. Only twice, matters that are not mentioned before in Kings are touched upon: Hezekiah's conduit, 2 Kgs 20.20, and Ahab's building activities, 1 Kgs 22.39. As is well known, a conduit is commemorated in the famous Siloam-inscription.[74] This makes Ahab's ivory house and cities the only indication of the possible existence of two sources comprising material that was not utilized by the author/compiler of the books of Kings, as indicated in the citation formula.[75] Redford calls attention to the possibility that the book of Amos was used as the source for this particular piece of information (Amos 3.15; Redford 1993: 331), and thus his scepticism seems well-founded: 'One can only conclude that a formal source that went under the rubric the 'Diurnal Deeds' never existed' (p. 332).

It is pivotal to the citation formula that the chronicles mentioned therein comprise יתר דברי המלך, the other events of the kings' reign, that is events that were not narrated in the books of Kings. As has been seen, these references to sources comprising more than the facts told by the Deuteronomist probably reflect a source-fiction. Redford puts the matter appositely: 'The slightest trace in his sources of an act that can be judged on the basis of his ethic, or construed as fulfillment of prophecy is bound to excite his penchant for editorializing. That he does not have any more events on which to comment than are now present in his work does not mean that he has been selective in his choice of materials, but rather that his material contained nothing more. He has given us all his sources gave him' (Redford 1993: 320).

DtrH is a theological commentary to the course of history. I do not agree with Mandell and Freedman that the source fiction of the

73. 1 Kgs 15.23 gives the information that Asa built cities—this is told in 15.22 as well. 1 Kgs 22.46 mentions Jehoshaphat's war reported in 22.29-37. Hezekiah's conduit is, apart from the reference in 2 Kgs 20.20, not mentioned in Kings. 2 Kgs 21.17 refers to Manasseh's sins narrated in the previous section. The remaining eleven references give no specific incidents: 1 Kgs 14.29; 15.7; 2 Kgs 8.23; 12.20; 14.18; 15.6; 15.36; 16.19; 21.25; 23.28; 24.5.

74. Text: Davies 1991: 68; translation: Pritchard 1969: 321.

75. A thirty-fourth instance of the citation formula is ספר דברי שלמה, 1 Kgs 11.41. It is not significantly different from the references to the annals of the kings of Judah and Israel.

Deuteronomist serves to bolster up an implied narrator as an historian. The very idea of an overriding implied narrator does not make
sense. Rather, the implied author purports to insert his work in an
existing written tradition. The kings concerned are literarily established as well-known characters. The *sefarim*, 'books', indicate that
the implied author builds on a written, not oral tradition. He does not,
like Herodotus, portray an overriding dramatized narrator, but of
course the citation formulas do contribute to the picture of the implied
author behind DtrH. Deuteronomy and the book of Joshua prepare the
stage for the genesis of the Solomonic kingdom, the book of Judges
demonstrates the consequences of disobedience to Yahweh, the books
of Samuel account for the origin of the monarchy, while the books of
Kings give the history of the monarchy. By means of the citation formulas, this history is inserted in an existing written tradition dating
back to Solomon. This creates the impression of a rich, national heritage in which Solomon represents the golden age of the nation. Quite
conveniently, the citation formulas start with Solomon (1 Kgs 11.41),
the ruler of the Israelite ideal kingdom, and they are repeated for
every king except Hoshea (2 Kgs 17) up to and including Jehoiakim
(2 Kgs 24.5) on the eve of disaster. Solomon represents the unity of
the kingdom, and with him the references to the annals start. They
reflect the continuity of history: From Solomon's ideal kingdom, the
monarchy is going downhill to face division and eventual destruction.

Tragedy in the Deuteronomistic Historical Work

DtrH confronts us with a series of themes that we also find in the
Herodotean tragedy. Five of these shared themes will be emphasized
here, followed by a closer description of tragedy in DtrH where these
themes are components. Finally, the deuteronomistic tragedy will be
compared to that of Herodotus.

Tragic Themes

First, the idea of *an immense distance between god and man* is
common to Herodotus and DtrH. The reasons for the deity's actions
are inscrutable. Yahweh chooses a people (Deut. 10.14-15) while
other peoples are left to worship the sun, moon, and stars (Deut. 4.19-
20; 29.25).[76] Yahweh also chooses individuals as his favourites whilst

---

76. True, Yahweh's choice appears to be explained by his covenant with Israel's

he rejects others without it being possible to fathom the reason for this. When Yahweh elected David to be Saul's successor, no reason was given for the actual choice of David (1 Sam. 16.1-13).[77] Nor does the prophet Nathan supply any other reason for David's good fortune than Yahweh's supreme choice (2 Sam. 7.8-17). The unfathomable ways of the deity are likewise in evidence when Yahweh punishes some individuals for a sin while refraining from punishing others who have committed the same sin. Both the sons of Samuel and the sons of Eli administer their positions as priests and judges badly (1 Sam. 2.12-17; 8.1-3), but only Eli and his house are punished (1 Sam. 2.27-36). The fate decreed by the deity cannot be changed by humans, but it may be delayed. When the prophet Isaiah foretells the impending death of King Hezekiah, the king reminds Yahweh that he has always been faithful to him and that he has been just. In this way, the prophesied death is postponed for 15 years (2 Kgs 20.1-11). Likewise, Josiah postpones the destruction of the kingdom of Judah by his just behaviour (2 Kgs 22.15-20) although he is unable to prevent it (23.25-27).[78]

Secondly, *man should keep to his proper place seen in relation to the deity* according to both Herodotus and DtrH. In DtrH, this is emphasized both generally and specifically. Generally speaking, one should be humble before Yahweh and not be proud (Deut. 8.17-18; 9.4-6). The deity saves the helpless and casts down the proud (2 Sam. 22.26-28). Specifically speaking, the Law (Deut. 5–26) states exactly what Yahweh demands of mankind (Deut. 26.16-19). If man is to prosper, he must take care not to overstep this precisely delineated

---

fathers (Deut. 4.31; 9.5 etc.), but the reason why the deity chose those very 'fathers' is all in the air. Even if we turn to texts outwith the deuteronomistic historical work, it does not, for instance, help to advance Abraham's faith as the reason for his election, as the faith he is credited with (Gen. 15.1-6) is faith in Yahweh's promise which was expressed beforehand.

77. It is perhaps possible to maintain that 1 Sam. 16.7 should be taken to mean that Yahweh chose David because he was good. This opinion may also be regarded as confirmed by 1 Kgs 11.34, which could, however, be termed a subsequent rationalization: Because David had been chosen, he had to have acted irreproachably. If David was chosen because he was good, one wonders why Yahweh did not show the same kind of discernment when electing Jeroboam king of the Northern Kingdom (1 Kgs 11.26-40; 12.26–13.34).

78. An obvious parallel is the story of Croesus in Herodotus (1.91), although it is Apollo, not Croesus himself, who achieves the postponement of Croesus' fate.

boundary between himself and the deity.

A third theme common to Herodotus and DtrH is the idea of the *deceptive deity* who leads humans to bring about their own misfortune. One of the consequences of the election of Israel and of Yahweh's promise of the land is that the deity hardens the hearts of the Canaanite peoples so that they attack Israel, thus giving Israel an excuse to annihilate them (Deut. 2.30; Josh. 11.19-20). Another example is the story of king Ahab of Israel's war against the Arameans (1 Kgs 22), where the prophets foretell an Aramean defeat because Yahweh has deceived the prophets by means of a lying spirit (v. 21). This deception of Ahab is Yahweh's punishment of Ahab's crime against Naboth, and it agrees with the curse pronounced by Elijah (1 Kgs 22.38; 21.19).[79] Earlier on, Yahweh's evil spirit had troubled Saul as a result of God's rejection of him (1 Sam. 16.14), and twice it had made him attempt to murder David (1 Sam. 18.10-11; 19.9-10). A third example is the story of Abimelech, the son of Gideon the judge, who was proclaimed king in Shechem after he had murdered his brothers. In order to avenge Abimelech's brothers, the deity sent an evil spirit to bring about an uprising against Abimelech (Judg. 9). There are a number of other examples of Yahweh having misled people or hardened their hearts to their own misfortune.[80] Israel is smitten by misfortune brought about by Yahweh, when the deity sets David against the people so that he carries out a census, an action for which God punishes him (2 Sam. 24).

A fourth theme met with in DtrH is one of *equilibrium*, often in the form of a *hubris–nemesis* motif. This may be found in the stories of Abimelech's reign and in the deity's misleading of Ahab. DtrH ends catastrophically with the exile as the punishment for the people's lack of faith towards Yahweh during many generations (Deut. 29.25-27; 2 Kgs 17.7-8; 17.19-20; 22.16-17). There is also a number of lesser

79. The connection is seen even more clearly in the LXX: compare LXX 3 Kgdms 20.19 with LXX 3 Kgdms 22.38.

80. Yahweh hardens the hearts of Eli's wrong-doing sons because he has decided that they should die (1 Sam. 2.12-17; 2.22-25). While fleeing from Absalom, David is cursed by Saul's kinsman Shimei. As this curse is due to Yahweh's instigation, David is forced to bow down to it (2 Sam. 16.5-13), but under Solomon, Shimei is put to death (1 Kgs 2.36-46). One of the methods employed by Yahweh in bringing David back to the throne after Absalom's uprising is also deceptive, as it is at Yahweh's instigation that Absalom rejects the respected Ahitophel's advice (2 Sam. 17.14; cf. 16.23).

stories containing the *hubris–nemesis* motif. The Arameans, for instance, insult Yahweh by calling him a mountain-god, whereupon a few Israelites beat more than 100,000 Arameans (1 Kgs 20.23-30). The year before, the Israelites had likewise been victorious after the Aramean king Ben-Hadad had overstepped all reasonable bounds for a suzerain's power (1 Kgs 20.1-21). There are, obviously, certain moral or metaphysical bounds that may not be overstepped without the deity's reacting by punishing the offender, or in other ways restoring equilibrium. As in Herodotus, this may likewise be seen when the balance of power between two opposing forces is strikingly unequal. An example is the story of Gideon's victory over the Midianites (Judg. 7–8), where on Yahweh's instigation no fewer than 120,000 Midianites fell at the hand of 300 Israelites.[81] When the deity's attitude to the strong is taken into consideration, any victory to the party with immense military might seems ominous. The account of Saul, who with no fewer than 300,000 Israelites and 30,000 Judaeans was victorious over the Ammonites may be considered an example of this (1 Sam. 11). The contrast to another of Yahweh's chosen, Gideon, is startling.

There are numerous examples of the fifth theme: *people are blessed or cursed by the deity on account of their lineage*. To take a few instances: The point is expressed paradigmatically in Deut. 5.9-10, where it is stated that Yahweh punishes a wrong-doer's guilt on up to three successive generations, whereas he shows solidarity (*ḥesed*)[82] with them that love him לאלפים, 'to the thousandth [generation]'. A curse on a lineage may be found in 1 Sam. 2.27-36 where Yahweh announces that he will cause all of Eli's lineage to die in the flower of their days. Solomon, on the other hand, is favoured and can ascend the throne due to Yahweh's blessing upon David's lineage. Solomon will be punished leniently if he should transgress against Yahweh (2 Sam. 7.12-15; 1 Kgs 3.6). Solomon's son Rehoboam is, however, affected by the curse incurred by Solomon in his old age (1 Kgs 11.9-13; 11.26-39; 12.1-19).

---

81. The story of the young David's fight against Goliath (1 Sam. 17) is another example of the weak winning over the strong with Yahweh's help. Yet another is the killing of twenty Philistines by Jonathan and his armour-bearer (1 Sam. 14.1-15).

82. This is the correct translation of the Hebrew word חסד—see Koehler and Baumgartner 1953: 318, s.v. According to LXX, however, God shows ἔλεος that is 'pity', 'mercy', or 'compassion'—LSJ: 532, s.v.

What Is a Tragedy?

In short, a tragic story has, according to A. Lesky (1958: 11-45) and
J.C. Exum (1992: 1-15), at least three elements: First, the tragic hero
usually experiences an irreversible disaster. Lesky is, though, of the
opinion that there are degrees of tragedy.[83] The most extreme form is
the utterly tragic understanding of the world in which the world
unconditionally, unavoidably, and incomprehensibly is destroyed by
opposing forces and values. An intermediary position is found in *the
tragic conflict*, represented by an incident being part of a greater
context which renders it meaningful. If man knows the rules that
govern the whole, the conflict is solved on a higher level, even when it
is apparently incomprehensible and meaningless. *The tragic situation*
in its turn also consists of opposing forces and of a person involved in
a hopeless conflict. However, due to fate's being favourable this
hopeless state ends all the same with rescue and reconciliation.

The second element in the tragic story consists of the fact that the
tragic hero is not subjectively but only objectively guilty. He offends
in good faith, due to the shortcomings of his limited, human cognition, and his misfortune is greater than his offence justifies. Thus he is
a victim of what Exum terms hostile transcendence (Exum 1992: 10,
41). Though lamentable, undeserved suffering is, however, not in
itself a tragedy. The tragedy contains a third element: The tragic hero
is fully aware of his misfortune and he makes every effort to combat
it, but in vain. 'Tragic heroes have the *hubris*—sometimes in authentic
greatness, sometimes in delusion—to defy the universe...in an insistence on their moral integrity' (Exum 1992: 12).

These characteristics of tragedy are not to be understood as a
definition but as a model that will be used heuristically in the following. In order to seek tragedy in a text, it is necessary to form some
idea of what we are looking for. The fact that the Herodotean
tragedies centred on Croesus, Cyrus, and Xerxes respectively can only
to a certain extent be fitted into Lesky's and Exum's model in no way
disassociates these stories from the Attic tragedy of the fifth century
BCE.[84] The story of Gyges and Candaules has three victims:
Candaules, the queen, and Gyges. Candaules is certainly not aware of

83. Lesky 1958: 27-28; cf. p. 11: 'Es ist in der komplexen Natur des Tragischen
bedingt, daß mit der wachsenden Annäherung an den Gegenstand die Aussicht auf
seine definitorische Erfassung sinkt.'

84. See Lesky's own examples, pp. 25-28.

his misfortune, but Herodotus clearly expressed a hostile transcendence with his *chren*, 'it was necessary'. The queen is a victim, but as she receives satisfaction for her humiliation, her disaster is not irreversible. Gyges is not worth a great deal as a tragic hero, as he is not forced into misfortune, nor does he have the moral integrity of a tragic hero. Candaules is actually the nearest to an ideal tragic hero in this story.

In the story of Atys and Adrastus, Croesus certainly experiences an irreversible disaster upon the death of his son. This misfortune had been foretold, and Croesus had made every attempt to prevent it. Here Croesus' guilt—he regarded himself as fortunate—is combined with hostile transcendence and tragical awareness. Croesus' punishment is far graver than the reader can be expected to find reasonable. Atys too experiences in his early death an irreversible disaster as the victim of his father's *hubris*. He is, though, disqualified as a tragic hero by his lack of awareness of the impending tragedy. Finally, Adrastrus, before he ever enters upon the scene, has experienced misfortune, but Croesus restored him to a fortunate position. When he suffers a new downfall, the first requirement of tragedy is fulfilled. Added to this, he is only objectively guilty as his spear throw accidently kills Atys, and his suicide demonstrates tragic awareness. His struggle with fate is, however, less marked than that of Croesus. Adrastus is thus a tragic hero to a greater extent than Atys, but to a lesser extent than Croesus.

Croesus' own downfall is irreversible, and both the ambiguous oracles and the Pythia's final interpretation of them remove all doubt: Croesus is certainly the victim of hostile transcendence. He insists too, in his questions to the Pythia after the disaster, upon his subjective innocence and the guilt of the gods. Thus he is shown as the most tragic of these heroes.

In the great Xerxes-*logos*, we once more find a downfall taking the form of an enormous humiliation, although the king does not lose his power. But he does become involved in ignominious intrigues within his palace. Hostile transcendence is shown even more clearly here, in Xerxes' deceptive dreams, the promising oracles, and the obvious blindness of both the king and the magi demonstrated by their total lack of ability when interpreting sinister dreams and omens. Like Croesus, Xerxes acts blindly, but in good faith in attacking Hellas. But Xerxes too is lacking as a tragic hero in so far as he, unlike Croesus, does not insist upon his innocence when once his misfortune is apparent.

We thus find greater and lesser tragedies in Herodotus. In particular, hostile transcendence characterizes the Herodotean tragedy. This is explicitly stated in the case of Candaules: 'Candaules necessarily fared ill' (1.8.2). It is also very marked in the Pythia's answer to Croesus: 'not even a god can avoid his pre-ordained fate' (1.91.1) and is perhaps most clearly seen before the Persian defeat at Plataea: 'no one can escape that which is ordained by a god...It is the worst human pain to be unable to act in spite of having the right intuition' (9.16.5). In considering the question of the tragedies in the Deuteronomistic historical work, I shall look for stories and statements that to a greater or lesser degree match the characteristics that constitute Lesky's and Exum's ideal tragedy: an irreversible disaster, hostile transcendence and tragic awareness.

The Tragic Leitmotif of the Deuteronomistic Historical Work

The Deuteronomistic historical work presents the history of Israel from the conquest of the promised land until the exile. The leitmotif is aetiological: why did Yahweh drive his chosen people out of the land he had promised it? The answer looks obvious at first, as we are frequently told that the people did not keep Yahweh's law and that they worshipped foreign gods.

From the very beginning, the conclusion of the story is hinted at, according to Deuteronomy, in the speeches which Moses held before the immigration. The normative, Deuteronomistic programme for the Israelites' existence in the promised land is expressed in these speeches (Deut. 5–28).[85] A warning to keep it strictly (Deut. 4.1-40) precedes the actual programme. In the course of this warning, Moses prophesies the coming apostasy and Yahweh's subsequent wrath, the people's expulsion from the land, and the fact that in exile the people will repent and Yahweh will show them mercy (Deut. 4.25-31). This is very much more than just a threat. The future *diaspora* is not a possibility but a fact. Not only is it certain that the present generation will get heirs in the land, but this posterity will make idols and offend Yahweh in other ways as well. Having declared his law, Moses names a number of rewards and punishments that will descend upon the people as the consequence of their obedience and disobedience,

---

85. Regarding this programme, see O'Brien 1989: 29, 56-62.

respectively. Judging by the number of curses and the wealth of detail, it seems that these are likewise part of a prophecy (Deut. 28). According to Deut. 28.45, the many curses are foretold *because*, not *if* Israel does not obey the law: כי לא שמעת בקול יהוה. The same is apparent in Joshua's speech, Joshua 23, where v. 16 declares that *when* Israel breaks the covenant that Yahweh has imposed upon them, they will be driven out of the land.[86] Finally, Deut. 31.27-29 states that misfortune will strike the people because they do evil in the sight of the Lord.

These texts (Deut. 4.25-31; Deut. 28; Deut. 31.27-29; Josh. 23.16) demonstrate Moses' and Joshua's foreknowledge that Israel will in the future incur guilt and be driven out of the promised land. This is foreknowledge and not necessarily predestination. The picture changes, though, in Deut. 29.1-5, for until now Yahweh has not given Israel the heart to understand, eyes that see, or ears that hear. The text is ambiguous, because actually Yahweh has already done what he could: he has demonstrated his power in Egypt and kept and taught the people for forty years in the wilderness. But at the same time, he has withheld the ability to understand his words. Much the same applies to the covenant in Shechem (Josh. 24) where the people upon Joshua's exhortation promise to worship Yahweh alone but are informed by Joshua that Israel is not able to do so. Yahweh is a jealous and passionate god who will not forgive Israel's transgressions and sins. *When*, not *if*, they forsake Yahweh, he will destroy them (Josh. 24.14-20). The Israelites are given a choice and they seal their own fate by choosing Yahweh who is holy and jealous and whom they are not capable of serving (v. 20). Thus the unavoidability of guilt is added to an account of objective guilt. The same point is made in Solomon's prayer at the sanctification of the temple. *When* the people sin against Yahweh, which is sure to happen as there is no one who does not sin, Yahweh will become angry and give the people into their enemy's hands, and the enemy will lead them captive to his own land. When the Israelites subsequently repent in the foreign land, Yahweh will

86. The infinitive construct in the phrase בעברכם את ברית יהוה אלהיכם...וחרה אף יהוה בכם should be translated as a temporal clause ('When you break...') as, for example, in the King James Version of the Bible ('When ye have transgressed...'), rather than as a conditional one ('If you break...'), as in many modern versions, for example *The Revised English Bible* (Oxford, 1989) ('If you violate...'). Cf. O'Brien 1989: 77 including n. 111.

forgive them (1 Kgs 8.46-51). This may be termed the tragic leitmotif in DtrH.[87]

According to M.A. O'Brien, the texts that constitute the tragedy are secondary, Deut. 28.45 being a possible exception.[88] All the same, they do follow the structure of O'Brien's DtrH. Here Moses declares the normative programme (Deut. 5.1–28.46) for Israel's existence in the promised land. By the time of Joshua's death, an important part of the implementing of it had been realized. Yahweh had given Israel the land and thereby fulfilled his promises (Josh. 21.43-45). The full realization of the programme takes place under Solomon (1 Kgs 8.56) whose kingdom represents the Deuteronomist's ideal state after the sanctification of the temple (O'Brien 1989: 288-89). The statements that constitute DtrH's tragic view of history are thus related to the Deuteronomistic programme, and to the most important milestones in its implementation: the conquest under Joshua, and Solomon's realization of the ideal state.

Exile is the unavoidable fate of Israel. In order to remain in the land, the people would have to show a degree of obedience to Yahweh far above the abilities of human beings. This is the reason for the exile. However, when the exiled people repent, Yahweh will be merciful, reverse the fate of the people, and lead them back to the land of their fathers. He will then 'circumcise' (*mul*) the hearts of the people,

---

87. This proposition of reading DtrH as a tragedy is partly inspired by Exum 1992. See p. 180 n. 65: 'One might view the Deuteronomistic History as the tragedy of the nation.'

88. O'Brien 1989. For Deut. 4.1-40, see p. 60 including n. 44. For Deut. 28, see p. 62 including n. 54. O'Brien divides Deut. 28 into three sections with 28.1-46* as part of DtrH. Verses 47-57 he isolates 'because of the shift from the conditional "if" (cf. v. 15) to a declaration of failure', while 58-68 'expresses different concerns to the preceeding two sections'. The asterisk in O'Brien's reference (Deut. 28.1-46*) shows that 'part of the material is not meant to be included in the reference' (p. xiii). Unfortunately, O'Brien does not mention which verses he thinks should be omitted. It seems strange to ascribe v. 45 and vv. 47-57 to different authors on the grounds of a presumed shift from a 'conditional "if"' to 'a declaration of failure'. בקול יהוה כי לא שמעת, v. 45, looks more like 'because' than 'if'. Talking of the future, Moses here declares that Israel will not listen to the voice of Yahweh, and for that reason a number of specified misfortunes will strike the land. In v. 15 there is, on the other hand, an 'if', as O'Brien rightly says. If Israel does not obey Yahweh, then such and such will happen. Here the possibility exists that they might obey. In v. 45 we are told that this possibility came to nothing. For Deut. 31.27-29, see p. 66; for Josh. 23–24, see pp. 75-79; for 1 Kgs 8.14-53, see pp. 153-58.

so that they afterwards love Yahweh with their whole heart and soul (Deut. 30.1-6). This is obviously a special kind of education: the people are not able to fulfill Yahweh's demands in the promised land; they are therefore to be exiled, but during the exile they will repent and then Yahweh will make them capable of fulfilling his demands.[89] Should one wish to ask why Yahweh could not have given his people this ability earlier, for instance when it declared to Joshua that it would serve Yahweh (Josh. 24.19-24), then the answer is lost in the fathomless mystery of the divine. It is possible to regard the 'circumcision of heart' in the exile as a result of the people's repentance and therefore as a reward for this repentance, and it is also possible to maintain that repentance is a necessary condition for circumcision of the heart, which again is necessary in order that one may serve the deity fully. The idea then would be that the people cannot repent until they are forced to it during the exile, where they face destruction.[90] Against this point of view, the passage from Joshua (Josh. 24.19-24) may be adduced as a suitable time to have carried out this circumcision. Another suitable time would have been when Solomon expressed the wish, after the sanctification of the temple, that Yahweh might turn the people's hearts and Solomon's heart towards himself, so that the people might remain faithful to the deity (1 Kgs 8.57-58). Subsequent history shows that Yahweh did not fulfill this wish, either for the people or for Solomon.

Joshua's prophecy, לא תוכלו לעבד את יהוה, 'you are not able to serve Yahweh' (Josh. 24.19), was perfectly true. The book of Judges is one long demonstration of the fact that Israel is not able to keep Yahweh's law. Here, however, the transcendence is mainly benign, as Yahweh is patient and does not destroy his people.[91] The story of the

---

89. Cf. le Déaut 1981: 181-82: 'C'est donc Dieu lui-même qui opère cette rénovation et qui crée en l'homme la capacité d'aimer...Cette circoncision du cœur permet d'obéir à la voix de Yhwh, de garder ses commandements et de revenir à lui "de *tout* son cœur et de *toute* son âme" (*vv.* 8-10).' See also p. 183: 'Le cœur circoncis est un cœur ouvert à son influence, obéissant à sa voix, malléable à son action.' It is interesting that ומל יהוה אלהיך את לבבך (Deut. 30.6), 'Yahweh, your God will circumcise your heart', is translated in LXX καὶ περικαθαριεῖ Κύριος τὴν καρδίαν σου, 'and the Lord will purge your heart', the verb מול being rendered by περικαθαρίξω rather than περιτέμνω.

90. le Déaut 1981: 181: 'Dieu promet à Israël repentant...de parfaire lui-même le processus de conversion.'

91. All the same, Judges has stories with tragical aspects, thus, to a lesser extent,

last of Israel's judges, Samuel, and the first king of Israel, Saul, is far more complicated. These two main characters differ from each other in the deity's different attitude to them. In the following, the story of Saul, where Saul and Samuel are leading characters, will be considered from the tragic point of view.

The Story of King Saul

This story begins, as D.M. Gunn has pointed out, with 1 Samuel 9, where Saul puts in his first appearance, and finishes with 1 Samuel 31, which tells of his death. 1 Samuel 8 may be regarded as the prologue and 1 Sam. 31.8–2 Sam. 2.7 as the epilogue.[92]

When Samuel's sons abuse their judgeships, the people demand a king (1 Sam. 8). This demand, and not the unjust behaviour of Samuel's sons,[93] provokes Yahweh's wrath. It seems a foregone conclusion that Samuel and his family are faultless,[94] whereas *the people* are blamed for demanding another form of government (1 Sam. 8.7; Gunn 1980: 59-65). All the same, Samuel at Yahweh's instigation gives in to the people and anoints Saul as king (1 Sam. 8–10). In this connection, Saul receives various instructions (1 Sam. 10.1-8). Upon the advent of certain signs, he is to do as the situation demands.[95] Then he is to go to Gilgal and wait seven days for Samuel's arrival. Samuel will sacrifice to Yahweh and tell Saul what he is to do. The signs come to pass, and Saul returns home (1 Sam. 10.9-16).

Samuel gathers the people so that they may choose a king (1 Sam. 10.17-27), and again he reproaches them because they reject their God by demanding a king. Saul is elected by lot, but some doubters deride the new king. However, when Jabesh is besieged by the Ammonites, Saul is able to muster 300,000 Israelites and 30,000 Judaeans and

the story of Samson (Judg. 13–16), and in greater degree that of Jephta (Judg. 11). On these, see Exum 1992: 18-60.

92. Gunn 1980: 18. As to the following, see also Exum 1992: 16-42; Good 1981: 56-80.

93. This may be compared with the damnation incurred by Eli's house on account of the unrighteous behaviour of *his* sons, 1 Sam. 2.12-36.

94. Samuel himself seems to be foremost among those holding this opinion (1 Sam. 12.1-5). The people's reaction (1 Sam. 12.5, 19) shows that they know it to be unwise to enter into discussions with Yahweh's prophet.

95. 'Do what the situation demands' is the interpretation of 1 Sam. 10.7b proposed by Fokkelman 1986: 35. This is the wording of the verse in question: עֲשֵׂה לְךָ אֲשֶׁר תִּמְצָא יָדֶךָ כִּי הָאֱלֹהִים עִמָּךְ, 'do whatever your hand finds, for God is with you'.

break the siege. This puts the doubters to shame, and Saul is acclaimed by all Israelites (1 Sam. 11). His victory over the Ammonites is, though, ambiguous, especially when one remembers the wars that Yahweh does not win conventionally.[96] When Saul, overshadowed by Yahweh's spirit (v. 6), uses such an extremely large force to combat the Ammonites, one is reminded of Herodotus' Xerxes who upon divine instigation (Hdt. 7.14-18) carried out his fatal attack on Hellas with a colossal force. After the victory when Saul enjoys the undivided acclaim of the people (1 Sam. 11.12-15), the feeling of something sinister to come is in no way lessened by Samuel's demonstrating with thunder and rain Yahweh's continuing displeasure at the people's demand for a king (1 Sam. 12.17-18).

Seen in the light of the ensuing events, Samuel's instructions to Saul are indeed unclear.[97] A possible interpretation is that Saul was left to deal with the first crisis on his own (1 Sam. 10.7), whereas he was to react to the second one by going to Gilgal to wait for Samuel.[98] The events in chs. 11 and 13 show that this was how Saul, quite rightly, understood Samuel.[99] As a king, he selects 3,000 men as a standing

96. Note the following examples: Gideon's victory with a force of 300 against 120,000 Midianites, Judg. 7–8; the 600 Israelites' victory over the Philistines, 1 Sam. 14; the little David's victory over Goliath the giant, 1 Sam. 17. Even in Judg. 4 where a large Israelite force fights Jabin, it is only a force of 10,000. Likewise the unorthodox strategy at Jericho, Josh. 6, and at Gibeon, Josh. 10.11.

97. Gunn (1980: 66-67) states that Samuel's instructions are ambiguous, as it is not clear whether Saul is to wait for seven days, or to wait until Samuel arrives. Actually, Samuel's order (1 Sam. 10.8) is quite clear on this point. Saul is to wait seven days, and then Samuel will arrive. Saul's dilemma is rather caused by the fact that Samuel breaks his own promise by not arriving at the end of seven days (1 Sam. 13.8).

98. Fokkelman 1986: 35: 'What follows in 10.8…is now linked by Saul with the next situation which faces him.'

99. According to Fokkelman (1986: 35 n. 13), the events told in 1 Sam. 10.10–13.22 agree with the chronology in 1 Sam. 10.2-8. I am more inclined to think we must accept that the chronological relationship between 1 Sam. 10.2-8 and the following events is unclear to the reader, but that this causes no problems for the actors in the story. Van Seters (1983: 257) gives a good example of the fact that the literary construction strikes the modern reader as artifical and highly illogical, as we are told in ch. 13 that Saul has an adult son, Jonathan, whereas we were told in ch. 10 that Saul was still a young man. Van Seters' conclusion that the events of 13.2–14.46 did not originally have any clear relationship to the foregoing is possible but not necessarily true. Van Seters is dealing with a redactor unable to see, as Van Seters does,

army and gives a thousand of them to his son, Jonathan. When the latter succeeds in defeating the governor of the Philistines, the next crisis occurs. Saul musters the army at Gilgal and obeying Samuel's orders, he stays there for seven days. During this time, more and more soldiers desert through fear of the enemy, and as Samuel still has not arrived, Saul makes the necessary sacrifices. No sooner has he done so than Samuel arrives with a judgment: if Saul had obeyed Yahweh, he would have obtained the deity's lasting favour. Instead, Yahweh has chosen another ruler for his people. After this tirade, Samuel leaves Gilgal, and Saul finds that his army has shrunk from two thousand to six hundred men (1 Sam. 13.2-15).

Samuel's curse must be caused by the fact that Saul, by sacrificing, has overstepped the bounds of his authority (Fokkelman 1986: 44). However, by delaying beyond the prefixed time, Samuel placed Saul in an unbearable dilemma. If Saul had waited any longer, the last six hundred men probably would have deserted too; because he did not wait, he lost Yahweh's favour which he intended to secure by sacrificing. Saul's intentions were good, he obeyed Samuel's orders, but Samuel broke his promise by not coming to make the sacrifices at the end of the seven days. It is again a foregone conclusion that Samuel is right, so *Saul* is judged. The question of why Saul is rejected must be discussed in conjunction with a query regarding what motives lie behind Samuel's and Yahweh's ignoring Saul's explanation. The supposition that the real reason for the rejection is to be found in Yahweh's attitude seems likely. Saul is, at one and the same time, chosen and rejected as a reaction to the people's unacceptable demand for a king.[100]

The killing of twenty Philistines by Jonathan and his armour-bearer (1 Sam. 14.1-23) is the beginning of a victorious battle against the Philistines. In the heat of battle, Saul demands that his soldiers fast until evening. Jonathan is unaware of this, and when he is reproached for breaking Saul's oath, he replies that Saul's oath rather than guaranteeing victory will result in a lesser victory. The tragic irony is

---

that his own literary construction is illogical. Why believe that an author would have thought more logically than a redactor? This is a typical way of solving problems in discussions on sources in traditional historical-critical scholarship. One simply creates new problems. The illogical author is superseded by the illogical redactor.

100. Gunn 1980: 33-44. Note the pun upon the name שָׁאוּל in Samuel's reproach (1 Sam. 12.17b): וּדְעוּ וּרְאוּ כִּי רָעַתְכֶם רַבָּה אֲשֶׁר עֲשִׂיתֶם בְּעֵינֵי יהוה לִשְׁאוֹל לָכֶם מֶלֶךְ.

fulfilled when the men later throw themselves upon the captured cattle thus breaking the Israelite taboo on blood (14.24-32). Saul tries to offer reparation for this by means of ritual slaughter (14.33-35), but actually this is unnecessary, as the people's sins did not consist of any lacking ritually slaughtering of the animals (Fokkelman 1986: 68-69). Saul bungles the situation even more when he, having forbidden the men to eat during the day, demands that they give up their night's sleep in order to pursue the Philistines. However, the oracle of Yahweh is silent, the pursuit has to be abandoned, and Jonathan's breaking of the oath imposed by Saul becomes publicly known. As Saul does not hesitate to pass sentence of death on Jonathan, the people have to ransom him (14.36-46).

In this story, Saul presumes the silence of the oracle to have been caused by a sin someone had committed, and he has lots cast to find the wrongdoer. Even if the sinner should prove to be Jonathan, Saul's own son, he must die (14.38-39). The lot is first cast between Saul and Jonathan together on one side against the people on the other (14.40-41). Saul obviously knows whom he is hunting, and this odd procedure guarantees that Jonathan's guilt is revealed as quickly as possible.[101] As J.P. Fokkelman (1986: 63-64) puts it, Saul's irrational behaviour demonstrates that 'he is certainly possessed of an evil spirit'. Perhaps this is an anticipation of ch. 16 onwards, where we are told that an evil spirit from Yahweh possesses Saul, leading him to behave recklessly.

1 Samuel 15 tells that Samuel sent Saul in Yahweh's name to curse the Amalekites. Saul obeys but spares the best cattle and the Amalekite king, Agag, to bring them to Yahweh's shrine at Gilgal. Yahweh is not slow to regret having made Saul king, but faced with Samuel's accusations that Saul has broken the divine command by not destroying the enemy utterly, the king replies that he has in fact obeyed Yahweh. The people intend to sacrifice the best of the cattle. In spite of Saul's explanation, Samuel curses him and declares that Yahweh has rejected him. Now Saul repents. He excuses himself saying that he feared the people and gave in to them. But Samuel is not to be moved, and the curse remains in force.

In this story, we are dealing with conflicting statements. Saul

---

101. This is also demonstrated by the fact that Saul is fully aware that Jonathan was not present when he imposed the fast upon the men (14.17). See Fokkelman 1986: 64, 71-72.

maintains he obeyed Yahweh. The fact that he brought the captives to Yahweh's principal shrine at Gilgal may be an indication that this is true and that Saul acted in good faith. According to 15.32, Agag believes himself to be released by Samuel's hand. Thus he had not expected anything but evil in Saul's hands.[102] This sin of Saul and the people seems to consist of their making no distinction between the ban (*herem*) that Saul has been ordered to effect and an ordinary sacrifice (*zebah*). From the point of view of Saul and the people, Yahweh's order *had* been obeyed.[103] Samuel points out immediately and sternly that *herem* and *zebah* are by no means the same thing. Once again, Saul's behaviour has proved inadequate. This is D.M. Gunn's interpretation of the situation, but J.P. Fokkelman disagrees. Fokkelman presumes that between the two sequences of events constituted by 1 Sam. 13.2–14.46 and ch. 15, Yahweh, to Samuel's astonishment, has reconsidered his decision and given Saul another chance. Saul makes poor use of this chance, and this annoys Samuel considerably.[104] Fokkelman's analysis of Saul's psychology is just as fanciful. This analysis is based on the fact that Saul erected a monument in celebration of his victory *before* going to Gilgal in order to make his sacrifice (15.12). Saul puts himself first, and his religious zeal is nothing but an expression of high-handedness (Fokkelman 1986: 92-93). In a thorough structuralistic analysis of the following dialogue between Saul and Samuel (vv. 13-33), Fokkelman states that Saul's stubbornness finally makes Samuel proclaim his ultimate rejection, this after Saul twice in the course of the discussion has had the opportunity of taking Samuel's criticism seriously (pp. 95-104). 'Saul...stubbornly repeats in v. 20 what he had already said in v. 15 and what he had already pretended in 13d' (p. 98).

Gunn's and Fokkelman's interpretations of the account of Saul's second rejection are thus diametrically opposed. According to Gunn, Saul acted in good faith (see also Exum 1992: 27-30), whereas

102. This interpretation is based on the Masoretic text (15.32b), וַיֹּאמֶר אֲגַג אָכֵן סָר מַר הַמָּוֶת, 'Agag said, truly the bitterness of death has passed away', which differs from LXX:... εἰ οὕτω πικρὸς ὁ θάνατος, '... is death thus bitter?' Cf. Stoebe 1973: 292 and Fokkelman 1986: 108 n. 37.

103. Gunn 1980: 45-55. See especially v. 21: 'The people took cattle and sheep from the booty, the best of what lay under ban, in order to sacrifice [it] to Yahweh, your God, at Gilgal.' Compare v. 15.

104. See particularly 15.11: '... Samuel became angry and called upon Yahweh all night'. Fokkelman 1986: 93-94.

Fokkelman holds that he acted in bad faith. While Fokkelman admits that Saul's rejection in ch. 13 rests on ambiguous grounds, he holds no brief for him in ch. 15, where the actions that Gunn takes to have been made in good faith are termed high-handedness by Fokkelman. Fokkelman's observations are usually shrewd, but he is perhaps also inclined to read a little too much between the lines so that his results become subjective. This might be the case in the detailed exposition of the subconsciousness and psychology of the protagonists based on an idea of a certain development in the inner Saul, this process being deemed to start on account of the decline in Saul's fortunes beginning in chs. 13–14 (Fokkelman 1986: 85).

Whatever attitude one holds to Gunn's and Fokkelman's readings, it is surprising that Saul is not forgiven. With his detailed knowledge of Saul's subconscious mind, Fokkelman has no difficulty in explaining this: 'His asking for forgiveness...is followed too quickly by a supplication which betrays dependence, "come back *with me*".' According to Fokkelman, Saul's repentance is not genuine. True, Saul can rightly be said to be taking the matter less seriously than Samuel. He realizes he has sinned, but the fact that he persuades Samuel to return and worship Yahweh with him (15.30) indicates that he does not take much notice of the prophet's pronouncement that Yahweh has rejected him as king (15.23, 26, 28). Even so, it is worth considering whether Saul does not view his sin in a manner that the reader too might find reasonable. Whether the booty and king Agag were despatched in one way or another, on the battlefield or in sacrifice at Gilgal, should not make so much difference that Saul, by infringing Yahweh's literal orders, would qualify for irreversible rejection. All the same, Saul *was* rejected, and this may point, as Gunn has it, to a hostile attitude to Saul on behalf of both Yahweh and his trusty Samuel that has little to do with this particular transgression.

Fokkelman advances a weighty argument for his idea of Saul's high-handedness when he mentions the monument that Saul erected at Carmel before going to Gilgal (15.12). However, one should not read too much into Saul's action here. There is nothing unusual in a king's celebrating a victory by erecting a monument, and it is therefore not necessarily a sign of high-handedness that could be taken to explain his rejection by the deity. Certainly, this action sounds ominous, but not, as Fokkelman has it, on account of Saul's psychology, but because the reader has already been made aware of Saul's rejection before the king erects his monument (15.11). Saul wins a great victory, erects a monument, and proceeds to Gilgal to sacrifice the booty to Yahweh. Just as he feels most successful, Samuel appears and announces that the wheel of fortune has turned again. Saul has been rejected as king and is facing his downfall. Thus Saul's monument serves to point to a contrast which may be read as herodotean (cf. Hdt. 1.207).

After the rejection of Saul, Samuel at Yahweh's command anoints a young shepherd, David (1 Sam. 16.1-13). ותצלח רוח יהוה, אל דוד מהיום ההוא ומעלה, 'and the spirit of Yahweh possessed David from that day on' (v. 13aβ). Correspondingly, we are told (v. 14a): ורוח יהוה סרה מעם שאול, 'the spirit of Yahweh left Saul', but the continuation of the verse is surprising (v. 14b): ובעתתו רוח רעה מאת יהוה, 'and an evil spirit from Yahweh dismayed him'. This evil spirit serves to place David the musician at Saul's court in order to relieve and entertain the king (16.14-23). All the same, we are given yet another account of how David entered Saul's service. In the second account, this happened during the war with the Philistines (ch. 17), and here David is shown as Yahweh's favoured warrior. David is associated with Saul's court both as a musician and as a commander, and returning together from warfare they are greeted by a song of victory (18.6-7): 'Saul slew thousands, David tens of thousands.' In this particular synonymous parallelism, the number used in the first half-verse is augmented by one unit in the second.[105] Here 'the largest (single) equivalent numerals available in Syro-Palestinian poetic diction; the fixed pair 'thousands'//'ten-thousands' are used.[106] The poem merely rejoices in the victory over the Philistines and contains no comparison of Saul's and David's deeds. Saul's interpretation of the poem (18.8) may thus be seen as the promptings of his evil spirit that make him regard David as a rival (Fokkelman 1986: 212-21).

David's stay at court is characterized by Saul's jealousy which Yahweh has awakened, but every move made by Saul against David only serves to increase David's fortune. Saul's efforts even cause dissension in his own family (Gunn 1980: 80-81). Saul's tragic insanity, his *áte*, is made plain when, once more possessed by the evil spirit (18.10-11), he hurls his spear at David. This having failed, in order to

105. Examples of this stylistic figure are Prov. 6.16; 30.15, 18, 21, 29.
106. Fokkelmann 1986: 214-15. Other examples may be found in Deut. 32.30; 33.17; Mic. 6.7; Ps. 91.7; Dan. 7.10. See likewise Fokkelman's Ugaritic examples (p. 214 n. 15).

get rid of his rival more discreetly, Saul then appoints him to the command of a thousand men—a dangerous appointment. However, Yahweh is with David, so he is successful and becomes increasingly popular with the people (18.12-16). Saul makes another couple of attempts (18.17-30): First he promises his daughter Merab in marriage to David, if David proves himself valiant in battle, but he then marries Merab off to someone else. He then offers his second daughter Michal in return for a hundred of the Philistines' foreskins. When David more than fulfils this condition, the king is forced to implement his promise. The irony here is that Michal was intended to bring about David's downfall but proved his rescue (19.11-17). From then on, Saul is forced to pursue David openly. However, Jonathan reasons with the king, and David is able to continue in Saul's service (19.1-8). When Yahweh's evil spirit ruptures this pleasant state of affairs, Saul again hurls his spear at David while David is playing for him. Helped by his wife Michal, David escapes, fleeing to the prophet Samuel. On three occasions Saul sends people after David in vain. Finally he goes after David himself, only to end in a humiliating frenzy (19.9-24).

In the following story of David's final departure from Saul's court, the king's son Jonathan chooses to be loyal to David rather than to Saul, exactly as Michal had done (1 Sam. 20). David's absence from court provokes Saul to order Jonathan to arrest David (20.30-31). Saul displays his knowledge of David's election by saying that David's very existence is a threat to his own monarchy (20.31) and thus to Jonathan's prospect of succeeding Saul (Fokkelman 1986: 330-37). Part of Saul's tragedy is that Jonathan moves away from him, identifying himself with David's interests. Even before David appeared, the passive Saul (14.2) seems to be in contrast to Jonathan who, along with his armour-bearer, showed courage equal to David's in the latter's fight with Goliath (14.1-15). This difference between father and son ends in Saul's attempt upon Jonathan's life (14.44). After David's arrival at court, Jonathan befriends him to such an extent that he even lends David his clothes and weapons (18.2-4). Later he pleads David's cause to the king (19.4-7). The second time he does so (ch. 20), Saul hurls his spear at Jonathan (20.33), as he had previously done at David. Jonathan has by now so thoroughly identified himself with David that his own father is no longer able to distinguish between them (Gunn 1980: 83-86).

When David flees and gathers some followers, Saul crazily accuses his own people of having joined David's and Jonathan's 'party' (1 Sam. 21.1–22.8). Saul presumes that David is acting as a king (22.7) and obviously expects the accession of a new king. When Saul discovers that the priest of Yahweh in Nob, Ahimelech, has given aid to David, he has all the priests of Yahweh in Nob slain. Ahimelech's son Abiathar alone escapes and flees to David (22.9-23). Thus the old curse upon Eli's house is brought to pass (1 Sam. 2.31-33).[107] Saul intended to be revenged upon Yahweh, but his action only brought about the fulfilment of the oracle regarding the house of Eli. At the same time, he practically makes David a present of the oracle of Yahweh (Fokkelman 1986: 407-410). Acting on the oracle's pronouncement, David later rids the town of Keilah of Philistines and evades Saul's planned attack upon it (23.1-13). By forcing David into exile, Saul gives him an advantage in the form of the control of the situation that Saul himself so desperately lacks.[108]

David goes out into the wilderness, where Saul pursues him. When Jonathan goes out to encourage his friend, he tells him what has already been indicated in the text, namely that Saul is acting in defiance of his realization that David is to become king (23.14-18). When David, during one of Saul's expeditions against him, is given the chance of slaying Saul, he refrains. Instead, he secures proof of his temporarily superior position (24.1-8). Afterwards, he confronts Saul openly, offers proof of his innocence and good will, and accuses Saul of pursuing him unjustly (24.9-16). Saul admits that David is right. Goodness may be attributed to David, whereas Saul has acted wrongly. Previously, the desperate and insane Saul had objected to David's election (18.8-9; 20.31). Now he seems resigned. He knows David will become king, and like Jonathan formerly (20.15), he begs him to spare his posterity (24.17-23; Fokkelman 1986: 469-72).

In the account of how David took Abigail to wife, Abigail prevents David from killing her ill-intentioned husband Nabal and his house and thus incurring blood-guilt (1 Sam. 25). Abigail is perfectly conversant with the fact of David's election and assures him that Yahweh himself will destroy David's enemies (25.26-31). This turns out to be

107. 1 Sam. 14.3 clearly shows Ahitub's relationship to Eli.
108. Here Yahweh's attitude to his followers is demonstrated in that David, during his flight, causes the priest Ahimelech to transgress a commandment (21.5-7, cf. Lev. 24.9), but this has no consequences for David himself, unlike Saul on a similar occasion. The consequences here were borne by Ahimelech and the other priests.

correct. Yahweh turns Nabal's evilness against him, and David is able to 'acquire' the willing widow (25.36-42). This story is sandwiched in between two episodes in which David has the chance of killing Saul (chs. 24 and 26). David refuses to avail himself of his opportunities, as he is unwilling to lay hands upon God's anointed (24.11; 26.9). He prefers Yahweh to judge between Saul and himself (24.13; cf. 26.23), a process that ends favourably for David and unfavourably for Saul (ch. 31). Thanks to Abigail, the same happens with Nabal. By leaving him to Yahweh, David avoids incurring blood-guilt. By his mockery of David and his men (25.10-11), Nabal denies David's election.[109] The same may be said of Saul when he continues to pursue David. In the same way as Saul, Nabal acts the king through false pride (25.36).

The next confrontation between David and Saul is brought about by David (1 Sam. 26). Once more, he protests his innocence and expresses his faith in Yahweh, and once again, Saul admits his guilt. He promises that he will no longer attempt to harm David and that he only wishes to bless him (26.13-25). The fact that Saul also asks David to return with him (26.21), links this episode to the scene of rejection in ch. 15 where Saul made the same request of Samuel (15.24-25 and 15.30). Saul has, thus, given in to both Samuel and the chosen David.[110] Moreover, the fact that Saul also admits he has acted foolishly (26.21) connects this scene to the first scene of rejection where Samuel made precisely the same accusation (13.13).

The final defence against his fate is put up by Saul in his visit to the witch of En-dor (1 Sam. 28.3-25). This story starts with the recapitulation of two important facts (28.3): Samuel is dead, and Saul has rid the land of necromancers (*'obot*) and sooth-sayers (*yidde'onim*). Thus Saul is in line with the later reform of Josiah (2 Kgs 23.24) as well as Yahweh's law (Lev. 20.27; Exod. 22.17, this last using the word *mekaššefah*). Saul is a faithful 'Yahwist'.[111] All the same, when faced

---

109. The fact that he may actually have known nothing about it does not matter here. Like Saul, he is punished for his *action*, regardless of whether this was carried out in good faith or not.

110. Fokkelman 1986: 547-48. See also 1 Sam. 19.18-24 which ends with Saul's falling into a frenzy at the feet of Samuel with whom David is staying at Ramah.

111. Fokkelman's doubts as to the purity of Saul's motives hardly seems convincing: '28,3d gives rise to the suspicion that Saul had a similar attack of religious zeal to that in Ch. 14... This rule may have been a renewed, late and weak attempt by him finally to obtain some access to, or confirmation from, Samuel' (Fokkelman 1986: 597).

by a new Philistine army, Saul finds the deity silent, unwilling to advise him either by dreams, *'urím* or prophecy (28.4-6).[112] Instead, Saul visits one of the forbidden sooth-sayers who conjures up the ghost of Samuel. When Saul complains that God has forsaken him, Samuel is hardly sympathetic as he merely reiterates this unhappy fact. Yahweh has acted against Saul in the manner he predicted, speaking through Samuel himself. He has torn the kingdom from Saul and given it to David because Saul had disobeyed the deity. 'Tomorrow', Saul and his sons will find themselves with Samuel, and Israel's army will be given over to the Philistines. Saul's illicit and desperate contact with Samuel is an expression of an impossible hope. He knows that God has forsaken him, and he has tried in vain to establish contact with him through prophets. This weakens any hope of Samuel's help, and thus it is not surprising that Samuel points out the superfluity of Saul's request, now that God has forsaken him and has become his enemy (28.15-16).

Samuel's words put Saul's defiant hope to shame, and all Samuel's authority only serves to confirm his worst fears (Fokkelman 1986: 611-18). J.C. Exum (1992: 23) rightly regards Saul's confrontation with his fate at En-dor as the tragic zenith of the story. 'Not content to let his tragic destiny unfold, the tragic hero stalks it. Like Oedipus, who relentlessly pushes for the full truth to be disclosed while the answers steadily close in upon him, Saul *must know*.' All that remains is to tell of his defeat in the war against the Philistines where his sons, Jonathan, Abinadab, and Malchishua are killed, whereupon Saul, in order not to fall to the Philistines, commits suicide as does his armour-bearer (1 Sam. 31.1-6).

In the text, the people's rejection of Yahweh[113] is formally linked to Yahweh's rejection of Saul.[114] From the beginning, Yahweh is a jealous god. He regards the people's desire for a king as disloyal, and Saul becomes the monarchy's scapegoat. Yahweh demonstrates the weakness of human rulers through Saul's alleged disobedience and he makes the people slaves again after the battle at Gilboah (1 Sam. 31). 'Thus God's initial hostility is vindicated and the way is open for him, freely now and out of his own gracious benevolence, to bestow king-

---

112. Fokkelman 1986: 599: 'He has reached the nadir of rejection, marked by the significant silence of his God.'

113. 1 Sam. 8.7: ‏לא אתך מאסו כי אתי מאסו ממלך עליהם‎...‏ויאמר יהוה אל שמואל‎.

114. 1 Sam. 15.23b: ‏יען מאסת את דבר יהוה וימאסך ממלך‎.

ship anew and on new terms.' In other words, Saul is the people's king, whereas David is Yahweh's king (Gunn 1980: 125).

> [I]n one set of (theological) terms, Saul's fall can be seen as part and parcel of the expiation of a sin, namely the people's demand for a king construed as the rejection of their 'true' king, Yahweh. Expressed in terms of a story of character and action, however, Saul falls victim to Yahweh's resentment at an imagined insult (the 'sin') and becomes the pawn (or scapegoat) in a process (the 'expiation') whereby Yahweh vindicates his shift of attitude towards the monarchy and buttresses his shaken self-esteem.[115]

The story of king Saul first presents his ascent to a secure position of power where the king is acknowledged by the entire people after a well-won war. Then his decline is shown as brought about by divine hostility. Saul is depicted as a scapegoat for the people who had rejected Yahweh by demanding a king. A tragical dilemma is forced upon Saul, and his reaction to it is *hubris* because he takes upon himself the role of the prophet, thus overstepping the bounds of his authority. This marks the beginning of his decline. During this sharp descent which ends in the king's suicide, Saul fights with all his strength against his unavoidable fate of which he is fully aware. As he is possessed of an evil spirit from Yahweh, it is also possible to find the motif of blindness. On its own, Saul's fate may look incomprehensible, but in a larger context it acquires the dimension of the scapegoat and becomes meaningful to a certain extent.

The Story of King David
The segment of the books of Samuel and Kings in which David appears, 1 Sam. 16.1–1 Kgs 2.11, may be divided into three sections: 'The rise of David', 1 Sam. 16–2 Sam. 9, 'the turning-point', 2 Sam. 10–12, and 'the decline of David', 2 Sam. 13.1–2 Kgs 2.11 (Exum 1992: 120-49; Whedbee 1988).

At the beginning, the transcendence is favourable. Yahweh chooses David to be king, gives him his spirit and generally paves his way to

---

115. Gunn 1980: 128. Another scapegoat in DtrH is Moses who in his own version of the reasons why he was not allowed to enter the promised land was apparently being punished, vicariously, for the people's refusal to conquer Canaan from Kadesh-barnea: Deut. 1.19-39; 3.24-27; 4.21-22. In Deut. 32.50-51 Yahweh states that the reason was Moses' and Aaron's unfortunate handling of the situation at Meribah-kadesh. According to Moses, he was punished though innocent, whereas Yahweh is quoted as saying that Moses is guilty.

success. In the first account of the start of David's career at Saul's court, the evil spirit that Yahweh has caused to come upon Saul is the reason for David's arrival at court (1 Sam. 16.14-23). In the second account, Saul gives David a place among his warriors because Yahweh has helped David defeat Goliath (ch. 17). The same divine support helps David to the top of the military tree, whereupon even the king's son regards David as his superior (18.1-5). When David's success arouses Saul's jealousy so that the king uses every measure to be rid of him, this merely becomes an added advantage for the parvenu (18.6-30). After Yahweh's evil spirit has prevented a reconciliation and has driven David away (19.1-10), Saul twice suffers the indignity of falling into David's hands, but David, being just, does not avail himself of this (chs. 24 and 26). In the story of Nabal and Abigail (1 Sam. 25) where David is just about to incur blood-guilt, he is even restrained from sin.

When Saul falls on the battlefield as a victim of Yahweh's curse (chs. 28 and 31), David has the messenger who boasts of having killed Saul put to death (2 Sam. 1.1-16). The Judaeans proclaim David king in Hebron (2.1-7), while Saul's cousin Abner proclaims Saul's son Ishbosheth king of all Israel (2.8-10). Both of these relatives of Saul are, however, killed without David being involved (3.6–4.12). David actually has the murderers of Ishbosheth put to death (4.12) and curses Joab and his house (3.28-29) because Joab murdered Abner, leaving it to Solomon to have him killed (1 Kgs 2.5-6). David makes the most of his anger and grief at Saul's death and Abner's murder (2 Sam. 1.17-27; 3.31-39), thus gaining the sympathy of the people (3.36-37). After this, he can march into Jerusalem and make this city his capital after having been proclaimed king by all Israelites (5.1-12). He defeats the Philistines (5.17-25), brings the ark of the covenant to Jerusalem (ch. 6), he is blessed by the prophet Nathan (ch. 7), and extends his kingdom to the Euphrates (chs. 8–12). All events are advantageous for David, and he piously leaves it to Yahweh to deal with his enemies. Others do the dirty work while David behaves blamelessly.

The exception to this blameless behaviour, the affair of Bathsheba (2 Sam. 11) which takes place at the climax of David's career, becomes the turning-point of his destiny. The episode occurs in the course of a war (chs. 10–12) during which the king had remained in Jerusalem, leaving Joab to subdue the rebellious Ammonites (10.7;

11.1). This could be interpretated as a hubristic attitude, which in turn
would explain the deity's characteristic absence during David's temp-
tation where the king is attracted by the beautiful Bathsheba—unfortunately, the lady is married. David's interest has consequences that
might have been predicted: the lady becomes pregnant, so David
recalls Uriah, the deceived husband, in the hope that this gentleman
will prove complaisant. Uriah shows not the slightest intention of
falling in with the king's wishes, so David is forced to take drastic
measures to ensure that he can marry the sorrowful widow, who duly
presents him with a son. At this juncture, the prophet Nathan
approaches David. He had previously pronounced Yahweh's eternal
blessing on David and his house (ch. 7). Now he tells a parable (12.1-
14): A rich man steals a poor man's only animal, a lamb, because the
rich man cannot bear to slaughter one of his own animals. David is
justifiably outraged and states that the rich man should be put to death
and that he must repay the lamb fourfold. Nathan then discloses the
true meaning of the parable and pronounces judgment on David: the
sword shall never depart from his house, misfortune will strike him
from his own family, and Yahweh will give his wives to another man.
At this, David expresses his repentance, and Nathan gives him
Yahweh's blessing: David will not die, but the son Bathsheba has born
him will.

The death sentence that David escapes here was not actually part of
the original punishment pronounced by Nathan. According to Nathan,
the sword would never depart from David's house (v. 10), and a misfortune, ra'ah, 'something evil' would strike him (v. 11). It is possible
that 'misfortune' here was meant as a euphemism for a violent death,
but it is more likely that Nathan's reaction to the king's repentance is
referring to the sentence that David pronounced against the rich man
of the parable (12.5b: 'death to the man who has done this') who was
actually himself (12.7a: 'Nathan said to David: You are the man!').
Now that the king has repented, this part of the sentence no longer
applies. Thus, Nathan's curse can be combined with David's judgment
on the sinner of the parable: The sin must be repaid fourfold, the
sword will never depart from David's house, 'something evil' will
strike the king from his own family, and David's wives will be given
to someone else. This series of curses is fulfilled in the following.
Firstly, David loses his first-born son by Bathsheba (12.14-23), and
both Amnon (ch. 13) and Absalom (18.9-17) die before Adonijah

becomes the loser in his and Solomon's struggle for power (1 Kgs 1) and is put to death after David's demise (2.12-25). The killing of Uriah is avenged fourfold with these four deaths. That the sword never departs from David's house is clearly shown both in the immediate sequel and in the account of the dynasty's future. After Nathan's curse and the conclusion of the war with the Ammonites (2 Sam. 12.26-31), misfortune does strike David from his own family with Amnon's rape of his sister Tamar, Absalom's revenge on Amnon, and later Absalom's revolt against David (chs. 13–18). During this revolt, Absalom makes himself king in Jerusalem and quite openly makes use of his father's harem (16.20-22).

The story of king David is not a tragedy. David possesses both subjective and objective guilt, but there are different nuances to his guilt. When David violates Bathsheba and thus Uriah, the *hubris* is aggravated as a result of the consequences of the act. These consequences are natural, true, but not *necessary*: Bathsheba becomes pregnant, and Uriah refuses to enjoy himself at home while his comrades in arms are still fighting the Ammonites (Exum 1992: 127-28). Thus, David is put into a dilemma. He must either incur even more *hubris* by getting rid of Uriah, or he must be prepared to have his transgression discovered. If David had resembled a tragic hero, he would have chosen the latter fate, but like Gyges or Xerxes[116] he chose the easy way out. However, the difference between Gyges or Xerxes in Herodotus and David in DtrH is evident: Gyges and Xerxes incurred *hubris* innocently, whereas David's dilemma was the result of his own *hubris*. Illicit intercourse was punished by a dilemma whereupon David chose the easier solution, thus further aggravating his *hubris*.

After the episode of Bathsheba, David's fate is a long decline with one misfortune after the other, and the king is at no time able to cope with the situation. He reacts inadequately to Amnon's rape of Tamar (2 Sam. 13.1-22), and Absalom takes the strong line, deciding to avenge her (13.23-39). The affair culminates in Absalom's revolt, David's flight from his own son Absalom, and Absalom's death (chs. 15–19).[117] After this, David's fate remains insecure. Everything

116. Herodotus' Xerxes is a parallel to David when he in his dream is faced with the choice of either attacking Hellas or losing his power immediately (Hdt. 7.14). As we have seen, he chose the former, thus incurring *hubris*.

117. See Exum (1992: 131-35) for a description of Absalom's death as a tragical climax.

goes wrong, he lives increasingly at the perimeter of events rather than at their centre and gives rise to competition and disturbances between the north and the south (Exum 1992: 135-36). When Sheba and the Israelites revolt against David, it is not Amasa, the commander appointed by David, who puts down the uprising, but Joab, taking the opportunity of getting rid of his rival Amasa at the same time (ch. 20).

The last account in the books of Samuel tells how Yahweh himself led David to sin, and then punished him for it (ch. 24). This story, like a tragedy, includes an irreversible disaster, 70,000 men die of plague (v. 15), as well as hostile transcendence (v. 1), and tragic awareness, shown by David's repentance (vv. 10 and 17). However, in a larger, metaphysical perspective, and in the context of David's entire fate, the story gains meaning as the conclusion of a process in which the relationship of the deity to David has gradually worsened. From the time of David's anointing until his assumption of power in Jerusalem, Yahweh's relationship to David may be termed as a divine presence. While David keeps warm at home in Jerusalem during the war with the Ammonites, the relationship is weakened into one of absence, and after David's sin with Bathsheba, the deity becomes utterly hostile to him. David is punished by a series of misfortunes culminating in the deity's imposing a new sin on David, for which God punishes Israel. From having been a blessing for Israel, a king under whom the land was greatly expanded, David became the curse of the nation. The closing chapters of David's life tell of an old, impotent king (1 Kgs 1.1-4) who can only take a passive interest in the intrigues, which are being carried out around him (1.5-53). Although the promise to David and his dynasty was unconditional before the episode of Bathsheba (2 Sam. 7.12-16), it is rendered as conditional in David's own repetition of it to Solomon (1 Kgs 2.3-4). The possibility of apostasy from Yahweh, even within David's own dynasty, must be taken into account to a far greater extent now than before David's sin (Exum 1992: 140-41).

Nevertheless, David is not rejected on account of his sins in the way that Saul was. The figure of David changes, but after Absalom's revolt David regains his power and keeps it until he dies as an old man. Apostasy, with which Samuel and Nathan reproach Saul and David, respectively, had by no means the same consequences for these first two kings of Israel.

The Story of King Solomon

The story of king Solomon is woven into the preceding stories of Saul and David. In Nathan's prophecy to David (2 Sam. 7.12-15), Solomon is seen as Saul's opposite: Yahweh will allow David's descendant to succeed him and establish his throne for eternity. Yahweh will be his father, and should he sin, Yahweh will punish him, but the deity will not break his solidarity (*ḥesed*) with him, as he did with Saul. Furthermore, Solomon is Bathsheba's second son by David, begotten as consolation for the loss of their first son. Yahweh loves him, we are told (2 Sam. 12.24-25).

Thus Solomon is ideally placed at the beginning of the story. Yahweh loves him, and according to Nathan's prophecy he will be a father to him. This enviable relationship is due to Yahweh's inexplicable and unconditional election of David (2 Sam. 7.8-16). After his decline, David refers to the divine promise from Nathan's prophecy, but now it is depicted as conditional (1 Kgs 2.1-4), and this is the case whenever the promise is mentioned in the story of Solomon (1 Kgs 6.12-13; 8.25-26; 9.4-5).[118] This story is told in 1 Kings 1–11, beginning with Solomon's and Adonijah's struggle for power, and ending with Solomon's death. If the king and his descendants are faithful to Yahweh, they will be fortunate and Yahweh will retain David's dynasty on the throne. From the beginning, the transcendent element is favourable to Solomon. Upon his ascension to his father's throne, Yahweh has secured his power and given him peace from his enemies (5.17-18).

However, from the very start of Solomon's reign, when once he has secured his power and settled events of the past (1 Kgs 1–2), there are hints of something sinister to come, for example, when it is said that he and the people sacrificed on the hilltops (3.2-3). Neither Saul nor David are said to have acted similarly. Sacrificing on the hilltops was the privilege of Samuel, and his sacrificing is depicted as in accordance with the will of Yahweh (1 Sam. 9.11-14). During one of Solomon's sacrifices, Yahweh appears to him and ask what he desires. Solomon only desires a 'heart that listens' (לב שמע), so that he can rule Yahweh's people and distinguish right from wrong. This modest desire is rewarded by Yahweh with the beginning of his immense wisdom, wealth and respect (1 Kgs 3.4-15). These blessings are

---

118. Solomon's promises to himself and his own dynasty as a reward for having implemented Yahweh's punishments can be ignored here (1 Kgs 2.33; 2.45).

demonstrated in great abundance during the course of the narrative. The sections on Solomon's wisdom and wealth (1 Kgs 3.16–5.14; ch. 10) flank the section on Solomon's building activities (5.15–9.28). As far as the temple is concerned, they represent the fulfilment of an old promise, given through Nathan (2 Sam. 7; 1 Kgs 6.12-13; 9.3-5). These building activities, however, could only be carried out by means of an extensive *corvée* (1 Kgs 5.27-30; 9.15-23) which incurred disastrous consequences when Solomon was succeeded by his son Rehoboam (12.1-19).

The ideal tale of Solomon is interrupted by the account of the king's idolatry. A good deal of Solomon's god-given wealth is spent upon a harem of no less than a thousand concubines who lead the king into idolatry in his old age. On this account, Yahweh curses Solomon's house: He will tear the kingdom away from Solomon's son and give it to another. However, for the sake of David, Solomon's son will be permitted to retain one of Israel's tribes (11.1-13). Immediately after this curse has been declared, Solomon's kingdom is reduced by the loss of Edom and Aram (11.14-25), and Jeroboam is chosen by Yahweh to be king of the ten tribes of Israel in the future, after Solomon's death. Solomon, like Saul before him, tries to prevent prophesied events from coming to pass. Jeroboam must flee to Egypt in order to avoid being killed by Solomon, and he remains there until after Solomon's death (11.26-40.)

The transcendence is favourable to Solomon all his life. He remains king until his death, even although he is punished by the loss of Edom and Aram, by Jeroboam's opposition, and by the knowledge of the approaching division of the kingdom. In this respect, Solomon is the absolute opposite of Saul (2 Sam. 7.14-15). Nevertheless, Solomon's prosperity brings misfortune down upon himself, his kingdom, and his successors. His many building enterprises necessitates forced labour in the form of a *corvée*, which has fatal consequences for Rehoboam, and the enormous harem Solomon is able to maintain proves his own undoing. Thus his advantages may be regarded as oxymoronic: his building enterprises and his wealth are expressions of Yahweh's blessing, but contain the seeds of disaster. In yet another way, Solomon must be said to be an ambiguous figure, as he clearly breaks the law of the king (Deut. 17.14-20) which states that the king may not acquire large numbers of horses, marry many wives who can lead his heart astray, nor collect silver and gold in great quantities.

These transgressions are emphasized in 1 Kgs 10.26–11.4. It is ironical that Yahweh himself gives Solomon the riches which cause his transgressions. Even though Solomon must be said to be guilty of transgressing, it seems obvious that the deity's attitude to him is ambiguous.

The story of Solomon cannot be called a tragedy, mainly because the king does not experience a downfall as such, but also because he is both subjectively and objectively guilty. Nevertheless, the story does contain tragic aspects. Solomon is warned of the impending misfortune and informed of his guilt, although, on the other hand, nothing indicates that Solomon's idolatry could be termed innocent, as there had been no lack of warnings from Yahweh (see particularly 9.6-9). Solomon's persecution of Jeroboam takes place after both Solomon and Jeroboam have been made aware by God of the impending misfortune (11.40). This points to the opposition to an unavoidable fate that often marks a tragic hero.

The Divided Monarchy
When Solomon's son Rehoboam becomes king, things fall out as had been foretold. Rehoboam becomes the victim of his father's guilt and thus a tragic figure (1 Kgs 12.1-25). In Shechem, the people offer Rehoboam their fealty if he is willing to lessen the forced labour that Solomon had extracted from them. The elders who had been in attendance on Solomon advise Rehoboam to accept this condition, but the young men in attendance advise him to demonstrate that his power is greater than Solomon's by increasing the people's burden. Blinded by Yahweh, Rehoboam makes the wrong choice and is therefore only acclaimed king in Judah. The Israelites choose Jeroboam who had come to Shechem from Egypt upon hearing of the impending election of a new king. The text emphasizes that Rehoboam had absolutely no choice (12.15, 24). His attempts at bringing the Israelites round are fruitless, and when Shemaiah tells him that what has happened is Yahweh's will, Rehoboam at first resigns himself to his fate (12.24b). However, we are also told that there was a continuous war between Rehoboam and Jeroboam (14.30; 15.6). Thus, Rehoboam does not cease fighting his fate, and the same seems to apply to his son, Abijam (15.7b).

Israel

Jeroboam receives a conditional promise of a lasting dynasty: Yahweh will build him a house which will stand as surely as the one he built David, if Jeroboam will keep his commandments (1 Kgs 11.38). Yahweh's unconditional promise to David (2 Sam. 7.16) is still in force. David's house may well be humbled, but not forever, and it will not be destroyed. On the contrary, it will remain in power in Judah (1 Kgs 11.36a; 11.39). Jeroboam is thus the opposite of David. When he sins, not only does his own lineage become the victims of Yahweh's curse, but the decline of all Israel is foretold as well (14.10-16).

The new Israelite king makes two local bull-calves and introduces his own cult (1 Kgs 12.26-33). For doing so, he is cursed by a man of god from Judah (13.1-10). Jeroboam's unauthorized cult brings guilt on his own house which is thereby doomed to utter destruction (13.33-34). When Jeroboam's son Abijah is taken ill, the prophet Ahijah who earlier had foretold Jeroboam's election as king curses the dynasty. The king's son will die and alone of Jeroboam's house be laid to rest in his grave. Jeroboam's house will be wiped out by a new king whom Yahweh will appoint. Yahweh will also strike Israel, uproot it from the land he gave the fathers of the present generation, and disperse it on the far side of the Euphrates. The nation will be abandoned on account of the sins Jeroboam has committed and which he seduced Israel into committing (14.1-18). However, apart from his son's death, it looks as if nothing bad will happen to Jeroboam himself (14.19-20).[119] Because of their evil deeds, with only one exception, the subsequent kings of Israel are condemned.[120] With regard to the kings' attitude to Jeroboam's sin, that is worshipping Yahweh in the

119. Ahija has much the same function in the story of Jeroboam as Nathan in the story of David. First, Ahija blesses Jeroboam, then when Jeroboam sins, Ahija curses him and his house. In both cases, a son dies as the result of the prophet's curse, while the recipient of the curse himself lives to an old age. Nathan, however, differs from Ahija in that he does not pronounce the total rejection of David and his house.

120. The exception is Shallum who ruled for a month and who ended the dynasty of Jehu in accordance with Yahweh's promise to Jehu (2 Kgs 15.13-15; cf. 10.30).

shape of the bull calves at Bethel and Dan,[121] the text is silent in only two cases.[122]

Jeroboam's son Nadab fell victim to Baasha's plot which completed Ahijah's curse (15.25-32). Yahweh himself makes Baasha king, but when he persists in Jeroboam's sin, one Jehu pronounces a curse upon him and his house. Baasha is cursed, strangely enough, both on account of his own sin and for being the instrument of Yahweh's punishment (15.33–16.7). The curse is fulfilled in the time of Elah, Baasha's son, when Zimri forms a conspiracy against Elah and slays all of Baasha's house. Zimri becomes king but only for a week. As a reaction to Zimri's *coup d'état*, the Israelite army appoints their leader Omri king (16.8-22).

Omri, like his predecessors, continues to sin in the manner of Jeroboam and indeed more than his predecessors, but this apparently goes unpunished. Unlike Jeroboam and Baasha, Omri's house is not cursed (16.23-28). However, when Omri's Son Ahab turns up, things change (16.29–22.40). He too behaves worse than his predecessors (16.29-33; 21.25-26). Yahweh sends a drought as punishment for the fact that Ahab and his father's house have turned away from Yahweh and worshipped Baal (18.18). The drought ends with a trial of strength between the prophet Elijah and the priests of Baal, where Elijah demonstrates that Baal is a false god and Yahweh the true god (chs. 17–18). Yahweh demonstrates his power further when a large Aramean army falls to a small army of seven thousand Israelites (20.1-21; compare vv. 10 and 15). When the Arameans offend Yahweh again the following year (20.23; 20.28), the deity again gives the victory to Israel (20.22-30), and once more the immense difference between the forces is emphasized (20.27). Ahab is merciful to Ben-hadad, the Aramean king (20.31-34), and is therefore condemned by one of Yahweh's prophets. Because Ahab gave a man whom Yahweh had placed under ban his freedom, he will pay with his life,

---

121. That these represent Yahweh is seen, firstly, by the fact that they were erected in order to obviate the necessity of the Israelites' travelling to Jerusalem in order to sacrifice to Yahweh there (1 Kgs 12.27). Secondly, Jeroboam himself identifies the calves with the god who brought Israel out of Egypt (1 Kgs 12.28; compare Aaron's calf, Exod. 32.4). Later, we are told of Jehu that he wipes out the worship of Baal in Israel (2 Kgs 10.18-28) but did not turn aside from Jeroboam's sin, in other words, worship of the calves (10.29, 31).

122. Shallum and the last king of Israel, Hoshea (2 Kgs 17).

and his people must pay for the Arameans (20.35-43). After the story of Ahab's appropriation of Naboth's vineyard, effected by the rightful owner's being charged with false accusations and stoned (21.1-16), Elijah curses Ahab's house, saying it will be wiped out of Israel (21.17-24). The curse is related to the king's crime against Naboth— where dogs licked the blood of Naboth, there too they will lick Ahab's blood (21.19). However, as we have seen, Ahab had been cursed prior to his crime against Naboth, and the judgment against him seems to be on account of his godless behaviour altogether (21.25-26). When Ahab repents, the fulfilment of the curse upon his house is postponed until his son's time (21.27-29), although the curse does touch Ahab himself in that Yahweh sends a lying spirit to his prophets and thereby causes the king to go to war against the Arameans in which connexion he is slain (22.1-40). Ahab's son Ahaziah continues the cultic practice of his parents (22.52-54) and becomes a victim of the curse on Ahab's house when he falls out of a window in his palace. He seeks advice of the god Baal-zebub, but is told by Yahweh's prophet Elijah that he must die because he has addressed himself to the wrong god (2 Kgs 1). His brother Jehoram becomes the next king (2 Kgs 3.1-27; 9.1-26). Certainly, he does wrong in the sight of the lord, but he is still an improvement upon his parents as he removed his father's image of Baal (3.1-3). Nevertheless, the curse on Ahab's house is fulfilled when Jehu is anointed king by Elijah and given the task of destroying Ahab's house (9.1-10).

Among the kings of the Northern kingdom, only Jehu has a reputation that may be called praiseworthy. He conspires willingly, obeys Elijah's orders faithfully (9.14–10.17), and destroys the cult of Baal (10.18-29). He is rewarded with a dynasty lasting four generations (10.30), even though, by adhering to Jeroboam's sin, he does not follow Yahweh's law (10.31). This latter fact might, though, be a reason why Israel loses the land east of the Jordan during Jehu's reign (10.32-33). Yahweh is favourably inclined to the kings of Jehu's house. They all do evil in his sight[123] but in spite of this, Yahweh rescues Israel from two crises which threaten to destroy the land during the reigns of Jehoahaz (2 Kgs 13.22-23) and Jeroboam II (2 Kgs 14.26-27). It is only in connection with kings of Jehu's line that we are told that Yahweh does not intend to destroy Israel as yet.[124]

123. Jehoahaz, 2 Kgs 13.2; Joash, 13.11; Jeroboam II, 14.24; Zachariah, 15.9.
124. Jehoahaz, 2 Kgs 13.22-23; Jeroboam II, 14.27.

The deity demonstrates two entirely different attitudes to his instruments of punishment, Baasha and Jehu. One reason for Baasha's damnation is that he acted as Yahweh's instrument of punishment by destroying Jeroboam's house (1 Kgs 15.29; 16.7), while Jehu, on the contrary, is rewarded for obeying Yahweh's order to destroy Ahab's house (2 Kgs 10.30). The text of the Books of Kings seems to make no distinction between these two kings with regard to their wrongdoings (compare 1 Kgs 15.34 and 16.2 with 2 Kgs 10.31). Jehu and Baasha were both the instruments of Yahweh's punishment and both broke Yahweh's law. In spite of the similarity, the deity treats them differently, punishing Baasha and rewarding Jehu.

The time-limit granted to Jehu's dynasty expires with Jehu's fourth descendant Zachariah, who falls victim to a conspiracy after a reign of only six months. The text indicates carefully that the story occurs as foretold in Yahweh's words to Jehu (2 Kgs 15.8-12). However, Zachariah's murderer and successor, Shallum, is only given a short time to enjoy his new power, as he is thrown down by Menahem at the end of a month (15.13-22). Being Yahweh's puppet is not necessarily felicitous. Three out of four kings in the period between Jehu's dynasty and Hoshea are murdered.[125] The exception is, strangely enough, Menahem, who slew Shallum, and who is described as the cruellest of Israel's kings. Of none of the others are we told that they ripped open the abdomens of pregnant women (15.16).[126] Notwithstanding, Menahem is the only king in the period between the dynasty of Jehu and Hoshea who is not killed due to a conspiracy.

Hoshea, like his predecessors, is condemned for doing evil in the sight of the lord (2 Kgs 17) although he is not judged as harshly as the others (17.2). Hoshea rebels against his Assyrian overlord and allies himself with the Egyptians. The Assyrian king retaliates by arresting Hoshea, conquering Samaria, and exiling the Israelites (17.3-6). The author equips these events with a lengthy explanation of why Yahweh allowed this to happen. It is Yahweh's punishment for Israel's idolatry and for continuing the sin that Jeroboam had led the entire land into (17.7-23). It looks as if the many sins committed in the course of time were regarded as having 'piled up', with each king adding to the pile.

125. Shallum, 2 Kgs 15.14; Pekahiah, 15.25; Pekah, 15.30.
126. On the other hand, the prophet Elijah prophesies something similar of the Aramean king Hazael (2 Kgs 8.12).

Thus they were both personally guilty and tainted by their predecessors' misdeeds.

Judah

Yahweh was favourably inclined towards Judah from the beginning. The country's fate was decided by the unconditional promise given on Yahweh's behalf by Nathan to David (2 Sam. 7.16). The promise was, as already mentioned, given before David's affair with Bathsheba and was next referred to after Solomon's downfall (1 Kgs 11.12-13, 32-36). Before that time, the references made to Nathan's promise are subjected to the proviso that Solomon observe Yahweh's commandments (1 Kgs 2.3-4; 6.12-13; 8.25; 9.4-5). After Solomon, unconditional references to Nathan's promise occur twice in connection with evil kings, Abijam (1 Kgs 15.4) and Joram (2 Kgs 8.19), and twice in connection with the just Hezekiah (2 Kgs 19.34; 20.6).

Due to David's just behaviour, Yahweh allows his dynasty to retain a *nir*, 'lamp',[127] in Jerusalem. The first three evil kings benefit from this lamp which is mentioned in connection with Rehoboam (1 Kgs 11.36) and his son Abijam (15.4). They were followed by two just kings, Asa who won peace with Israel by buying support from the Aramean king Ben-Hadad (15.9-24), and Jehoshaphat who managed to remain at peace (22.41-51). After Jehoshaphat, Joram, the third of the evil kings, ascended the throne (2 Kgs 8.16-24). For David's sake, Yahweh still did not destroy Judah (8.19). Up to this point, there has been favourable transcendence shown in the account of Judah's history. In spite of the sins of the kings and the people, Yahweh does not destroy the country on account of David.

However, it seems as if the transcendence changes in the time of Joram. After him, David's lamp is no longer mentioned, and not even the just kings are free from misfortunes. Under Joram, Edom and Libnah break away from Judah's rule (8.20-22), and Joram's evil son Ahaziah is murdered when he makes an alliance with the Israelites' king Joram, son of Ahab, against the Aramean king Hazael. He and the Israelite king fall victims to Jehu's rebellion and the curse on Ahab's house (9.1-29). The next ruler, Ahaziah's mother Athaliah, is executed (11.1-16). The following four just kings are likewise unfortunate. The exemplary Joash is murdered (12.21), and Amaziah attacks

---

127. For possible explanations of this abstruse word, see Nelson 1981: 108-109.

Israel in his overweening pride[128] and is defeated (14.7-14). Later, he becomes the victim of a conspiracy (14.19). Of Azariah and Jotham who reign for 52 (15.2) and 25 years (15.33), respectively, practically nothing except misfortunes are told. Azariah is afflicted by leprosy (15.5) and Jotham is attacked by an Israelite–Aramean coalition (15.37). Apart from this, we only learn the kings' names, some chronological data, and the fact that they were just in the sight of the lord. The evil Ahaz, however, is responsible for the misfortunes that afflicted him. He lost Elath (16.6) and in order to escape from an Israelite siege, he became an Assyrian vassal (16.7-9). The righteous Hezekiah and the evil Manasseh both received similar sad prophecies about a misfortune that was to strike their successors (20.16-19 and 21.1-18 respectively). Not even the most righteous of all, Josiah, is able to avert the predicted misfortunes, even by means of his exemplary reform (chs. 22–23). In contrast to the just kings whom misfortune strikes in spite of their faithfulness to Yahweh, there were two good kings who ruled before Joram: Asa and Jehoshaphat. They are not mentioned in connection with misfortunes, and Asa even entered into a successful coalition with the Aramean king against Israel's king Baasha (1 Kgs 15.9-24; 22.41-51).

With Joram, a change occurs in the divine guidance of history. David's 'lamp' in Jerusalem is no longer mentioned, and even the good kings are struck by misfortune. It is no coincidence that Joram is the turning-point. His wife belongs to the accursed house of Ahab (2 Kgs 8.18), and Athaliah, the mother of Joram's son Ahaziah, is a descendant of Omri (8.26) and thus related to Ahab as well. Ahaziah, too, married a woman of the house of Ahab.[129] Thus the author had good grounds for making him and his mother the victims of the curse upon Ahab's house. Once the royal house of Judah had contaminated itself by marriage with Ahab's house, the transcendence becomes hostile. Judah is now unavoidably moving towards disaster.[130] That

---

128. See particularly the Israelite king's message to Amaziah, 14.10a: הכה הכית את אדום ונשאך לבך, 'You have beaten Edom, and your heart lifts you up.'

129. 2 Kgs 8.27b, according to MT: כי חתן בית אחאב הוא. The corresponding passage is not found in LXX.

130. This is the answer to a qustion that occurs frequently in scholarly works advocating the idea of a pre-exilic DtrH being edited and updated in the exile: '[H]ow can [a single work] encompass unconditional promises for a Davidic dynasty, yet drive the final nail into the coffin of that dynasty with 2 Kings 25.27-30...?' (Nelson 1981: 120).

the very mention of Ahab in connection with either Joram or Ahaziah is ominous, is a fact clearly demonstrated in the condemnation of Manasseh in 2 Kgs 21.3, where this, the worst of Judah's kings whose sins resulted in the exile, is compared to Ahab.

Hezekiah is praised (2 Kgs 18–20) nearly as highly as Josiah (23.25). Hezekiah brings about a comprehensive reform on behalf of Yahweh, destroying the hill shrines which had been used by all his predecessors since the time of Solomon. At no other time does Judah experience a king who has kept faith with Yahweh to the same extent or who has kept the commandments given to Moses so well. Therefore Yahweh has been with Hezekiah. When he rebels against his overlord, the Assyrian king Sennacherib, and Sennacherib retaliates by taking Judah's fortified towns, Yahweh rescues the righteous king (2 Kgs 18–19).[131] When Hezekiah is taken ill and expects to die, he succeeds in obtaining 15 more years of life from Yahweh. Having recovered from his illness, Hezekiah proudly shows all the costly treasures contained in his palace and kingdom to a friendly Babylonian deputation. However, the prophet Isaiah, hearing about this, tells Hezekiah Yahweh's words: One day everything in his palace will be taken to Babylon, and his descendants will be courtiers in the king of Babel's palace. Hezekiah interprets this optimistically, that is as a sign that there will be peace in his lifetime (2 Kgs 20.1-19).

As mentioned, two unconditional references to the promise to David are seen in connection with Hezekiah. With reference to the Assyrian crisis, Isaiah states that Yahweh will protect and save Jerusalem for David's sake (19.34). After this, Yahweh's angel kills no fewer than 185,000 Assyrians, thus forcing Sennacherib to stop the siege of Jerusalem. The second time the promise is mentioned (20.6) is in connection with the 15 extra years of life granted Hezekiah. It is thus possible that the promise was specifically related to these 15 years in the same way as it referred to a certain Assyrian crisis in 19.34. The promise expresses the deity's favourable attitude to the righteous Hezekiah in both of these particular situations. During Hezekiah's

---

131. In DtrH, the Assyrian Sennacherib may be regarded as a parallel to Herodotus' Xerxes. As already mentioned, Xerxes' death is not actually recounted by Herodotus, although the trend of his history seems to require it. Similarly, the Deuteronomist shows the deity as hostile to Sennacherib, whose death is shown as *nemesis* caused by his attack on Israel which was ruled by the righteous Hezekiah (2 Kgs 19.6-7, 35-37).

reign, Yahweh protects Jerusalem on account of David. But the same Hezekiah is also told of Jerusalem's future destruction.

It is obvious that Hezekiah's display of wealth reflects his pride or *hubris* that was punished many years later by the Babylonian exile. Hezekiah's descendants were thus punished for their ancestor's sin.[132] The fact that Hezekiah to a certain extend misunderstands the oracle which he interprets favourably can be compared to the blindness, *áte*, that strikes tragic heroes. Following this interpretation, it is evident that the disaster which is later prophesied to Manasseh has already been foretold to the innocent Hezekiah. There is also a certain effectiveness attached to the fact that it is in connection with a visit from a Babylonian deputation that Elijah prophesies the destruction of Judah. Hezekiah was secure and content at this time as he had been healed by Yahweh and had been protected by him from the Assyrians. However, just at this point Isaiah troubles him with a warning.

If Hezekiah can be called the most exemplary king of Judah so far, then his son and successor Manasseh must be considered the worst (2 Kgs 21.1-18). Manasseh reversed the cultic reforms (21.3-8), an action that earned him the reputation of behaving worse than the peoples whom Yahweh had driven out of the promised land (21.9, 11). The author's indignation overflows when he recounts how Manasseh places an image of Asherah in Yahweh's temple, while referring to Yahweh's promise to Solomon (1 Kgs 9.3-7) which stated that Yahweh had chosen and named this temple as his and that he would not drive Israel out of the promised land as long as the children of Israel kept his commandments (2 Kgs 21.7-8). This transgression, combined with the fact that Manasseh filled Jerusalem with innocent blood (21.16), makes him the 'anti-Yahwistic climax' of the kings of Judah. In all, only three Judaean kings are compared to the peoples who had been driven out,[133] and Manasseh is the only one of them who is said to have behaved worse than the ousted people. Yahweh makes his prophets announce that on account of Manasseh's many sins, he will bring disaster upon Jerusalem and Judah comparable to the misfortune that had already struck Samaria (2 Kgs 17) and Ahab's house (1 Kgs 21.20-29; 2 Kgs 9–10) and that he will reject the remnant of his chosen people (2 Kgs 21.10-15). However, Manasseh reigns for 55 years (21.1) without apparently suffering any hardships.

---

132. This explanation does not contradict Isaiah's reading it as a parable.
133. The others being Rehoboam (1 Kgs 14.24) and Ahaz (2 Kgs 16.3).

His son Amon, however, fares worse. He continues in his father's evil ways but has only ruled for two years when he falls victim to a conspiracy (21.19-26).

A new climax in the books of Kings is reached with the account of Amon's successor, the completely righteous Josiah and his reform (2 Kgs 22.1–23.30). During repairs to the temple, the high priest finds a book of laws which convinces the king that Yahweh's wrath has been kindled by the fact that the forefathers of the people have not kept his law. Asked for her opinion, the prophetess Huldah confirms the statements in the book: Yahweh will bring all misfortunes named in the book down upon 'this place and its inhabitants' because they have forsaken and offended the lord. Because Josiah humbled himself before Yahweh when he heard his threats, misfortune will not, however, strike in Josiah's lifetime (2 Kgs 22.3-30). Josiah carries out a reform which is even more comprehensive than the one Hezekiah had authorized, and he makes a covenant with the people, agreeing to keep the book of the covenant (23.1-3). All illicit cult-objects and places are destroyed in accordance with the old prophecy made to Jeroboam (1 Kgs 13.2; 2 Kgs 23.1-18), also in the former Northern kingdom, and the celebration of the passover is initiated in the manner specified in the book of the covenant (23.4-24). Josiah is thus the most faithful king to Yahweh ever seen (23.25), but this does not mitigate Yahweh's anger against Judah which Manasseh had caused. In a reference to the promise to Solomon (1 Kgs 9.3), we are told that both Judah and Jerusalem will be rejected (2 Kgs 23.26-27). Even although he is righteous, Josiah is not free from misfortunes. When the Egyptians make war upon the Assyrians, Josiah recklessly intervenes and dies a righteous death (23.28-30).

Judah's succeeding kings, Jehoahaz (23.31-34), Jehoiakim (23.34–24.7), Jehoiachin (24.8-17), Zedekiah (24.17–25.21) and Gedaliah (25.22-26) are deprecated, and all of them suffer misfortunes. Once the Babylonian exile had come to pass, Jehoiachin was pardoned 37 years after his capture and spent the rest of his life as a respected official of the Babylonian court (25.27-30). In this way, the downfall of David's house, which in some ways resembles the downfall of Saul's house, is accomplished, and Jehoiachin's fate in Babylon is similar to that of Mephibosheth in Jerusalem under David (2 Sam. 9; Exum 1992: 149).

The Question of the Leitmotif in the Deuteronomistic Historical Work
According to M. Noth, DtrH is intended to show 'God's just retribu-
tive action'. By the Babylonian exile, the people are punished for disobedience to Yahweh.[134] However, as we have seen, many scholars
insist upon there being an original DtrH from the pre-exilic era. This
assumption is principally based upon the fact that Josiah's reform is an
indisputable climax in the work and therefore, presumably, its original conclusion. S.L. McKenzie (1991: 122-26) advances three themes
in support of this point of view: the promise to David, Jeroboam's sin,
and Manasseh's sin.

We have seen that Yahweh's promise to the house of David is given
in both a conditional and an unconditional form. It is argued that
when Solomon's son is given one tribe so that David may always have
a 'lamp' in Jerusalem (1 Kgs 11.36), no end to the Davidic dynasty
was envisaged, and thus the text may be dated to the pre-exilic era
(Provan 1988: 94-97). The Davidic theme culminates with Josiah's
reform (2 Kgs 22.1–23.25). Josiah is the last of the kings to be compared to David (22.2), indeed only Josiah and Hezekiah comported
themselves as perfectly as David (2 Kgs 18.3; 22.2). Josiah surpasses
Hezekiah in his eagerness for reform. His cultic reforms include both
Judah and Israel, and he even succeeds in ridding them of Jeroboam's
sin (23.15-20). Judging from the eulogy in 23.25, Judah's future can
only be regarded as favourable.

The closing chapters of Kings blame Manasseh for the exile (21.1-
15; 23.26-27; 24.3-4) as his sins had been so grave that not even
Josiah's reform could prevail upon Yahweh to forgive Judah. F.M.
Cross (1973: 285-87) calls this theme 'a kind of afterthought' which
confirms that Josiah was the principal character in the original DtrH.
Before the time of Manasseh, nothing indicates that Judah was moving
towards an unavoidable disaster. On David's account, Jerusalem is
preserved from disaster even under the rule of an evil king (1 Kgs
11.12, 31-39; 15.4; 2 Kgs 8.19). However, due to the irreversible
judgment given on account of Manasseh's rule, the narrative of Josiah
becomes an anticlimax. 'The pessimism of this Manasseh theme, con-
trasts sharply with the positive tone of the Hezekiah and Josiah

---

134. Noth 1943: 100. Cf. p. 91: 'Mit den abschließenden geschichtlichen Kata-
strophen vor Augen hat Dtr... mit großer Konzequenz die Linie des ständig
zunehmenden Verfalls durch das Ganze hindurchgeführt und diese Linie sogleich in
den Anfängen der von ihm dargestellten Geschichte einsetzen lassen.'

accounts which surround it and suggests that the Manasseh theme is a later addition'.[135]

A series of expressions and hints connects Josiah, DtrH's final hero, with Moses, its first hero, and supports the idea that Josiah and his reform represented the climax of the story (McKenzie 1991: 128-31; Friedman 1981: 7-10): The book of laws found during Josiah's repairs to the temple can well be associated with the book of laws that Moses directs the levites to lay by the ark of the covenant (Deut. 31.36) and which had been totally disregarded in the interval between Moses and Josiah. Josiah is the only person to follow the Deuteronomistic call to love Yahweh with all one's heart, soul, and might (Deut. 6.5), or to obey Moses' command to read the law for all Israel (Deut. 31.11; 2 Kgs 23.2). Josiah tears down Jeroboam's altar in Bethel (2 Kgs 23.15) in correspondence to Moses' destroying the golden calf (Deut. 9.21), and by his destruction of all idolatrous cult-objects (2 Kgs 23.6, 12), Josiah obeys the ruling of Deuteronomy in Deut. 12.3; 7.25. The expression that one should deviate neither to the right nor to the left from the divine commandments occurs frequently in Deuteronomy (5.32; 17.11; 17.20; 28.14) as well as in the book of Joshua (Josh. 1.7; 23.6). Apart from these instances, the Hebrew bible only uses it in connection with Josiah (Lisowsky 1958: 1375–76), of whom it is said that he deviated neither to the right nor to the left from David's way (2 Kgs 22.2; 2 Chron. 34.2).[136] The correlation between Moses, Joshua, and Josiah is once again to be found in the covenant Josiah makes with the people (2 Kgs 23.2-3) and which is actually a renewal of Yahweh's covenant with Israel and Moses, the subject of Deuteronomy being an account of a renewal of the covenant in the plains of Moab (Deut. 28.69; 29.9-16). In DtrH, only Moses, Joshua (Josh. 24.25), and Josiah are associated with a covenant.

To make the prospects of DtrH bright, one has to disregard the passages that indicate the exile, thus omitting the tension between the

---

135. McKenzie 1991: 126. In support of this point of view, Friedman (1981: 10-11) observes that all of Manasseh's sins in 2 Kgs 21.1-7 are corrected by Josiah according to 2 Kgs 23. Where 21.7 refers to the unconditional Davidic promise, this is made conditional upon obedience to the law of Moses in v. 8, which thus refers to the exile. On this account, Friedman understands 2 Kgs 21.8-15, which blames Manasseh for the exile, as an exilic addition.

136. Apart from Josiah, only Hezekiah is compared positively to David (2 Kgs 18.3) although he does not reach the same degree of excellence as Josiah.

optimistic themes and the themes of exile. However, these two different themes taken in conjunction express something very important
about the exile. At the very climax of the narrative after Josiah's
reform, Judah's decline begins and thus the tragedy is set off very
clearly. In the wording of T.R. Hobbs (1985: xxv), 'the important
point about the reign and reform of Josiah is their failure'. A curse
from the time of Manasseh rests upon the people, and Josiah's ener-
getic, but fruitless efforts may be compared to the Herodotean *elpís*-
motif. Thus the exile is delineated as an unavoidable tragedy which is
merely emphasized by Josiah's reform.[137] It therefore seems to me
that the exile, rather than the reform of Josiah, is the actual, tragic
climax of DtrH.[138]

The Deuteronomistic Tragedy

If the Deuteronomistic history is a tragedy, then who is the tragic
hero? I would suggest that the people of Israel should be regarded as
the tragic hero of the Deuteronomistic history. To such a phenomenon
I find a literary-historical parallel as well as a contrast in the Jewish
tragedian Ezekiel who in the second century BCE wrote a tragedy,
Exagoge, on the events of the exodus recounted in Exodus 1–15.[139] In
H. Jacobson's words, 'The *Exagoge* is a drama about the Jewish people
and as such it does not have a "tragic hero" in the familiar sense'
(Jacobson 1983: 4). Similarly, the Deuteronomistic history, being the

---

137. Contra O'Brien 1989: 21-22, where it is stated that hypotheses which date the
account of Josiah to the exile are 'unable to give a satisfactory reason for the obvious
importance of the account'. Further to this, McKenzie 1991: 149: 'It makes no sense
for Dtr to present such a positive picture of Josiah correcting all of Manasseh's
wrongs and then to blame Manasseh for the exile.'

138. It is only possible to say that there is nothing in the work indicative of the
impending destruction of Judah, if one deletes all passages referring to it. This is
actually what Cross 1973: 285-87 does, cf. McKenzie 1991: 7 including n. 11: Deut.
4.27-31; 28.36-37; 28.63-68; 29.27; 30.1-10; Josh. 23.11-13; 23.15-16; 1 Sam.
12.25; 1 Kgs 2.4; 6.11-13; 8.25b; 8.46-53; 9.4-9; 2 Kgs 17.19; 20.17-18; 21.2-15;
22.15-20, whereas Deut. 30.11-20 and 1 Kgs 3.14 are suspect. McKenzie does
include 1 Kgs 8.46-50a which speaks of the exile as inavoidable due to the fact that
all human beings sin. See the summary, pp. 151-52. Regarding 1 Kgs 8, see
pp. 138-40. Noth (1943: 108) is in no doubt that the entire passage in 1 Kgs 8.44-53
belongs in DtrH.

139. Critical edition: Snell 1971. Text, translation and commentary: Jacobson
1983; Robertson 1985; Holladay 1989. For a readily accessible introduction to
Ezekiel the Tragedian, see Horst 1992.

history of the Jewish people, does not contain a single, overriding tragic hero. Instead, the people might be regarded as such a hero. But whoever might have been a tragic hero in Ezekiel's work, of which only fragments quoted by Euseb are extant,[140] it is certainly not the Israelite people. Thus, Ezekiel the Tragedian furnishes a parallel as well as a contrast to the Deuteronomistic history.

In the following, I intend to examine whether the Deuteronomistic history from the time of the Israelites' coming to the promised land until the exile can be said to resemble the Herodotean tragedy. There are certain differences in the latter, but it is nevertheless possible to demonstrate a general pattern:

1) The hero occupying an apparently secure position characterized by power, wealth, or happiness, or by any combination of these, is deluded so that a course of events is initiated which he, mistakenly, believes will be to his advantage. 2) Due to his delusion, the hero behaves *hubristically* by crossing a metaphysical, physical, or moral boundary. 3) The overstepping of the boundary is *expiated*. The hero who has too much power, wealth, or happiness suffers a misfortune of commensurate dimensions. A conquest may fail, thus involving fatal consequences for the hero, or it may be that the moral offence is revenged. The depth of the hero's downfall is often emphasized by the *elpís*-motif, that is the efforts he has made to avoid the impending misfortune that he has become aware of. 4) At this point, the hero may become *conscious* of his tragic situation and realize that he has acted wrongly and that the gods, or fate, are against him. 5) The theme of *adynaton–apophygein* shows that what has happened is the will of fate which no one can avoid. 6) Seen as isolated events, the episodes of Herodotus' tragic stories may seem unreasonable, but in the *larger, metaphysical context* they acquire meaning. Croesus, for instance, loses his son because he regarded himself as fortunate, and his downfall was caused by Gyges' transgression, five generations earlier.

If we regard the people of Israel as the tragic hero of the Deuteronomistic history, it is possible to regard the main trend of the Deuteronomistic history as conforming to the pattern delineated

140. In his *Praeparatio evangelica*, 9.28-29, Euseb, quoting Alexander Polyhistor, gives 269 verses. Text and translation: Places 1991. A few verses are also quoted by Clement of Alexandria and Pseudo-Eustathius—see Robertson (1985: 803) and Holladay's list of all the fragments (Holladay 1989: 338-43).

above. The secure position was attained when Yahweh gave the people the promised land. A set of conditions were then established in the form of a law. This law had to be obeyed if the people were to continue in the promised land. The difficulty here is that the people are not able to fulfil the conditions, but will unavoidably sin. On the face of it, the deity seems favourably inclined to the people of Israel. However, his attitude is ambiguous in that, to use biblical terms, he does not circumcise the hearts of the people thus enabling them to serve him truly, until they have suffered deeply. The people believed that the action initiated by the establishing of the deity's conditions was to their advantage, so they declared that they would serve Yahweh. But Joshua's reply (Josh. 24.19) showed clearly that it is dangerous to serve this deity and that actually no one is able to do so. If the people accept the conditions that they are not actually able to comply with, their failure will eventually result in their being driven out of the promised land. The people's declaration that they will serve Yahweh and the deity's declaration that the people are his (Deut. 26.18-19) result in the people behaving hubristically when they unavoidably break Yahweh's law and thus overstep the boundaries decreed by the deity.

This transgression is punished by the problems that are visited upon the people and which culminate in the exile. However, *nemesis* brings about a renewal of the balance between god and man. In this instance, the renewal is accomplished by circumcision of the heart so that the people become able to serve Yahweh properly. As a consequence of this circumcision, the people will regain the land. The tragic awareness, too, may be found during the exile, when the people realize what is wrong and repent. Then Yahweh will perform his circumcision of their hearts. Thus here, there is a discrepancy seen in relation both to the Herodotean tragedy and to tragedy in general, as the misfortune of Israel is reversible. The children of Israel can expect to return to the promised land (Deut. 30). It is thus only the process leading to the exile that is irreversible. The *elpís*-motif may be seen when Josiah, having consulted the prophetess Huldah, carries out his reform in order to prevent the misfortune that Huldah has foretold, whereas the *adynaton–apophygein* motif occurs in 2 Kgs 23.26-27 where Josiah's efforts are said to be unavailing, as Yahweh is determined upon the destruction of Judah and the rejection of Jerusalem and its temple.

This course of events is meaningful in the larger, metaphysical context where it is shown as an educational process intended to lead the people to repentance. This is a necessary condition for Yahweh's circumcision of their hearts, which in its turn enables them to serve him. The reason that Yahweh did not find the condition for circumcision to have been fulfilled either when the people declared they would serve him (Josh. 24.19-24), or when Solomon's temple was sanctified and the king prayed Yahweh turn the peoples' hearts towards him (1 Kgs 8.57-58), is lost in the divine mystery. It would be possible to employ one's imagination and say that the people did not honestly mean their declaration, but this cannot be ascertained from the text, which merely says that the people are not able to comply with Yahweh's conditions, however much they may want to. Thus, it is not the entire course of events that can be explained. The real reason why Israel has to suffer so much before Yahweh enables the people to serve him truly—and this is clearly shown to be his intention—is lost in the unfathomable distance between god and man.

Tragedy is only explicitly stated a few times in the work, but the context of the three occasions serves to emphasize them. In a series of speeches, Moses gives the grounds for the following historical presentation in the form of a programme that the successive leaders must fulfil: the Israelites are to conquer the land Yahweh has promised them, obey his law, which is meticulously specified, and worship him alone. In return for this, Yahweh will protect Israel, give the people prosperity, and guarantee their continued existence in the land. Joshua succeeds Moses and begins the conquest, which is completed by David (2 Sam. 8.1-14). The climax in the completion of the Deuteronomistic programme is reached when Solomon sanctifies Yahweh's shrine in Jerusalem (1 Kgs 8). There are thus three main figures involved in the implementation of the Deuteronomistic programme (O'Brien 1989: 288-89), and it is these three who express the tragic leitmotif of the historical exposition. Moses knows that Yahweh does not let his people Israel learn from their experiences (Deut. 29.1-5), Moses' successor Joshua declares that the people are not able to serve Yahweh and that he therefore will destroy them (Josh. 24.19-20), and Solomon, addressing Yahweh, states that the people will undoubtedly sin, as no one is capable of never sinning, and that Yahweh will therefore, equally unavoidably, allow the enemies of Israel to lead the people into exile (1 Kgs 8.46).

The first king of Israel, Saul, fully lives up to the general criteria for a tragic hero advanced by A. Lesky and J.C. Exum as well as the specific Herodotean tragedy. First, he is given a secure position of power by the deity and is acclaimed by the people. In the first narrative of rejection, he is then placed in a tragic dilemma because Samuel does not keep his promise. In his dilemma, Saul acts in an apparently sensible manner, but this is later shown to have been the beginning of his downfall. In the second narrative of rejection, he again attempts to act as wisely as possible, which again proves in vain and conducive of his own ruin, when he brings the booty from the Amalekites to Yahweh's shrine at Gilgal instead of sacrificing it on the battlefield. These actions are hubristic, and Samuel therefore foretells Saul's downfall. In spite of Saul's awareness of his misfortune, he still continues to fight his fate with all the means at his command. This *elpís*-motif emphasizes that Saul's downfall is both considerable and irreversible, and the fact that there is no escape for him is shown even more clearly in his encounter with the ghost of Samuel at Endor. This encounter also serves to emphasize the theme of *adynaton–apophygein*. Apart from informing Saul of the exact hour of his death, the ghost tells him nothing new, but by his reaction to the ghost's revelation, Saul demonstrates that he, at this point, is more fully aware of his tragedy than he has been previously (1 Sam. 28.15-20). Finally, Saul's tragedy acquires meaning in the greater, metaphysical context, which is likewise customary in Herodotus, if Saul is regarded as a scapegoat for the people's unacceptable demand for a king.

Likewise, David's story contains tragic elements which may be compared to the Herodotean pattern. First, it is only after David has been acclaimed as king by all Israel and has conquered Jerusalem, making it his capital, that his downfall begins, due to an infatuation. He commits *hubris*, and is thus struck by *nemesis* in the form of various misfortunes, although he only loses his royal power for a very short interval. However, as David was both subjectively and objectively guilty, his story cannot be regarded as a tragedy as such. It does have tragic consequences for his family, and at the end of the story there is a tragedy in which the deity makes David act hubristically and then punishes him for doing so. As the tragic climax of an exposition in which the relationship between David and the deity has gradually been aggravated because David committed *hubris* with Bathsheba, this latter tragedy acquires meaning in the greater metaphysical context.

The story of Solomon is less tragic, but still has tragic aspects which may be compared with Herodotus. To start with, Solomon is the deity's favourite and is gifted with immense power, wisdom, and riches. These gifts tempt him to transgress Yahweh's law, due to his infatuation with his many foreign wives and concubines. That the many gifts of the deity lead Solomon into misfortune is, perhaps, the most tragic aspect of his story. Obvious Herodotean parallels are the tale of Polycrates' ring (Hdt. 3.39-43; 3.120-25) and Artabanus' speech to Xerxes (7.46), though the fact that Herodotus' Polycrates is innocent constitutes a considerable difference to Solomon, who is guilty of transgressing the prohibition against worshipping other gods than Yahweh. The story of Solomon gains tragic importance principally due to its consequences for the king's son, Rehoboam.

Rehoboam is a tragic figure. Just as he is about to assume the government of his late father's kingdom, he is blinded by the deity and misled into making unreasonable demands of his subjects. He is punished by the division of Solomon's kingdom: Rehoboam must make do with becoming king of Judah. It is emphasized that Rehoboam's fate has been decided by Yahweh, but he nevertheless combats it throughout his life, as we are told there was constant war between the kingdoms of Judah and Israel. Nor is the metaphysical aspect missing in the story of Rehoboam, as his misfortune is also due to Solomon's idolatry.

In Israel, Jeroboam transgresses by idolatry, and the destruction of his house and of Israel is foretold both on this account and because the succeeding generations continued in Jeroboam's sinful ways (1 Kgs 14.15-16). This dichotomy is repeated throughout Israel's history. Jeroboam is blamed, but with only one exception his successors are all condemned individually because of their participation in Jeroboam's sin. Thus, Israel's downfall cannot be considered a tragedy, as it is a just punishment for continuing to sin like Jeroboam. A tragic aspect cannot, however, be entirely ignored, as each king is both personally guilty and tainted as well by his predecessors' misdeeds. Sin accumulates in the course of time.

In Israel, the transcendence could be called neutral—if Jeroboam keeps Yahweh's law, the deity will be with him, but as he does not fulfil this condition, he is rejected. Because his successors continued to sin as he had done, both they and the kingdom were rejected as well. It was otherwise with Judah. In Judah, the transcendence was benign to start with. The reason that God did not reject this kingdom and its dynasty, in spite of their sinfulness, was his promise to David. The deity is lenient to the first of the evil kings, but when the dynasty contaminates itself through contact with one of the accursed dynasties from the north, that of Ahab, the deity's attitude towards the southern kingdom becomes reserved in that a number of misfortunes strike Judah—not even the good kings go free. Hezekiah is one of the most righteous kings, and oddly enough the destruction of the Judaean kingdom is first foretold during Hezekiah's reign. In other words, there was good reason to expect Judah's destruction even before the advent of Manasseh, who is usually blamed for it (2 Kgs 21.10-15; 23.26-27).

Josiah is even more righteous, but not even his reform towards a pure cult of Yahweh can avert misfortune. Thus, Hezekiah and Josiah both have their tragic aspects. Yahweh had just shown his favour to Hezekiah by settling the Assyrian crisis and restoring the king to health after a serious illness (2 Kgs 18.3–20.11), when the destruction of the kingdom was foretold to him (20.12-19). But the mere fact that Hezekiah does not understand the situation shows a lack of tragic awareness that disqualifies him as a tragic hero. Naturally, this observation is confirmed in that the disaster does not strike him personally. Josiah is wiser. Fully aware of the impending, unavoidable misfortune (2 Kgs 22.3-20), he carries out his reform (23.1-27), thus postponing the disaster (22.19-20). However, even in spite of these *elpís-* and *adynaton–apophygein* motifs, Josiah is not a tragic hero. Misfortune does not even strike him, on the contrary, he dies a heroic death in warfare (23.28-30). Nor are the succeeding kings, all of whom were evil, tragic figures. Nevertheless, the impression of tragic aspects remains, as the misfortunes culminating in Judah's destruction are brought about by their wicked predecessor Manasseh (2 Kgs 24.2-4) in conjunction with the accumulated sins of the past (2 Kgs 22.16-27).

Chapter 4

CONCLUSION

Starting from J. Van Seters' idea (1983: 326) that 'the first Israelite historian... was the Deuteronomistic historian' and his statement that the Deuteronomistic historical work is unique in the ancient Near Eastern context but is markedly similar to the earliest, complete history extant in Greek, written by Herodotus (Van Seters 1983: 354-62), I have compared these two historical works with special reference to the tragic mode of presentation. It is obvious that Herodotus was influenced by the literary conventions of his time, but his work does demonstrate something completely new: an endeavour to write a corporate and causal history. Herodotus' intention was to write the history of *all* the Greeks during the great Hellenic–Persian conflict, define the reasons for this conflict, and describe its outcome in 479 BCE. Being a piece of corporate and causal historiography, DtrH likewise represents something new in its Near-Eastern context. Certainly, DtrH is influenced by the literary conventions of the Near East,[1] but the nearest comparable work is not found in the historiographic texts from Ḥatti, Mesopotamia, Egypt, or Persia. The comparable method of writing history is to be found in the early Greek writers, especially in Herodotus.

Both Herodotus and DtrH represent independent, literary versions of what was in part already existing material. The collection of frequently disparate traditions to be found in DtrH has not been fitted together quite as well as Herodotus' sources. Herodotus had undeniable advantages in his use of source fiction. It is particularly noticeable that DtrH by comparison with Herodotus lacks the aspect of

1. Van Seters (1983: 356-57) mentions the king lists, the royal incriptions in their many variants, and most important of all, the chronicle. However, it is impossible to ascertain whether the small nations of Western Asia 'and Israel in particular' (p. 357) had chronicles in any way comparable to the Babylonian Chronicle Series.

rational evaluation as well as the geographical and ethnographic interests that characterize Herodotus and his Ionian background. The geographical interest in DtrH is mainly confined to the description and division of the promised land, especially in the book of Joshua. However, both works are expressions of an antiquarian interest in the past, characterized by the collecting of the greatest possible number of traditions on the subjects represented in the respective works, these subjects being then treated according to a given philosophy which includes a tragic interpretation of the course of history. No effort has been made to establish or verify a redaction-history of DtrH, as any such attempts would necessarily rest upon subjective criteria. Instead, I have attempted to demonstrate a leitmotif in the tradition as it has been compiled, although I realize that, to quote W. Booth (1961: 73), 'most works worth reading have so many possible "themes", so many possible mythological or metaphorical or symbolic analogues, that to find any one of them, and to announce it as what the work is *for*, is to do at best a very small part of the critical task'.

It is possible that DtrH and Herodotus represent the earliest attempts in literary history at writing an historical account that is corporate, causal, and didactic. The nation, rather than the king and his dynasty, is the centre of the historical account that connects the recent past with the distant past in a chain of cause and effect. Herodotus intended to explain how a small and divided people were able to withstand the united hostile powers of Asia, whereas DtrH's intention was to answer the question of why Yahweh's chosen people lost the land that they had been given by Yahweh. The success of the Hellenes was, according to Herodotus, due not only to their bravery and their good leaders, but also to the fact that they fought for their liberty as Greek *nomos* decrees. The Israelites' faithlessness towards Yahweh accounts in DtrH for their fiasco. However, in both cases the inscrutable workings of the deity must also be taken into account. In Herodotus, the deity is inimical to the enemies of the Hellenes, while the deity in DtrH is hostile to the Israelites' foes as well as equivocal towards the Israelites themselves. The tragedy in Herodotus is the tragedy of 'the others', whereas in DtrH it is 'our tragedy'.[2] On the other hand, 'we'

2. For a remarkable example of the reverse, to wit a tragedy applying to 'the other' in Jewish literature of antiquity, see the Jewish tragedian Ezekiel's work *Exagoge* (second century BCE). In this drama, an Egyptian messenger tells of the Egyptian disaster in the Red Sea in a manner very much like the Persian messenger in

in DtrH may confidently expect restitution towards the end of the story, whereas 'the others' in Herodotus do not have this possibility.

As has been pointed out by T.L. Thompson (1992: 381-82), the redaction of the Old Testament's collection of traditions was motivated by contemporary needs rather than an interest in the past. The tragic view of the course of history serves here, as in Herodotus, as a way of implementing these desires. This is seen in DtrH by the presence of various tragic motifs, amongst which the most important is the idea of the deceptive deity. Tragedy can be found as either corporate, dynastic, or individual. The Israelite disaster is unavoidable, and the process leading up to it is irreversible, but as the misfortune is later mitigated, the corporate history cannot be described as an ideal tragedy. The dynastic tragedy dominates in the books of Samuel and Kings. There are numerous examples of people who are cursed on account of their ancestors' misdeeds. Eli's dynasty is exterminated on account of the misdeeds of his sons; Saul's dynasty is eliminated because of his rejection; four of David's sons die unhappy deaths due to their father's guilt; Rehoboam loses half the kingdom on account of his father's idolatry; three Israelite kings, Nadab, Elah, and Joram, fall victim to the curse upon their ancestors, while Zachariah, the fourth descendant of Jehu, is the victim of Yahweh's words to Jehu that his lineage will sit on the throne of Israel for four generations. Finally, we see the deity's attitude to Judah becoming hostile after the royal house has contaminated itself through contact with Ahab's dynasty. Various individual tragedies occur as well: Jephthah

---

Aeschylus' *Persai*. Ezekiel may have been dependent on some Septuagint version of Exodus, but a more precise analysis of the nature of such a Greek text on which Ezekiel could have based his work is a *desideratum*—cf. Robertson 1985: 805.

However, the said difference between Herodotus and DtrH should not be pressed too far. According to Mandell and Freedman 1993: 55-57, '[Herodotus'] depiction of the Greeks at the pinnacle of success was necessitated by the need to render their impending fall, be it imminent or delayed, the more precipitous' (p. 57). 'Greece, like Persia, can and must fall, and that fall must be from a vertiginous height' (pp. 56-57). The battle of Marathon, representing the first major Greek triumph, 'is clearly the dramatic high point before the fall. As such it renders the situation of "All Greece" analogous to that of a culture hero or "great man" such as the victorious Agamemnon, at the height of his prowess, returning home to be murdered basely after the fall of Troy' (p. 57).

(Judg. 11.29-39),[3] Saul, David (2 Sam. 24), Shimei (2 Sam. 16.5-13; 1 Kgs 2.8-9, 36-46) and Rehoboam (1 Kgs 12.1-24).

There are likewise various tragic motifs in Herodotus, and as is the case in DtrH, the idea of the deceptive deity is prominent. The Herodotean tragedy is dynastic or individual, but not corporate. Croesus suffers due to being king five generations after Gyges,[4] while Xerxes suffers as the last link in a tragic chain comprised of the four Achaemenian kings, Cyrus, Cambyses, Darius and Xerxes. The individual tragedies in Herodotus are those of Candaules (1.8-12), Croesus (1.34-45; 1.46-91), Adrastus (1.34-45), Cyrus (1.205-214), Polycrates (3.39-43; 3.120-28) and Xerxes. The two narratives that resemble each other most closely in Herodotus and DtrH, respectively, are perhaps those that tell of a godfearing king who, in spite of his piety, is thrown down at the zenith of his power, due to the hostile attitude of the deity or fate: Herodotus' Croesus, DtrH's Saul.

The fact that the similarities between the Herodotean and the Deuteronomistic historiography also include the tragic ornamentation of the course of history supports the assumption that the Hellenic literary tradition, which Herodotus was part of, influenced the Deuteronomistic history. Thus it becomes probable that DtrH was written at a time and in a milieu where the Hellenistic influence was important in the Israelite or more correctly, the Jewish tradition.

3.   The tragedy is set in motion when Jephthah makes his fatal vow after the spirit of Yahweh has come upon him.

4.   The resemblance to Jehu's dynasty, which likewise consisted of five generations, is unmistakable.

BIBLIOGRAPHY

Ahn, G.
1992   *Religiöse Herrscherlegitimation im achämenidischen Iran: Die Vor-
        aussetzungen und die Struktur ihrer Argumentation* (Acta Iranica, 31;
        Leiden: Brill).
Albrektson, B.
1967   *History and the Gods: An Essay on the Idea of Historical Events as
        Divine Manifestations in the Ancient Near East and in Israel*
        (ConBOT, 1; Lund: Gleerup).
Aly, W.
1969   *Volksmärchen, Sage und Novelle bei Herodot und seinen Zeit-
        genossen: Eine Untersuchung über die volkstümlichen Elemente der
        altgriechischen Prosaerzählung* (Göttingen: Vandenhoeck & Ruprecht,
        2nd edn).
Armayor, O.K.
1978a   'The Homeric Influence on Herodotus' Story of the Labyrinth', *CB*
        54: 68-72.
1978b   'Did Herodotus Ever Go to the Black Sea?', *HSCP* 82: 45-62.
1978c   'Did Herodotus Ever Go to Egypt?', *JARCE* 15: 59-73.
1980   'Sesostris and Herodotus' Autopsy of Thrace, Colchis, Inland Asia
        Minor and the Levant', *HSCP* 84: 51-74.
1985   *Herodotus' Autopsy of the Fayoum, Lake Moeris and the Labyrinth of
        Egypt* (Amsterdam: J.C. Gieben).
Avery, H.
1979   'A Poetic Word in Herodotus', *Hermes* 107: 1-9.
Balcer, J.M.
1987   *Herodotus and Bisitun: Problems in Ancient Persian Historiography*
        (Historia: Einzelschriften, 49; Stuttgart: Steiner).
Baumgarten, A.I.
1981   *The Phoenician History of Philo of Byblos: A Commentary* (EPRO, 89;
        Leiden: Brill).
Berge, K.
1990   *Die Zeit des Jahwisten: Ein Beitrag zur Datierung jahwistischer
        Väterexte* (BZAW, 186; Berlin: de Gruyter).
Blume, H.-D.
1979   '2. Ps.Longinos', in Ziegler and Sontheimer 1979: III, col. 733-34.
Bockisch, G.
1984   'Herodot—Geschichten- und Geschichtsschreiber', *Klio* 66: 488-501.

Bolin, T.M.
    1996   'When the End is the Beginning: The Persian Period and the Origins
                of the Biblical Tradition', *SJOT* 10: 3-15.
Booth, W.
    1961   *The Rhetoric of Fiction* (Chicago: University of Chicago Press).
Breasted, J.H.
    1906–07   *Ancient Records of Egypt: Historical Documents from the Earliest
                Times to the Persian Conquest* (5 vols.; New York: Russell & Russell).
Brinkman, J.A.
    1977   'Mesopotamian Chronology of the Historical Period', in A.L.
                Oppenheim, *Ancient Mesopotamia: Portrait of a Dead Civilization*
                (Chicago: University of Chicago Press, 2nd edn): 335-48.
Burn, A.R.
    1962   *Persia and the Greeks: The Defense of the West, ca. 546–478*
                (London: Arnold).
Cancik, H.
    1976   *Grundzüge der hethitischen und alttestamentlichen Geschichts-
                schreibung* (ADPV; Wiesbaden: Otto Harrassowitz).
Chekhov, A.
    1965   *Letters on the Short Story, the Drama and Other Literary Topics:
                Selected and edited by Louis S. Friedland* (London: Vision; 1st edn
                New York, 1924).
Chiasson, C.
    1982   'Tragic Diction in Herodotus: Some Possibilities', *Phoenix* 36: 156-61.
Cobet, J.
    1974   Review of Fehling 1971, *Gnomon* 46: 737-46.
Cross, F.M.
    1973   'The Themes of the Book of Kings and the Structure of the
                Deuteronomistic History', in F.M. Cross, *Canaanite Myth and Hebrew
                Epic: Essays in the History of the Religion of Israel* (Cambridge, MA:
                Harward University Press): 274-89.
Dandamaev, M.A., and V.G. Lukonin
    1989   *The Culture and Social Institutions of Ancient Iran* (Cambridge:
                Cambridge University Press).
Davies, G.I., *et al.*
    1991   *Ancient Hebrew Inscriptions: Corpus and Concordance* (Cambridge:
                Cambridge University Press).
Davies, P.R.
    1992   *In Search of 'Ancient Israel'* (JSOTSup, 148; Sheffield: JSOT Press).
Déaut, R. le
    1981   'Le théme de la circoncision du cœur (DT. XXX 6; Jér. IV 4) dans les
                versions anciennes (LXX et Targum) et à Qumran', in J.A. Emerton
                (ed.), *Congress Volume: Vienna 1980* (VTSup, 32; Leiden: Brill):
                178-205.
Dietrich, W.
    1972   *Prophetie und Geschichte: Eine redaktionsgeschichtliche Unter-
                suchung zum deuteronomistischen Geschichtswerk* (FRLANT, 108;
                Göttingen: Vandenhoeck & Ruprecht).

Donner, H., and W. Röllig
1962–64   *Kanaanäische und aramäische Inschriften* (3 vols.; Wiesbaden: Otto
           Harrassowitz).
Egermann, F.
1965   'Herodot—Sophokles: Hohe Arete', in W. Marg, *Herodot: Eine
           Auswahl aus der neueren Forschung* (WdF, 26; Darmstadt:
           Wissenschaftliche Buchgesellschaft, 2nd edn): 249-55.
Erbse, H.
1961   'Tradition und Form im Werke Herodots', *Gym* 68: 239-57.
Evans, J.A.S.
1982   *Herodotus* (TWAS, 645; Boston: Twayne).
1991   *Herodotus, Explorer of the Past: Three Essays* (Princeton, NJ:
           Princeton University Press).
Evelyn-White, H.G.
1914   *Hesiod: The Homeric Hymns and Homerica* (LCL, 57; London:
           Heinemann).
Exum, J.C.
1992   *Tragedy and Biblical Narrative: Arrows of the Almighty* (Cambridge:
           Cambridge University Press).
Fehling, D.
1971   *Die Quellenangaben bei Herodot: Studien zur Erzählkunst Herodots*
           (UaLG, 9; Berlin: de Gruyter).
1989   *Herodotus and his 'Sources': Citation, Invention and Narrative Art*
           (Arca, 21; Liverpool: Cairns).
Finkelstein, I.
1988   *The Archaeology of the Israelite Settlement* (Jerusalem: Israel Explora-
           tion Society).
Fohl, H.
1913   *Tragische Kunst bei Herodot: Inaugural-Dissertation zur Erlangung
           der Doktorwürde der hohen philosophischen Fakultät der Universität
           Rostock* (Borna–Leipzig: Buchdruckerei Robert Noske).
Fohrer, G.
1965   *Einleitung in das Alte Testament* (Heidelberg: Quelle & Meyer, 12th
           edn).
Fokkelman, J.P.
1986   *Narrative Art and Poetry in the Books of Samuel: A Full Interpretation
           Based on Stylistic and Structural Analyses*. II. *The Crossing Fates
           (I Sam: 13–31 & II Sam 1)* (Assen: Van Gorcum).
Fornara, C.W.
1971   'Evidence for the Date of Herodotus' Publication', *JHS* 91: 25-34.
1983   *The Nature of HISTORY in Ancient Greece and Rome* (Berkeley:
           University of California Press).
Fowler, H.N.
1936   *Plutarch: Moralia in Sixteen Volumes: Volume X: 771E–854D* (LCL,
           321; London: Heinemann).
Freedman, D.N.
1990   'The Formation of the Canon of the Old Testament: The Selection and
           Identification of the Torah as the Supreme Authority of the Postexilic

Community', in E.B. Firmage, B.G. Weiss, and J.W. Welch (eds.), *Religion and Law: Biblical–Judaic and Islamic Perspectives* (Winona Lake, IN: Eisenbrauns): 315-31.

Friedman, R.E.
1980   'From Egypt to Egypt: Dtr[1] and Dtr[2]', in B. Halpern and J.D. Levenson (eds.), *Traditions in Transformation: Turning Points in Biblical Faith* (Winona Lake, IN: Eisenbrauns): 167-92.
1981   *The Exile and Biblical Narrative: The Formation of the Deuteronomistic and Priestly Works* (HSM, 22; Chico, CA: Scholars Press).

Fritz, K. von
1967a   *Die griechische Geschichtsschreibung. I. Von den Anfängen bis Thukydides* (Berlin: de Gruyter).
1967b   *Die griechische Geschichtsschreibung. I. Von den Anfängen bis Thukydides: Anmerkungen* (Berlin: de Gruyter).

Frye, R.N.
1984   *The History of Ancient Iran* (HAW: Abteilung 3.7; Munich: Beck).

Fyfe, W.H.
1995   *Longinus: On the Sublime*, in S. Halliwell *et al.*, *Aristotle: The Poetics; Longinus: On the Sublime; Demetrius: On Style* (LCL, 199; Cambridge, MA: Harvard University Press): 160-307.

Garbini, G.
1988   *History and Ideology in Ancient Israel* (New York: Crossroad).

Gardiner, A.H.
1959   *The Royal Canon of Turin* (Oxford: Oxford University Press).
1961   *Egypt of the Pharaohs: An Introduction* (Oxford: Clarendon Press).

Godley, A.D.
1922–38   *Herodotus* (LCL; 4 vols.; Cambridge, MA: Harvard University Press): 117-20.

Gomme, A.W.
1954   *The Greek Attitude to Poetry and History* (Sather Classical Lectures, 27; Berkeley: University of California Press).

Good, E.M.
1981   *Irony in the Old Testament* (Bible and Literature Series, 3; Sheffield: Almond Press, 2nd edn).

Götze, A.
1933   *Die Annalen des Muršiliš* (MVAeG, 38: Hethitische Texte in Umschrift mit Übersetzung und Erläuterungen, 6; Leipzig: Hinrichs).

Gould, J.
1989   *Herodotus* (London: Weidenfeld & Nicolson).

Grabbe, L.
1991   'Reconstructing History from the Book of Ezra', in P.R. Davies (ed.), *Second Temple Studies. I. Persian Period* (JSOTSup, 117; Sheffield: JSOT Press): 98-106.

Gray, J.
1970   *I & II Kings: A Commentary* (OTL; London: SCM Press, 2nd edn).

Grayson, A.K.

1975a   *Babylonian Historical–Literary Texts* (Toronto Semitic Texts and Studies, 3; Toronto: University of Toronto Press).

1975b   *Assyrian and Babylonian Chronicles* (TCS, 5; Locust Valley, NY: J.J. Augustin Publisher).

1980   'Histories and Historians of the Ancient Near East: Assyria and Babylonia', *Or* 49: 140-94.

1983   'Königslisten und Chroniken. B. Akkadisch', in D.O. Edzard *et al.* (eds.), *Reallexikon der Assyriologie und vorderasiatischen Archäologie* (Berlin: de Gruyter): VI: 86-135.

Grene, D.

1961   'Herodotus: The Historian as Dramatist', *JPh* 58: 477-88.

Groningen, B.A. van

1949   *Herodotus' historiën met inleiding en commentaar. II. Tekst* (Grieksche en Latijnsche Schrijvers met Aanteekeningen; Leiden: Brill).

Gunn, D.M.

1980   *The Fate of King Saul: An Interpretation of a Biblical Story* (JSOTSup, 14; Sheffield: JSOT Press).

Gurney, O.R.

1981   *The Hittites* (Harmondsworth: Penguin Books, 2nd edn).

Güterbock, H.G.

1938   'Die historische Tradition und ihre literarische Gestaltung bei Babyloniern und Hethitern bis 1200: Zweiter Teil: Hethiter', *ZA* 10: 45-145.

1956   'The Deeds of Suppiluliuma as Told by His Son, Mursili II', *JCS* 10: 41-68; 75-98; 107-130.

1967   'The Hittite Conquest of Cyprus Reconsidered', *JNES* 26: 73-81

Hauvette, A.

1894   *Hérodote: Historien des guerres médiques* (Ouvrage couronné par l'Académie des Inscriptions et Belles-lettres; Paris: Librairie Hachette).

Hawkins, J.D.

1982   'The Neo-Hittite States in Syria and Anatolia', in CAH, III.1: 372-441.

Hayes, W.C.

1970   'Chronology: I: Egypt—to the End of the Twentieth Dynasty', in CAH, I.1: 173-93.

Helck, W.

1956   *Untersuchungen zu Manetho und den agyptischen Königslisten* (UGAÄ, 18; Berlin: Akademie Verlag).

1979   'Manethon: 1', in Ziegler and Sontheimer 1979: III: col. 952-53

Hellmann, F.

1934   *Herodots Kroisos–Logos* (Neue philologische Untersuchungen, 9; Berlin: Weidmann).

Hignett, C.

1963   *Xerxes' Invasion of Greece* (Oxford: Clarendon Press).

Hinz, W.
    1976   *Darius und die Perser: Eine Kulturgeschichte der Achämeniden* (Holle
                vergangene Kulturen; Baden-Baden: Holle Verlag).
Hobbs, T.R.
    1985   *2 Kings* (WBC, 13; Waco, TX: Word Books).
Hoffmann, H.-D.
    1980   *Reform und Reformen: Untersuchungen zu einem Grundthema der
                deuteronomistischen Geschichtsschreibung* (ATANT, 66; Zürich:
                Theologischer Verlag).
Hoffner, H.A.
    1980   'Histories and Historians of the Ancient Near East: The Hittites', *Or*
                49: 283-332.
Holladay, C.R.
    1989   *Fragments from Hellenistic Jewish Authors.* II. *Poets* (SBLTT, 30:
                Pseudepigrapha Series, 12; Atlanta: Scholars Press).
Horneffer, A.
    1971   *Herodot: Historien. Deutsche Gesamtausgabe* (KTA, 224; Stuttgart:
                Alfred Kröner Verlag, 4th edn).
Horst, P.W. van der
    1992   'Ezekiel the Tragedian', in ABD, II: 709.
How, W.W., and J. Wells
    1928   *A Commentary on Herodotus: With Introduction and Appendixes*
                (2 vols.; Oxford: Clarendon Press, 2nd edn).
Huber, L.
    1965a   'Religiöse und politische Beweggründe des Handelns in der
                Geschichtsschreibung des Herodot', (Tübingen: Inaugural-Dissertation
                zur Erlangung des Doktorgrades einer hohen philosophischen
                Fakultät der Eberhard-Karls-Universität zu Tübingen).
    1965b   'Herodots Homerverständnis', in H. Flashar and K. Gaiser (eds.),
                Synusia: Festgabe für Wolfgang Schadewaldt zum 15. März 1965
                (Pfullingen: Neske): 29-52.
    1969   'Nachwort', in Aly 1969: 317-28.
Huizinga, J.
    1936   'A Definition of the Concept of History', in R. Klibansky and
                H.J. Paton (eds.), *Philosophy and History: Essays Presented to Ernst
                Cassirer* (Oxford: Clarendon Press): 1-10.
Immerwahr, H.R.
    1966   *Form and Thought in Herodotus* (Philological Monographs, 23;
                Cleveland: The Press of Western Reserve University).
    1985   'Herodotus', in P.E. Easterling and B.M.W. Knox (eds.), *The
                Cambridge History of Classical Literature.* I. *Greek Literature* (Cam-
                bridge: Cambridge University Press): 426-41.
Imparati, F., and C. Saporetti
    1965   'L'autobiografia di Hattusili I', *SCO* 14: 44-55.
Jacobson, H.
    1983   *The* Exagoge *of Ezekiel* (Cambridge: Cambridge University Press).

Jacoby, F.
1913   'Herodot', in W. Kroll (ed.), *Paulys Realencyclopädie der classischen Altertumswissenschaft: Supplementband II* (Stuttgart: Alfred Druckenmüller Verlag): col. 205-520.
1923   *Die Fragmente der griechischen Historiker*. I. *Genealogie und Mythographie* (Berlin: Weidmann).
1949   *Atthis: The Local Chronicles of Ancient Athens* (Oxford: Clarendon Press).

Jones, H.L.
1917   *The Geography of Strabo*. I. (LCL, 49; London: Heinemann).

Kent, R.G.
1953   *Old Persian: Grammar, Texts, Lexicon* (AOS, 33; New Haven: American Oriental Society, 2nd edn).

Keyes, C.W.
1928   *Cicero: De re publica; De legibus* (LCL, 213; London: Heinemann).

Kirk, G.S., J.E. Raven, and M. Schofield
1983   *The Presocratic Philosophers: A Critical History with a Selection of Texts* (Cambridge: Cambridge University Press, 2nd edn).

Koch, K.
1981   'Das Profetenschweigen des deuteronomistischen Geschichtswerks', in J. Jeremias and L. Perlitt (eds.), *Die Botschaft und die Boten: Festschrift für Hans Walter Wolff zum 70. Geburtstag* (Neukirchen–Vluyn: Neukirchener Verlag): 115-28.

Koehler, L., and W. Baumgartner
1953   *Lexicon in Veteris Testamenti Libros* (Leiden: Brill, 2nd edn).

Kuenen, A.
1890   *Historisch–kritische Einleitung in die Bücher des Alten Testaments hinsichtlich ihrer Entstehung und Sammlung*. I. *Zweites Stück: Die historischen Bücher des Alten Testaments* (Leipzig: O.R. Reisland).

Lambert, W.G.
1957   'Three Unpublished Fragments of the Tukulti-Ninurta Epic', *AfO* 18: 38-51.
1970   'History and the Gods: A Review Article', *Or* 39: 170-77.
1972   'Destiny and Divine Intervention in Babylon and Israel', *OTS* 17: 65-72.

Laroche, E.
1971   *Catalogue des Textes Hittites* (EeC, 75; Paris: Editions Klincksieck).

Lateiner, D.
1989   *The Historical Method of Herodotus* (Phoenix: Supplementary Volume, 23; Toronto: University of Toronto Press).

Lehmann-Haupt, C.F.
1938   'Berossos', in E. Ebeling and B. Meissner (eds.), *Reallexikon der Assyriologie* (Berlin: de Gruyter): II: 1-17.

Lemche, N.P.
1991   *The Canaanites and their Land: The Tradition of the Canaanites* (JSOTSup, 110; Sheffield: JSOT Press).
1993   'The Old Testament—A Hellenistic Book', *SJOT* 7: 163-93.

1996   'Clio is also Among the Muses! Keith W. Whitelam and the History of Palestine: A Review and a Commentary', *SJOT* 10: 88-114.

Lesky, A.
1958   *Die griechische Tragödie* (KTA, 143; Stuttgart: Alfred Kröner, 2nd edn).
1963   *Geschichte der griechischen Literatur* (Bern: Francke, 2nd edn).
1977   'Tragödien bei Herodot?', in K.H. Kinzl (ed.), *Greece and the Eastern Mediterranean in Ancient History and Prehistory: Studies presented to Fritz Schachermeyr on the Occasion of his Eightieth Birthday* (Berlin: de Gruyter): 224-30.

Levi, P.
1985   *A History of Greek Literature* (Harmondsworth: Viking).

Levin, C.
1993   *Der Jahwist* (FRLANT, 157; Göttingen: Vandenhoeck & Ruprecht).

Licht, J.
1983   'Biblical Historicism', in H. Tadmor and M. Weinfeld, *History, Historiography and Interpretation: Studies in Biblical and Cuneiform Literatures* (Jerusalem: Magnes): 107-120.

Lisowsky, G.
1958   *Konkordanz zum hebräischen Alten Testament* (Stuttgart: Württemberg).

Liverani, M.
1973a   'Memorandum on the Approach to Historiographic Texts', *Or* 42: 178-94.
1973b   'Storiografia politica Hittita. I. Šunaššura, ovvero: Della reciprocità', *OrAnt* 12: 267-97.
1977   'Storiografia politica Hittita. II. Telipinu, ovvero: Della solidarietà', *OrAnt* 16: 105-131.
1990   'Hattushili alle prese con la propaganda ramesside', *Or* 59: 207-217.

Lloyd, A.B.
1975–88   *Herodotus: Book II* (EPRO, 43; 3 vols.; Leiden: Brill).

Long, B.O.
1984   *1 Kings with an Introduction to Historical Literature* (FOTL, 9; Grand Rapids: Eerdmans).

Machinist, P.B.
1976   'Literature as Politics: The Tukulti–Ninurta Epic and the Bible', *CBQ* 38: 455-82.
1978   'The Epic of Tukulti-Ninurta I: A Study in Middle Assyrian Literature' (PhD Dissertation; authorized facsimile in the Royal Danish Library, Copenhagen; Ann Arbor: University Microfilms International, 1983).

Mandell, S., and D.N. Freedmann
1993   *The Relationship between Herodotus'* History *and Primary History* (South Florida Studies in the History of Judaism, 60; Atlanta: Scholars Press).

Marincola, J.
1987   'The Sources of Herodotus', *Arethusa* 20: 26-35.

Mayes, A.D.H.
1983   *The Story of Israel between Settlement and Exile: A Redactional Study of the Deuteronomistic History* (London: SCM Press).

Mayrhofer, M.
1978   *Supplement zur Sammlung der altpersischen Inschriften* (SÖAW.PH, 338; Veröffentlichungen der iranischen Kommision, 7; Vienna: Verlag der österreichischen Akademie der Wissenschaften).

McKenzie, S.L.
1991   *The Trouble with Kings: The Composition of the Books of Kings in the Deuteronomistic History* (VTSup, 42; Leiden: Brill).

Mejer, J.
1985   'Det klassiske Athen (ca. 500–300 f.Kr.)', in H. Hertel (ed.), *Verdens litteratur–historie*. I. *Oldtiden* (Copenhagen: Gyldendal): 147-217.

Meriggi, P.
1967–75 *Manuale di eteo geroglifico*. II. (Incunabula Graeca, 14-15; 2 vols.; Rome: Edizioni dell'Ateneo).

Meyer, E.
1953   *Geschichte des Altertums*. II. *Zweite Abteilung: Der Orient vom zwölften bis zur Mitte des achten Jahrhunderts* (5 vols.; Stuttgart: J.G. Cotta'sche Buchhandlung Nachfolger, 3rd edn).
1954   *Geschichte des Altertums*. III. *Erste Abteilung: Das Perserreich und die Griechen bis zum Vorabend des peloponnesischen Krieges* (5 vols.; Stuttgart: J.G. Cotta'sche Buchhandlung Nachfolger, 5th edn).

Miller, M.
1974   'The Moabite Stone as a Memorial Stela', *PEQ* 106: 9-18.

Momigliano, A.
1958   'The Place of Herodotus in the History of Historiography', *Hist* (L) 43: 1-13.
1972   'Tradition and the Classical Historian', *History and Theory* 11: 279-93.
1978   'Greek Historiography', *History and Theory* 17: 1-28.
1981   'Biblical Studies and Classical Studies: Simple Reflections upon Historical Method', *ASNSP* 11: 25-32.
1990   'Persian Historiography, Greek Historiography, and Jewish Historiography', in A. Momigliano, *The Classical Foundations of Modern Historiography* (Sather Classical Lectures, 54; Berkeley: University of California Press): 5-28.

Müller, R.
1984   'Herausbildung und Formen des Geschichtsdenkens in Griechenland', *Klio* 66: 334-65.

Murray, A.T.
1924–25 *Homer: The Iliad* (LCL, 170-71; 2 vols.; Cambridge, MA: Harvard University Press).
1919   *Homer: The Odyssey* (LCL, 104-105; 2 vols.; Cambridge, MA: Harvard University Press).

Myres, J.L.
1953   *Herodotus: Father of History* (Oxford: Clarendon Press).

The Tragedy in History

Nagy, G.
 1987   'Herodotus the *Logios*', *Arethusa* 20: 175-84
Nelson, R.D.
 1981   *The Double Redaction of the Deuteronomistic History* (JSOTSup, 18;
          Sheffield: JSOT Press).
Neu, E.
 1974   *Der Anitta-Text* (Studien zu den Boğazköy-Texten: Herausgegeben
          von der Kommission für den Alten Orient der Akademie der Wissen-
          schaften und der Literatur, 18; Wiesbaden: Otto Harrassowitz).
Nicholson, E.W.
 1967   *Deuteronomy and Tradition* (Oxford: Basil Blackwell).
Nickau, K.
 1990   'Mythos und Logos bei Herodot', in W. Ax (ed.), *Memoria rerum
          veterum: Neue Beiträge zur antiken Historiographie und alten
          Geschichte: Festschrift für Carl Joachim Classen zum 60. Geburtstag*
          (Palingenesia, 32; Stuttgart: Franz Steiner): 83-100.
Noth, M.
 1943   'Das deuteronomistische Werk (Dtr)', in M. Noth,
          *Überlieferungsgeschichtliche Studien: Die sammelnden und bearbeit-
          enden Geschichtswerke im Alten Testament* (Schriften der Königs-
          berger gelehrten Gesellschaft: Geisteswissenschaftliche Klasse, 18;
          Halle: Niemeyer): 45-152.
 1948   *Überlieferungsgeschichte des Pentateuch* (Stuttgart: Kohlhammer).
O'Brien, M.A.
 1989   *The Deuteronomistic History Hypothesis: A Reassessment* (OBO, 92;
          Freiburg: Universitätsverlag).
Olmstead, A.T.
 1948   *History of the Persian Empire* (Chicago: University of Chicago Press).
Oppenheim, A.L.
 1960   'The City of Assur in 714 BC', *JNES* 19: 133-47.
Panofsky, H.
 1885   *Quaestionum de historiae Herodoteae fontibus pars prima* (Berlin);
          non vidi.
Pearson, L.
 1939   *Early Ionian Historians* (Oxford: Clarendon Press).
Peckham, B.
 1985   *The Composition of the Deuteronomistic History* (HSM, 35; Atlanta:
          Scholars Press).
Places, E. des
 1991   *Eusèbe de Césarée: La préparation évangélique: Livre IX*, in G.
          Schroeder and E. des Places, *Eusèbe de Césarée: La préparation évan-
          gélique: Livres VIII–IX–X* (SC, 369; Paris: Cerf): 182-345.
Pohlenz, M.
 1937   *Herodot: Der erste Geschichtschreiber des Abendlandes* (Neue Wege
          zur Antike: Reihe 2, 7-8; Leipzig; repr. Darmstadt: Wissenschaftliche
          Buchgesellschaft, 1961).

Polzin, R.
1980   *Moses and the Deuteronomist: A Literary Study of the Deuteronomic History*. I. *Deuteronomy, Joshua, Judges* (New York: Seabury).
1989   *Samuel and the Deuteronomist: A Literary Study of the Deuteronomic History*. II. *1 Samuel* (San Fransisco: Harper & Row).

Pritchard, J.B.
1969   *Ancient Near Eastern Texts relating to the Old Testament* (Princeton, NJ: Princeton University Press, 3rd edn).

Pritchett, W.K.
1982   'Some Recent Critiques of the Veracity of Herodotus', in W.K. Pritchett, *Studies in Ancient Greek Topography IV* (UCP.CS, 28; Berkeley: University of California Press): 234-85.
1993   *The Liar School of Herodotos* (Amsterdam: J.C. Gieben)

Provan, I.W.
1988   *Hezekiah and the Books of Kings: A Contribution to the Debate about the Composition of the Deuteronomistic History* (BZAW, 172; Berlin: de Gruyter).

Rad, G. von
1938   *Das formgeschichtliche Problem des Hexateuch* (BWANT, 4.26,; Stuttgart: Kohlhammer), in von Rad 1958: 9-86.
1944   'Der Anfang der Geschichtsschreibung im alten Israel', *AKuG* 32: 1-42.
1947   'Die deuteronomistische Geschichtstheologie in den Königsbüchern', FRLANT NS 40: 52-64, in von Rad 1958: 189-204.
1957   *Theologie des Alten Testaments*, I (EETh, 1; Munich: Chr. Kaiser Verlag).
1958   *Gesammelte Studien zum Alten Testament* (TBü, 8; Munich: Chr. Kaiser Verlag).
1984   'The Deuteronomic Theology of History in I and II Kings', *The Problem of the Hexateuch and Other Essays* (London: SCM Press).

Raubitschek, A.E.
1939   '*Erga megala te kai thomasta*', *REA* 41: 217-22, in Raubitschek 1991: 270-74.
1955   'Gyges in Herodotus', *CW* 48: 48-51.
1957   'Die schamlöse Ehefrau (Herodot 1, 8, 3)', *RhM* 100: 139-40, in Raubitschek 1991: 330-31.
1989   'What the Greeks Thought of their Early History', *The Ancient World* 20: 39-45.
1991   *The School of Hellas: Essays on Greek History, Archaeology, and Literature* (New York: Oxford University Press).

Redfield, J.
1985   'Herodotus the Tourist', *CP* 80: 97-118.

Redford, D.B.
1986   *Pharaonic King-Lists, Annals and Day-Books: A Contribution to the Study of the Egyptian Sense of History* (Publication of the Society for the Study of Egyptian Antiquities, 4; Mississauga: Benben Publications).

1993 *Egypt, Canaan, and Israel in Ancient Times* (Princeton, NJ: Princeton University Press).

Regenbogen, O.

1930a 'Die Geschichte von Solon und Krösus. Eine Studie zur Geistes-geschichte des 5. und 6. Jahrhunderts', *HGym* 41: 1-20, in Regenbogen 1961: 101-124.

1930b 'Herodot und sein Werk: Ein Versuch', *Antike* 6: 202-248, in Regenbogen 1961: 57-100.

1933 'Thukydides als Politischer Denker', *HGym* 44: 2-25, in Regenbogen 1961: 217-47.

1961 *Kleine Schriften* (Munich: Beck).

Rendtorff, R.

1977 *Das überlieferungsgeschichtliche Problem des Pentateuch* (BZAW, 147; Berlin: de Gruyter).

Rieks, R.

1975 'Eine tragische Erzählung bei Herodot (*Hist.* 1,34-45)', *Poetica: Zeitschrift für Sprach- und Literaturwissenschaft* 7: 23-44.

Robertson, R.G.

1985 'Ezekiel the Tragedian (Second Century BC): A New Translation and Introduction', in J.A. Charlesworth (ed.), *The Old Testament Pseudepigrapha* (2 vols.; London: Darton, Longman & Todd): II: 803-819.

Roccati, A.

1986 'Turiner Königspapyrus', in W. Helck and W. Westendorf (eds.), *Lexikon der Ägyptologie*. VI. (Wiesbaden: Otto Harrassowitz): col. 809-810.

Rogerson, J.W.

1992 *W.M.L. de Wette: Founder of Modern Biblical Criticism: An Intellectual Biography* (JSOTSup, 126; Sheffield: JSOT Press).

Rollinger, R.

1993 *Herodots babylonischer Logos: Eine kritische Untersuchung der Glaubwürdigkeitsdiskussion* (*IBKW*.S, 84; Innsbruck: Verlag des Instituts für Sprachwissenschaft der Universität Innsbruck).

Rosén, H.B.

1962 *Eine Laut- und Formenlehre der herodotischen Sprachform* (Indogermanische Bibliothek, Reihe 1: Lehr- und Handbücher; Heidelberg: Carl Winter).

Rosenmeyer, T.G.

1982 'History or Poetry? The Example of Herodotus', *Clio (M)* 11: 239-59.

Rost, L.

1926 *Die Überlieferung von der Thronnachfolge Davids* (BWANT, 3.6; Stuttgart: Kohlhammer), in L. Rost, *Das kleine Credo und andere Studien zum Alten Testament* (Heidelberg: Quelle & Meyer, 1965): 119-240.

Saggs, H.W.F.

1978 *The Encounter with the Divine in Mesopotamia and Israel* (JLCR, 12; London: Athlone Press).

Sasson, J.M.
1981   'On Idrimi and Šarruwa, the Scribe', in M.A. Morrison and D.I. Owen,
            *Studies on the Civilization and Culture of Nuzi and the Hurrians: In
            Honor of E.R. Lacheman* (Winona Lake, IN: Eisenbrauns): 309-324.
Sayce, A.H.
1883   *The Ancient Empires of the East: Herodotus I–III. With Notes, Intro-
            ductions and Appendices* (London: Macmillan).
Schmid, H.H.
1976   *Der sogenannte Jahwist: Beobachtungen und Fragen zur Pentateuch-
            forschung* (Zürich: Theologischer Verlag).
Schmid, W.
1934   *Geschichte der griechischen Literatur: Die griechische Literatur in der
            Zeit der attischen Hegemonie vor dem Eingreifen der Sophistik* (HAW,
            7.1.2; Munich: Beck).
Schnabel, P.
1923   *Berossos und die babylonisch–hellenistische Literatur* (Leipzig:
            Teubner).
Schuler, E. von
1964   'Staatsverträge und Dokumente hethitischen Rechts', in G. Walser
            (ed.), *Neuere Hethiterforschung* (Historia: Einzelschriften, 7; Wies-
            baden: Franz Steiner): 34-53.
Skafte Jensen, M.
1992   *Homer og hans tilhørere* (København: Gyldendal).
Smend, R.
1971   'Das Gesetz und die Völker: Ein Beitrag zur deuteronomistischen
            Redaktionsgeschichte' in H.W. Wolff (ed.), *Probleme biblischer Theol-
            ogie: Gerhard von Rad zum 70. Geburtstag* (Munich: Chr. Kaiser
            Verlag): 494-509.
1978   *Die Entstehung des Alten Testaments* (ThW, 1; Stuttgart: Kohlhammer).
Smith, C.F.
1928   *Thucydides. I. History of the Peloponnesian War: Books I and II*
            (LCL, 108; London: Heinemann, 2nd edn).
Smith, S.
1924   *Babylonian Historical Texts Relating to the Capture and Downfall of
            Babylon* (London: Methuen).
1949   *The Statue of Idri-Mi* (Occasional Publications of the British Institute
            of Archaeology in Ankara, 1; London: The British Institute of Archae-
            ology in Ankara).
Snell, B.
1971   '128 Ezechiel', in Snell *et al.* 1971: I: 288-301.
1973   'Gyges und Kroisos als Tragödien-figuren', *ZPE* 12: 197-205.
Snell, B. *et al.*
1971–81   *Tragicorum Graecorum Fragmenta* (4 vols.; Göttingen: Vandenhoeck
            & Ruprecht).
Sommer, F., and A. Falkenstein
1938   *Die hethitisch–akkadische Bilingue des Ḫattušili I. (Labarna II.)*
            (ABAW.PH, 16; Munich: Verlag der bayerischen Akademie der
            Wissenschaften).

Spoerri, W.
    1979   'Beros(s)os', in Ziegler and Sontheimer 1979: I, col. 1548.
Stahl, H.-P.
    1968   'Herodots Gyges–Tragödie', *Hermes* 96: 385-400.
Stoebe, H.J.
    1973   *Das erste Buch Samuelis* (KAT, 8.1; Gütersloh: Gütersloher Verlagshaus)
Storr, F.
    1912–13 *Sophocles: With an English Translation* (LCL, 20-21; 2 vols.; London: Heinemann)
Strasburger, H.
    1972   *Homer und die Geschichtsschreibung* (SHAW.PH, 1972.1; Heidelberg: Carl Winter).
Sturtevant, E.H., and G. Bechtel
    1935   *A Hittite Chrestomathy* (William Dwight Whitney Linguistic Series; Philadelphia: Linguistic Society of America, University of Pennsylvania).
Thomas, R.
    1996   'Review Article I: Herodotus', *JHS* 116: 175-78.
Thompson, T.L.
    1992   *Early History of the Israelite People: From the Written and Archaeological Sources* (SHANE, 4; Leiden: Brill)
    1995   'The Intellectual Matrix of Early Biblical Narrative: Inclusive Monotheism in Persian Period Palestine', in D.V. Edelman (ed.), *The Triumph of Elohim: From Yahwisms to Judaisms* (Kampen: Kok): 107-124.
Torrey, C.C.
    1896   *The Composition and Historical Value of Ezra–Nehemiah* (BZAW, 2; Giessen: J. Ricker'sche Buchhandlung).
Trenkner, S.
    1958   *The Greek Novella in the Classical Period* (Cambridge: Cambridge University Press).
Van Seters, J.
    1975   *Abraham in History and Tradition* (New Haven: Yale University Press).
    1983   *In Search of History: Historiography in the Ancient World and the Origins of Biblical History* (New Haven: Yale University Press).
    1992   *Prologue to History: The Yahwist as Historian in Genesis* (Louisville, KY: Westminster/John Knox Press).
    1994   *The Life of Moses: The Yahwist as Historian in Exodus–Numbers* (Contributions to Biblical Exegesis and Theology, 10; Kampen: Kok).
Veijola, T.
    1975   *Die ewige Dynastie: David und die Entstehung seiner Dynastie nach der deuteronomistischen Darstellung* (AASF; Series B, 193; Helsinki: Suomalainen Tiedeakatemia).
    1977   *Das Königtum in der Beurteilung der deuteronomistischen Historiographie: Eine redaktionsgeschichtliche Untersuchung* (AASF; Series B, 198; Helsinki: Suomalainen Tiedeakatemia).

Waddell, W.G.
1940   *Manetho* (LCL, 350; London: Heinemann).
Walbank, F.W.
1960   'History and Tragedy', *Hist* 9: 216-34.
Waters, K.H.
1985   *Herodotos, the Historian: His Problems, Methods and Originality* (London: Croom Helm).
Weinfeld, M.
1972   *Deuteronomy and the Deuteronomic School* (Oxford: Clarendon Press).
Weippert, H.
1972   'Die "deuteronomistischen" Beurteilung der Könige von Israel und Juda und das Problem der Redaktion der Königsbücher', *Bib* 53: 301-339.
1985   'Das deuteronomistische Geschichtswerk: Sein Ziel und Ende in der neueren Forschung', *TRu* 50: 213-49.
Weir Smyth, H.
1922   *Aeschylus*. I. (LCL, 145; Cambridge, MA: Harvard University Press).
Weissbach, F.H.
1911   *Die Keilinschriften der Achämeniden* (VAB, 3; Leipzig: Hinrichs).
Wellhausen, J.
1889   *Die Composition des Hexateuchs und der historishen Bücher des Alten Testaments* (Berlin: Georg Reimer, 2nd edn).
1905   *Prolegomena zur Geschichte Israels* (Berlin: de Gruyter, 6th edn).
Westermann, C.
1994   *Die Geschichtsbücher des Alten Testaments: Gab es ein deuteronomistisches Geschichtswerk?* (TBü, 87; Gütersloh: Chr. Kaiser/ Gütersloher Verlagshaus).
Wette, W.M.L. de
1805   *Dissertatio critico–exegetica qua Deuteronomium a prioribus Pentateuchi Libris diversum, alius cuiusdam recentioris auctioris opus esse monstratur* (Jena), in W.M.L. de Wette, *Opuscula Theologica* (Berlin: Georg Reimer, 1830): 149-68.
1817   *Lehrbuch der historisch–kritischen Einleitung in die Bibel Alten und Neuen Testaments*. I. *Die Einleitung in das A.T. enthaltend* (Berlin: Georg Reimer).
1852   *Lehrbuch der historisch kritischen Einleitung in die kanonischen und apokryphischen Bücher des Alten Testamentes* (Berlin: Georg Reimer, 7th edn).
Whedbee, J.W.
1988   'On Divine and Human Bonds: The Tragedy of the House of David', in G.M. Tucker, D.L. Petersen, and R.R. Wilson (eds.), *Canon, Theology, and Old Testament Interpretation: Essays in Honor of Brevard S. Childs* (Philadelphia: Fortress Press): 147-65.
Wilson, R.R.
1977   *Genealogy and History in the Biblical World* (YNER, 7; New Haven: Yale University Press).

Wolff, H.W.
     1961   'Das Kerygma des deuteronomistischen Geschichtswerks', *ZAW* 73:
                   171-86.
Ziegler, K., and W. Sontheimer (eds.)
     1979   *Der kleine Pauly: Lexikon der Antike in fünf Bänden* (5 vols.; Munich:
                   Deutscher Taschenbuch Verlag).

INDEXES

INDEX OF REFERENCES

OLD TESTAMENT

INDEX OF AUTHORS